AWARD EDITION

HOUGHTON MIFFLIN

The Literature Experience

READING

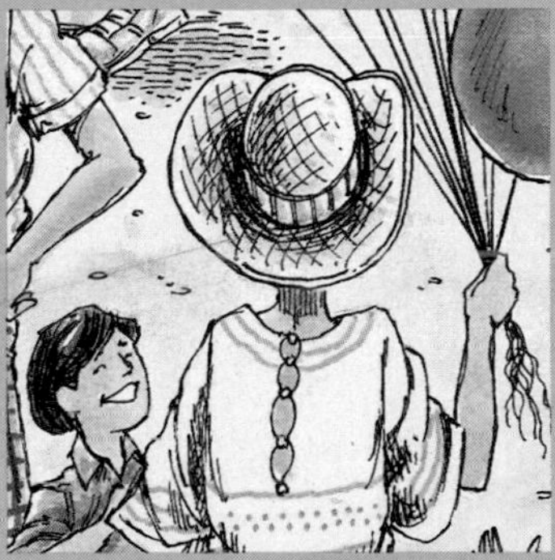

Celebrate Reading with us!

Acknowledgments appear on page 527.

Printed in the U.S.A.

ISBN: 0-395-61088-5

3456789-VH-96 95 94 93

DINOSAURING

Senior Author
John J. Pikulski

Senior Coordinating Author
J. David Cooper

Senior Consulting Author
William K. Durr

Coordinating Authors
Kathryn H. Au
M. Jean Greenlaw
Marjorie Y. Lipson
Susan E. Page
Sheila W. Valencia
Karen K. Wixson

Authors
Rosalinda B. Barrera
Edwina Bradley
Ruth P. Bunyan
Jacqueline L. Chaparro
Jacqueline C. Comas
Alan N. Crawford
Robert L. Hillerich
Timothy G. Johnson
Jana M. Mason
Pamela A. Mason
William E. Nagy
Joseph S. Renzulli
Alfredo Schifini

Senior Advisor
Richard C. Anderson

Advisors
Christopher J. Baker
Charles Peters
MaryEllen Vogt

HOUGHTON MIFFLIN COMPANY BOSTON
Atlanta Dallas Geneva, Illinois Palo Alto Princeton Toronto

THEME 1

FOLKTALES

Award Winner

THEME 2

NONFICTION

91

THEY WALKED THE EARTH

THEME 4

FANTASY

225

Fantasy Close to Home

THEME BOOKS

THEME 5

MYSTERY

THEME 6

BIOGRAPHY

The Dreamers

THEME 7

FICTION

427

Dear Diary

THEME BOOKS

READING SOCIAL STUDIES

READING SCIENCE

FOLKTALES

THEME 1

Battle of Wits

Watch as these tricksters attempt to outwit, outfox, and outsmart their opponents, using only their brains!

Contents

The Boy of the Three-Year Nap

retold by Dianne Snyder ◆ illustrated by Allen Say

On the banks of the river Nagara, where the long-necked cormorants fish at night, there once lived a poor widow and her son.

All day long the widow sewed silk kimonos for the rich ladies in town. As she worked, her head bobbed up and down, up and down, like the heads of the birds hunting for fish.

"What next? What next?" she seemed to say, as if the work would never end. Her only son, Taro, was, oh, such a clever lad and as healthy as a mother could wish. But, alas! He was as lazy as a rich man's cat. All he did was eat and sleep, sleep and eat.

If he was asked to do any work, he would yawn and say, "After my nap."

It was said that if no one woke him, Taro would sleep three years at a stretch. And so he was called "The Boy of the Three-Year Nap."

When Taro was nearly grown, a rice merchant moved to town and built a mansion. It had twenty rooms with sliding doors that opened onto the most exquisite garden. In the center was a pond filled with golden carp. And at the end of the garden was a teahouse where one could sit in the cool of the evening and gaze at the moon.

The merchant's wife and daughter wore elegant kimonos with obis of gold brocade. The merchant himself carried a cane made of ivory and smoked a pipe with a bowl of solid gold.

Taro was impressed with his fine new neighbors and began to sneak into the garden between his naps. Everything he saw enchanted him — the magnificent house, the elegant daughter, the fat carp in the pond.

When the merchant counted out his sacks of rice with a tap of his cane, Taro would sigh. "Ah, what a life!"

As the months passed, Taro grew even more lazy. His mother began to pester him, first in one ear, then the other.

"I hear the merchant is looking for a boy to work for him," she told Taro.

"What does he need a boy for?" Taro asked.

"To haul rice sacks, what else?" said the mother.

"Hauling rice sacks!" Taro laughed. "I pity the fool who takes the job. His back will get bent like an old man's."

"How can you sit here and do nothing?" she cried. "The roof leaks like a basket, the walls are crumbling, the rice sack is empty. I don't know how we shall live. I don't know how!"

"Cheer up, Mother. I have a plan."

"How you talk! What you need is a job, not a plan!"

"Don't worry, but you must make me a black kimono and hat like a priest wears."

"What will you do with them?"

"Oh, they are part of my plan." That was all he would say.

"Maybe he is planning to become a priest," Taro's mother thought. But the priests she knew got up before dawn, ate only one meal a day, and never took naps. Try as she might, she could not imagine her son doing that. Still, she decided to make the kimono and hat, for she did not know what else to do.

The next evening, Taro put on the new clothes. Then, with a piece of charcoal, he blackened his brows and drew scowl lines on his forehead and on each side of his nose. When he was done he looked as fierce as a samurai warrior.

"Taro, is it really you?" his mother cried out.

"Don't be alarmed, Mother," said Taro. "It's all part of my plan. Now, don't say a word of this to anyone."

Before she could say more, he ran out of the house.

At sundown, the merchant came out of his house for his evening walk.

"Good evening, madam," he called to Taro's mother. "I suppose that lazy son of yours is still in bed."

"He's a little tired tonight, sir," said the widow.

"Ha! You are a soft one. What he needs is a good smack on his back and a kick on his bottom. Napping at dusk, indeed!"

The merchant went on his stroll until he came to a shrine by the roadside. It was the shrine of the ujigami, the patron god of the town. As he stopped to make an offering, a black figure appeared before him, scowling like a goblin.

"Wh— who are you?" asked the startled merchant.

"I am the ujigami," a fierce voice bellowed.

"What do you want of me? What did I do?" cowered the merchant.

"It is time for your daughter to take a husband," said the ujigami. "You must wed her at once to that fine lad who lives on your street."

"What fine lad, my lord?"

"That fine young man called Taro."

"Taro!" The merchant rubbed his ears. "You mean 'The Boy of the Three-Year Nap,' *that* Taro?"

"The same!"

"Oh, no! There must be some mistake!"

"Gods do not make mistakes!"

The merchant began to tremble. "Surely there must be someone else my daughter can marry. Anyone but Taro — "

"Not a one," growled the ujigami. "It has been decreed, ordained, and sanctified!"

"Oh, my lord, grant me time to think about this. Couldn't we wait a year or two?"

"Impudent mortal!" the ujigami thundered. "How dare you bargain with me! If you delay my command, I shall turn your daughter into a cold clay pot! See if she can find a husband then!"

"No, no!" wailed the merchant. "My child, a pot? Have mercy!"

Falling on his knees, the merchant beat his fists against the ground and sobbed until he was quite worn out.

By then, however, the god had disappeared.

Quite early the next morning, the merchant came knocking on the widow's door. His eyes were red and his face was drawn, as though he had cried all night.

"Madam, I come on the most urgent business," he said grimly. "It seems that my daughter must marry your . . . ah . . . son."

The poor woman's mouth fell open.

"Yes, your son," the merchant repeated. "The ujigami appeared to me last night, and that is his command."

"But the ujigami has never appeared to anyone before," the widow exclaimed.

"That was so, until last night. I am ruined."

"Tell me, honorable sir, what did the god look like?"

The merchant shivered. "In dress, he is like a priest. But in manner, he is more like a goblin. His face is as black as coal and as fierce as a warrior's."

The widow saw at once what her son was up to. Her head began to bob up and down, up and down — like a cormorant about to dive after a fish. Still, she did not want to seem too eager.

So she said to the merchant, "We are humble folk, my good sir. My Taro could never marry a lady as fine as your daughter."

"Agreed," the merchant cried. "But unfortunately what we think matters not. We must do as the god commands or he will turn my daughter into a clay pot."

"How terrible!" The widow widened her eyes. "But, sir, even if they are to marry, your daughter could never live in this wretched house. Why, the roof leaks in a hundred places, and the walls have so many cracks the wind blows right through."

The merchant frowned. He had not thought of that.

"Very well then, I will send a man to mend the cracks and leaks," he said.

First thing the next morning, a plasterer came to repair the house.

"Fine work, fine work," Taro mumbled from his bed.

In the evening the merchant said to the widow, "Now will you consent to the marriage?"

"Alas, how can I, sir?" The widow bowed. "As you can see, our house has but one room. Your daughter would be ashamed to live in a place as small as this."

"True," muttered the merchant. "All right, I will send carpenters to build you many rooms."

After the merchant left, Taro chuckled. "Splendid. My plan is working!"

When the widow's house was finished, the merchant asked, "Now will you consent to the marriage?"

"I fear, sir, that your daughter will still not find happiness here."

"What is it now?" cried the merchant. "Speak your mind or my daughter will turn into a clay pot!"

"My Taro has no job," said the widow. "How can he keep your daughter in luxury and comfort?"

"Surely this is the end of me," groaned the merchant. "All right, your son shall manage my storehouse. But I warn you, madam, he will have no time for naps at my place. Now do you consent to the marriage?"

Taro's mother tossed her head like a cormorant that has caught a large fish. "You have my consent," she said.

No sooner had the merchant left than the widow hurried to tell Taro the news. "The merchant has made a most wonderful offer," she cried.

Taro sat up in bed, ho-hum, stretching and yawning like a satisfied cat.

"It was all part of my plan, Mother. I hope you accepted the offer."

"Indeed I have," said his mother. "You start work first thing tomorrow morning."

"Work!" Taro leaped out of bed. "What do you mean? That was not part of my plan!"

"Ha! Do you think you are the only one who makes plans?" his mother answered.

The wedding ceremony was the finest the townfolk had ever seen. And as it turned out, the marriage is a happy one.

The ujigami must be pleased, for he has never shown himself again. And the merchant's daughter has shown no signs of turning into a pot.

As for Taro, he does a good job keeping count of the rice for his father-in-law, which is no easy task. If he is not the busiest man in town, neither is he the laziest.

It has been a long time since anyone has called Taro "The Boy of the Three-Year Nap." Perhaps everyone has forgotten by now.

Write Another Tricky Ending

What if this story had ended another way? Suppose this had happened: It's the morning of Taro's wedding to the merchant's daughter — but Taro has overslept! Write another ending to this story, telling how Taro tries to talk his way out of this one. Read your new ending to your classmates.

Dianne Snyder

Dianne Snyder, the author of *The Boy of the Three-Year Nap*, had some practice playing the part of the *ujigami*, the same part Taro played in the story. One Halloween while growing up in Japan, Snyder, like Taro, painted her face with *sumi*, the black ink used in traditional Japanese art. As a child Snyder also heard many folktales and trickster stories told by Japanese storytellers who traveled from village to village. *The Boy of the Three-Year Nap*, her first book, is one of those stories.

Above: Snyder (kneeling) with friends in Niigata, Japan, 1953

Snyder doing homework, with her mother and sister in Japan in 1954

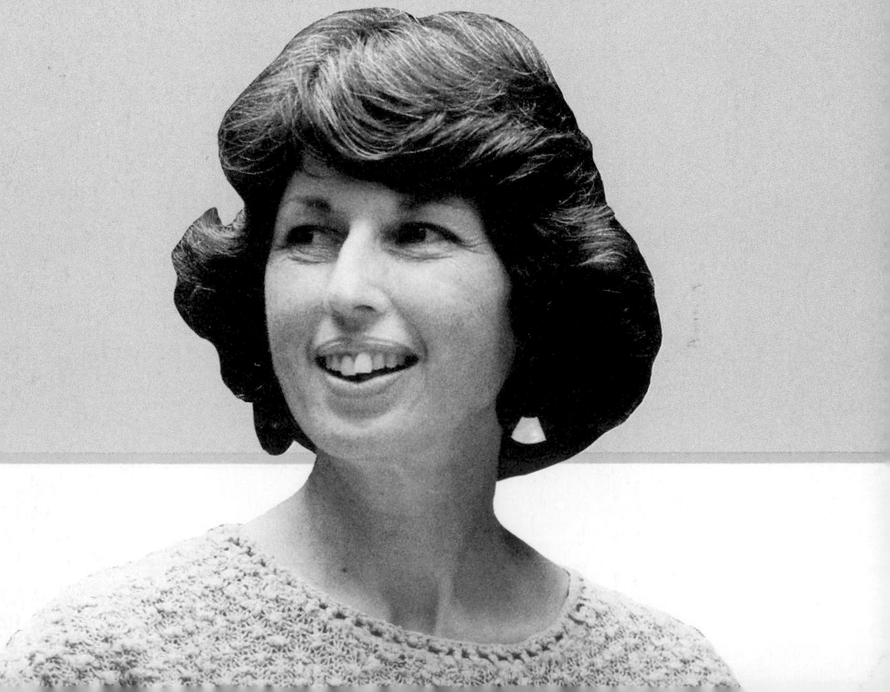

Allen Say

Above:
A scene from The Bicycle Man, *a story about Say's childhood in Japan*

After working as an illustrator for years, Allen Say decided to put down his paintbrushes and write novels. In fact, when he was asked to illustrate a children's folktale by Dianne Snyder, he said no.

But finally Say agreed to illustrate the book — and something amazing happened. "I locked myself in my room, I took out my old paint box, and I began working," he says. "It gave me an intense joy." That book was, of course, *The Boy of the Three-Year Nap*.

Now Say is happily back to writing and illustrating children's books, including *A River Dream*, which begins on page 246 of this book.

Iktomi and the Boulder

a Plains Indian story

retold and
illustrated by Paul Goble

About Iktomi

Iktomi is the hero of many amusing stories. Iktomi (pronounced eek-toe-me*) is his Sioux name; he stars in similar stories from all over North America and is known by various names: Coyote, Sinti, Old Man Napi, Nanabozo, Sinkalip, Wihio, Veho, and others. Iktomi, or Ikto, is very clever, with unusual magical powers, but he is also very stupid, a liar, and a mischief-maker. He is forever trying to get the better of others but is himself usually fooled. The mention of Iktomi's name makes people smile, for he is always up to no good and always getting himself into trouble. He is beyond the realm of moral values. He lacks all sincerity. Tales about Iktomi remind us that unsociable and chaotic behavior is never far below the surface. We can see ourselves in him.*

Iktomi is also credited with greater things: in many of the older stories the Creator entrusts him with much of Creation. People say that what seem to be the "mistakes" and "irrational" aspects of Creation, such as earthquakes, floods, disease, flies, and mosquitos, were surely made by Iktomi.

There is no single "correct" version of these stories; story-tellers kept to certain familiar themes and wove variations around them. Tales with a moral, but without any sermon, they were told in informal language, because Iktomi has no respect for the precise use of words. All the stories start in the same way: "Iktomi was walking along . . . " The words suggest right from the start that Iktomi is idle and aimless, with nothing better to do than to cause mischief for our amusement.

Iktomi was walking along. . . .
Every story about Iktomi starts this way.

Iktomi was walking along.
It was a beautiful morning.
Iktomi was going to visit
his friends and relations
in the next village.

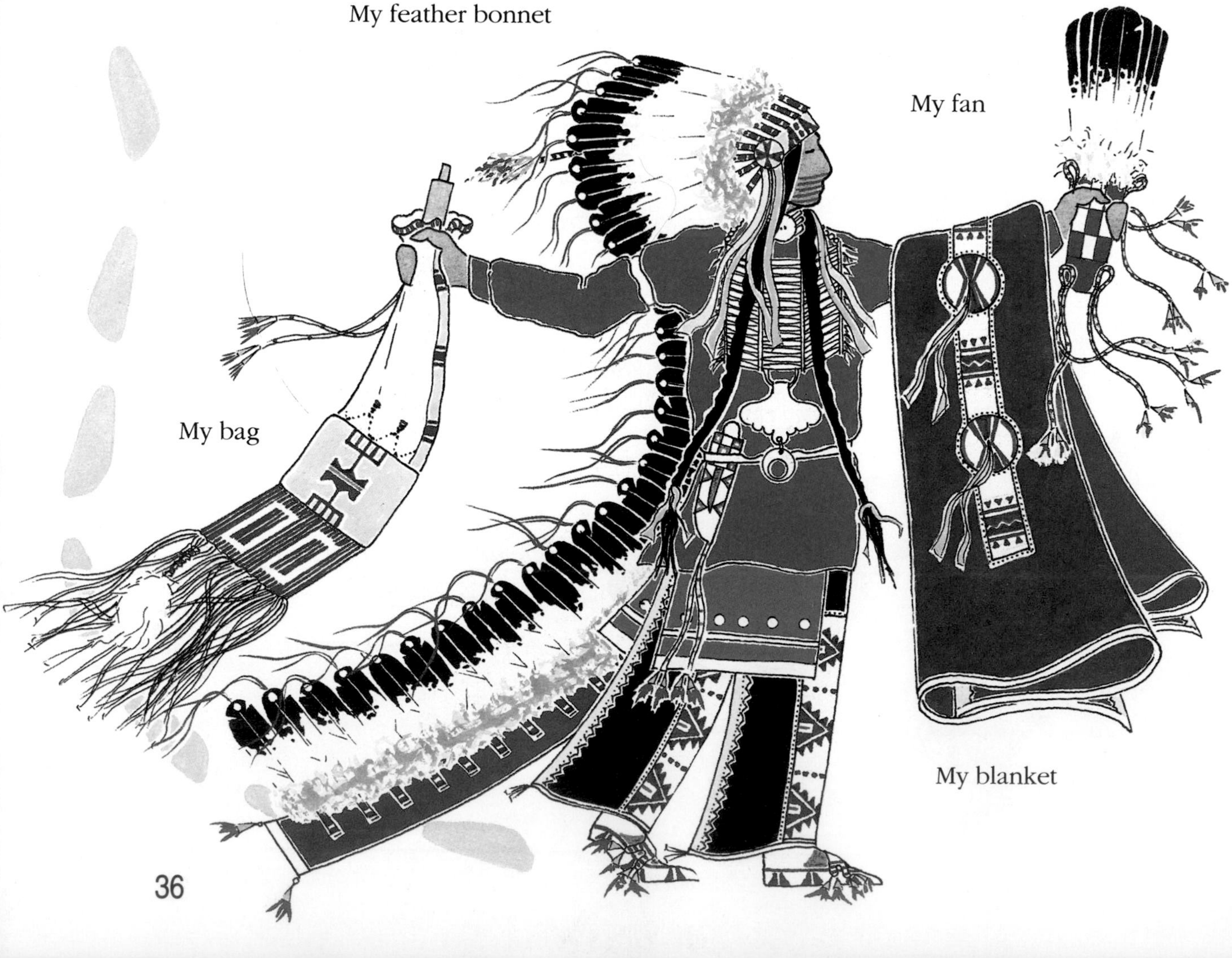

I bet the birds wish
they had all my feathers.
I'll look great at the
dance tonight.

He was feeling happy with himself.
He had painted his face
and was wearing all his very best clothes.
Doesn't he look like a dandy?

I really am very
good-looking. I look
like a real chief.

"How handsome I look," he was thinking.
"Everyone will be impressed.
All the girls
will want me to notice them."
Iktomi is forever showing off — and then always getting into trouble.
He never learns.
The birds and animals
stopped to look as he passed.
Iktomi was feeling much too important
to notice them.
He never noticed
that they were laughing at him!

The sun rose higher in the sky.
Iktomi was getting hot.
He had a l-o-n-g walk ahead of him.
His face-paint started to feel sticky,
and he wished he had not put on
so many clothes.

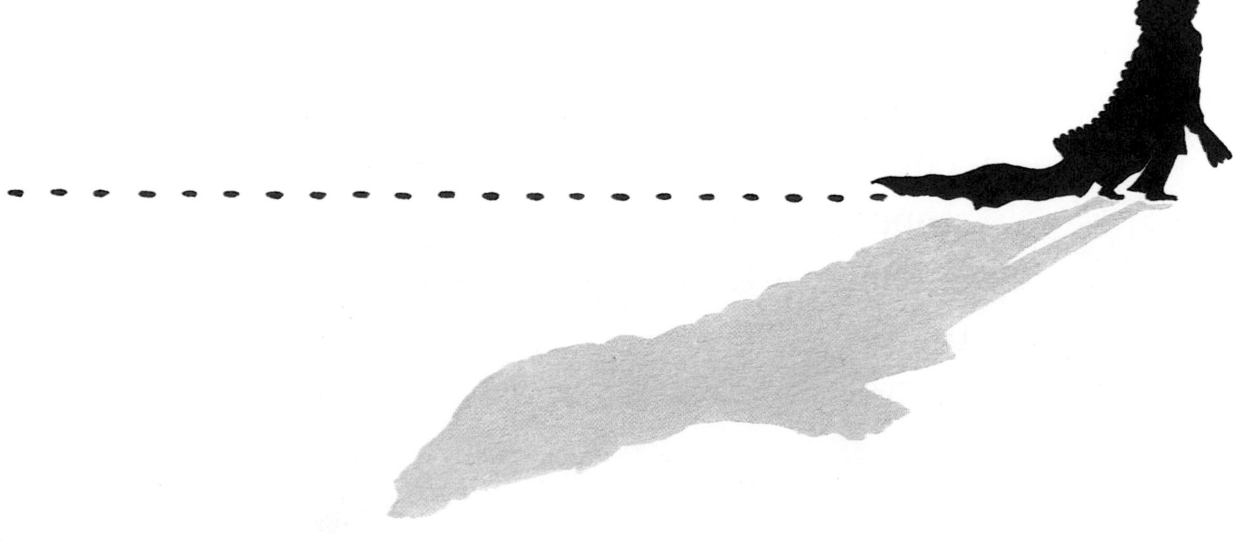

Feeling more and more uncomfortable,
he sat down at last to rest
in the shade of a great boulder.
"What a hot day!" Iktomi thought.
"Why did I bring my blanket?
I'll never need it.
I can't be bothered to carry it any further."

I'll pick it up again
on my way back.

"Grandfather," he said to the boulder,
"Grandfather Boulder, I feel sorry for you.
You are terribly sunburnt
from sitting here so long in the sun.
You have given me shade.
I'm generous, too.
I give you my blanket
to keep the sun off you. Take it."
He wasn't really generous at all, was he?

Iktomi spread his blanket over the boulder,
and went on his way.

After a while he noticed
dark thunder clouds gathering
like mountains behind him.
"I might need my blanket after all,"
he thought. "Rain would spoil
my beautiful clothes."

"I did give it," he said to himself
as he walked back.
"A gift is a gift. Still,
I need it. Anyway, it's much too nice
a blanket just to leave on a rock."

"Boulder," he said,
"you don't need my blanket.
You are only a rock.
The sun can't burn you any more.
I was only lending it to you."
That's not true, is it?

Iktomi snatched the blanket off the boulder.

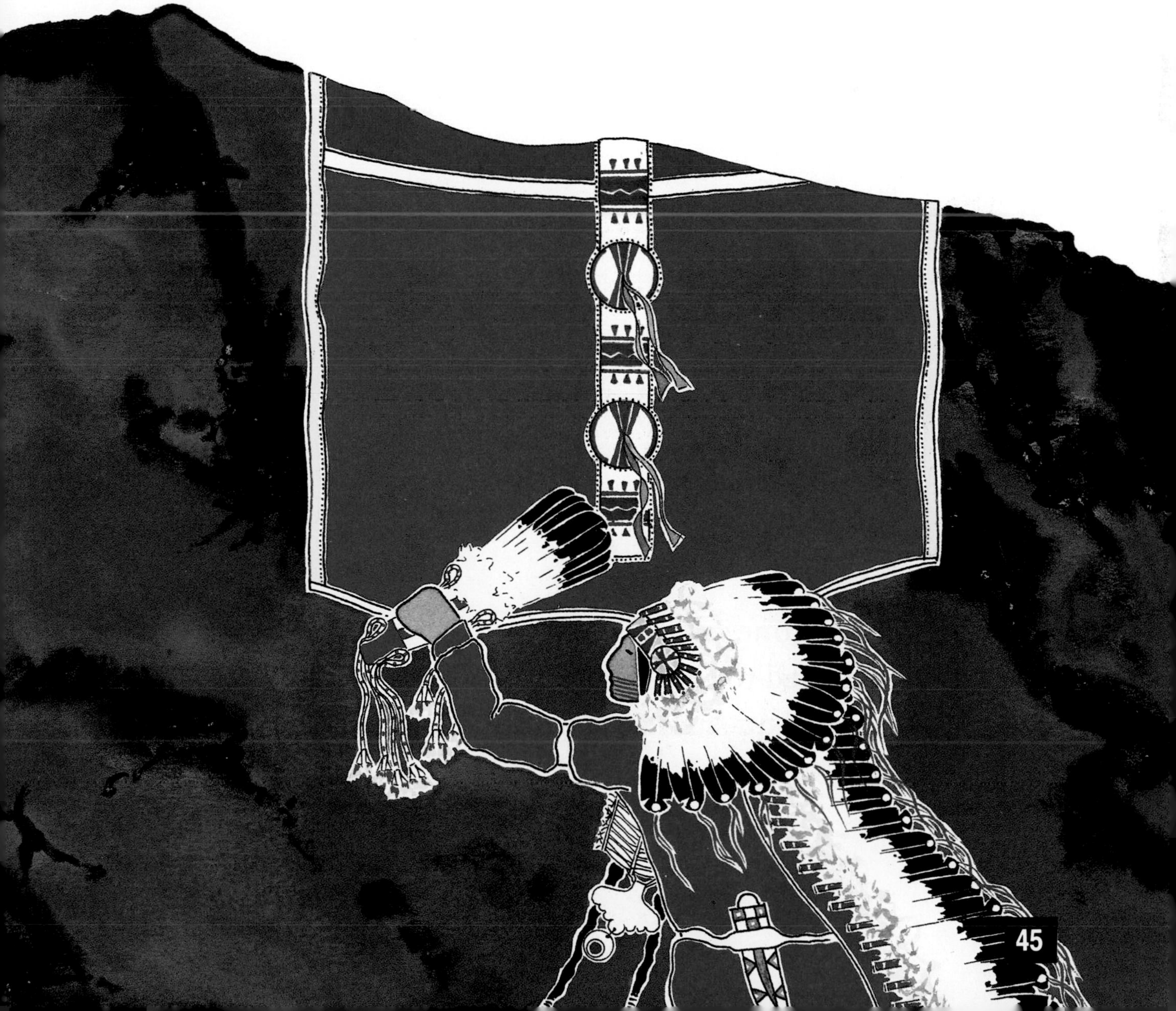

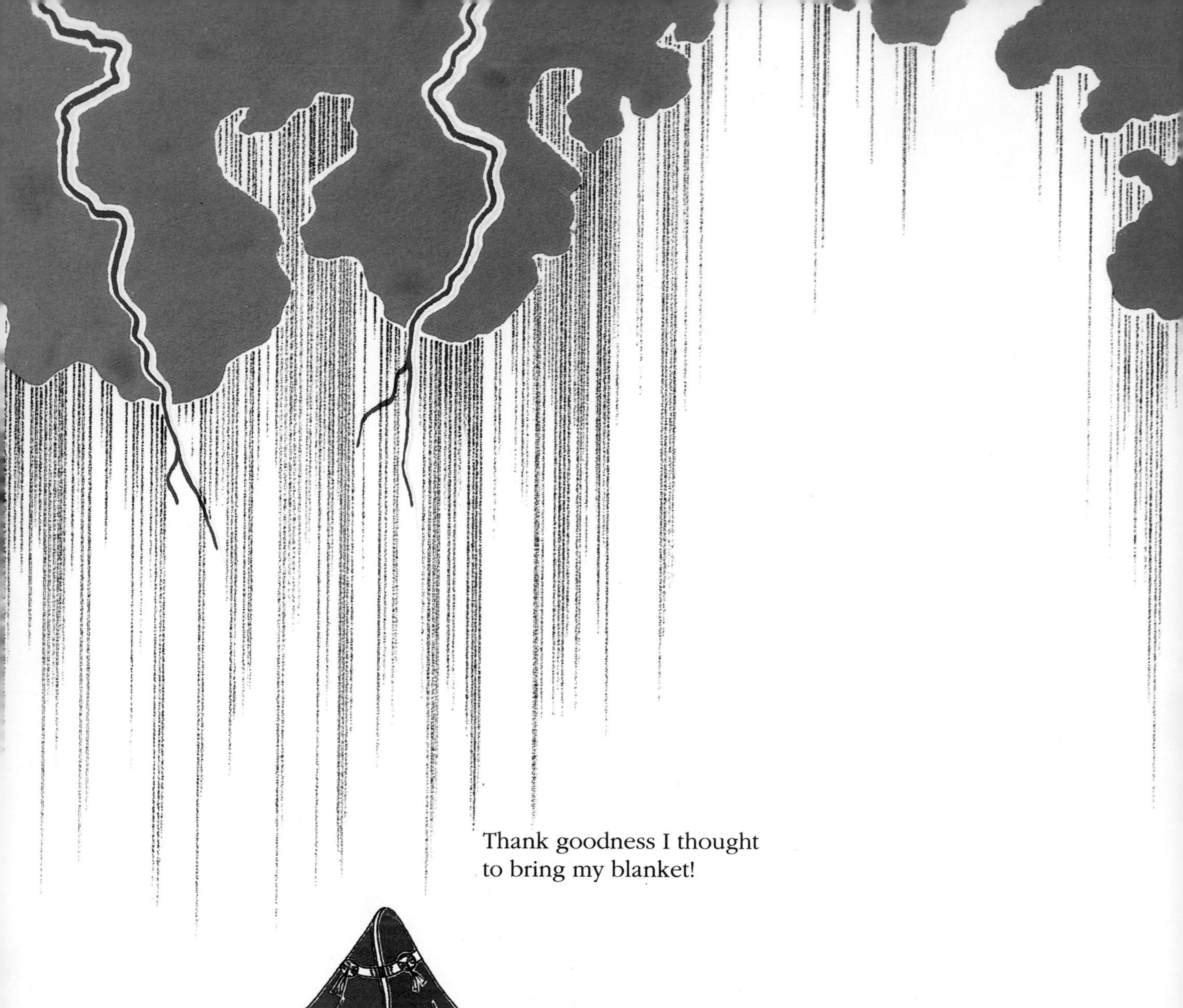
Thank goodness I thought
to bring my blanket!

He had not gone far
when it started to thunder and rain.
He sat down and sheltered
under his blanket.

Soon, above the rumble of thunder,
he heard a different sound:
it seemed to shake the earth —
a regular *thump-crash-bump-*
thump-bump-crash —
"That doesn't sound like thunder,"
he thought.

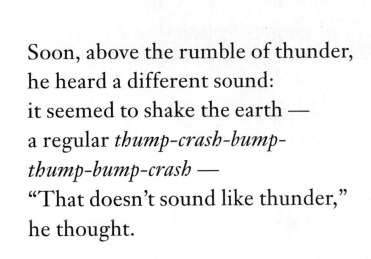

He peeped out from under his blanket;
that great boulder was bouncing
and crashing across the prairie
straight toward him!

Iktomi dropped his blanket
and ran in absolute terror.

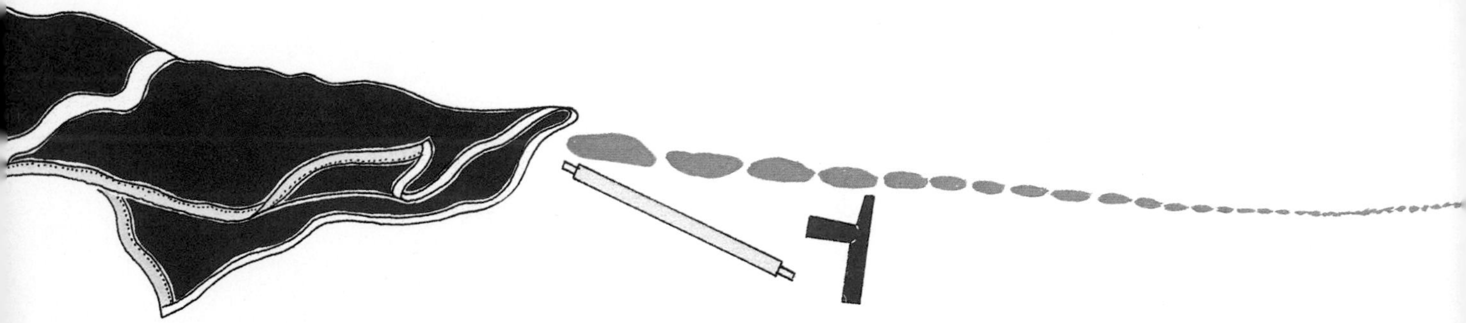

"I must get to the top of the hill,"
he muttered.
"The boulder cannot go uphill."
He was wrong!
The boulder pounded end over end
right to the top.

"I must get across the river,"
he panted.
"That boulder will get stuck in the mud."
Iktomi ran down toward the river,
the boulder bounding and thumping
close at his heels.

Anyone can outwit a rock!

That rock has a terrible temper.

He ran this way.
He ran that way.

He just could not escape
from the boulder.

He splashed across the river,
gasping for breath,
and scrambled out on the far bank
and fell down exhausted.
The boulder jumped the river
in one mighty bound.
Before Iktomi could get up again,
the boulder rolled on top of his legs,
and stopped.

Now what is Iktomi going to do?
Is it the end of the story?

Help!
Get off me! Do you hear?
What are you doing?

Now what do I do?

Iktomi could not move.
He struggled. He screamed.
He hit the boulder. He pleaded.
He cried. It made no difference;
the boulder did not move.

Some buffaloes heard Iktomi
and came to have a look.
"My younger brothers," Iktomi said.
Iktomi has no respect.
He calls everyone "younger brother."
"Younger brothers," he said
to the buffaloes, "please help me.
I was just climbing around on this boulder
when it rolled over onto my legs.
See, I cannot move. Roll it off me."

That wasn't true, was it?

The bulls got their horns underneath
and h-e-a-v-e-d and s-h-o-v-e-d,
but they could not move the boulder
even a little bit.
The elk, the antelope and the bears
saw what was happening.
They came to help.

Come on — *push*!
Don't be so feeble.

Even the prairie dogs and the smallest
of the four-legged ones joined in.
They could not roll the boulder
off Iktomi's legs.

They gave up
and wandered off.

What's the matter with you?
For goodness sake, *push*!

What else can I tell them?
They'll believe anything I say.

Darkness came, and the bats appeared
with the rising moon.
"Ho! My younger brothers!"
Iktomi called out to the bats.
"This boulder has been saying rude things
about you.
He said you are so ugly
that you don't dare show yourselves
during the daytime.
He said that you sleep upside-down
because you don't know your 'up side'
from your 'down side.'
He said some other things,
but I simply cannot repeat them."

Of course Iktomi was making up stories again, wasn't he?

It made the bats cross.
More and more of them gathered.
"I told this boulder that he ought
to know better than to insult
his good-looking relatives.
He even said that you don't know whether
you are birds or animals,
two-legged or four-legged.
'Furry Birds,' he called you.
What a dreadful thing to say — "

The bats were furious.
Suddenly they started hitting the boulder.
They darted this way and that,
and each time they struck,
pieces of the boulder broke off.
"Yes! *Furry Birds* he called you,"
Iktomi shouted.

Bats and pieces of rock flew in every direction.

Ha! That's done it!
I always knew I could get even
with that stupid rock!

"Don't know your 'up side'
from your 'down side'!"
Iktomi yelled.
The bats swooped at the boulder
and knocked off pieces
until there was nothing left but little chips.

"That's right," Iktomi said to the bats.
"You taught that boulder a lesson."

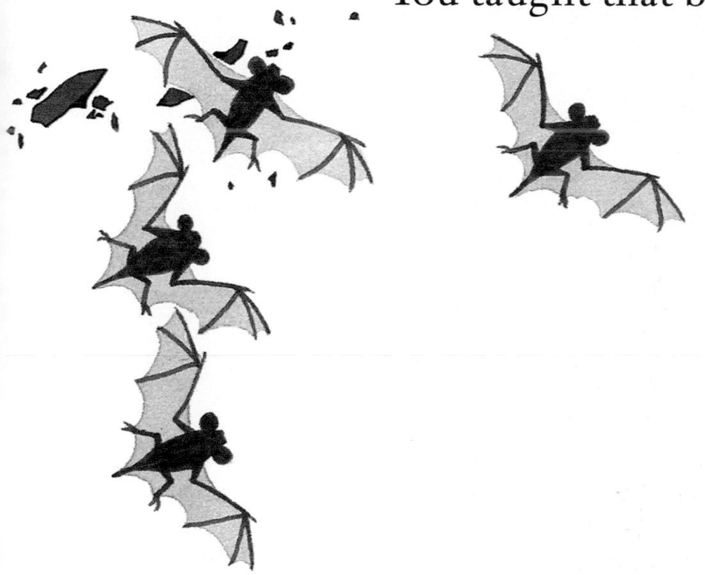

Iktomi went on his way again. . . .

What do you think
Iktomi will get up to next?

Let me think:
what shall I do now?

This story also explains why
bats have flattened faces,
and why there are rocks
scattered all over the Great Plains.

No Native American myth or tale is seen as something which happened long ago. . . . Even today, people with bad traits are likened to Iktomi.

He lives.

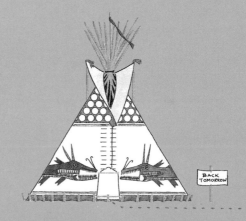

Performing the Story of Iktomi

What should we do first?

Great idea!

Read what it says below!

Working with a group, perform the story of Iktomi as a dramatic reading.

Have one person read the part of Iktomi. Iktomi's spoken lines could be the small print next to the pictures, as well as the lines in quotation marks.

Assign the lines that look like this *to a narrator.*

Lines **that look like this** *could be performed by a chorus of students. The chorus should add their own comments about Iktomi since this is the way Iktomi stories are actually told by the Plains Indians.*

Practice reading the lines smoothly. Then give your reading for your classmates.

Paul Goble

Over thirty years ago, long before Paul Goble began writing, he heard his first Iktomi story. It was during a visit to Pine Ridge, South Dakota, that Goble sat and listened to Edgar Red Cloud, great-grandson of the famous Chief Red Cloud, tell Iktomi stories. "I was watching and listening to storytelling in a truly ancient oral tradition," Goble says.

Today, when working on an Iktomi book, Goble can almost hear Red Cloud's voice and see his expressive hand movements and twinkling eyes. Goble tries to capture these things in his books.

Goble has retold and illustrated many Native American legends, including these other books about the trickster, Iktomi: *Iktomi and the Buffalo Skull*, *Iktomi and the Berries*, and *Iktomi and the Ducks*.

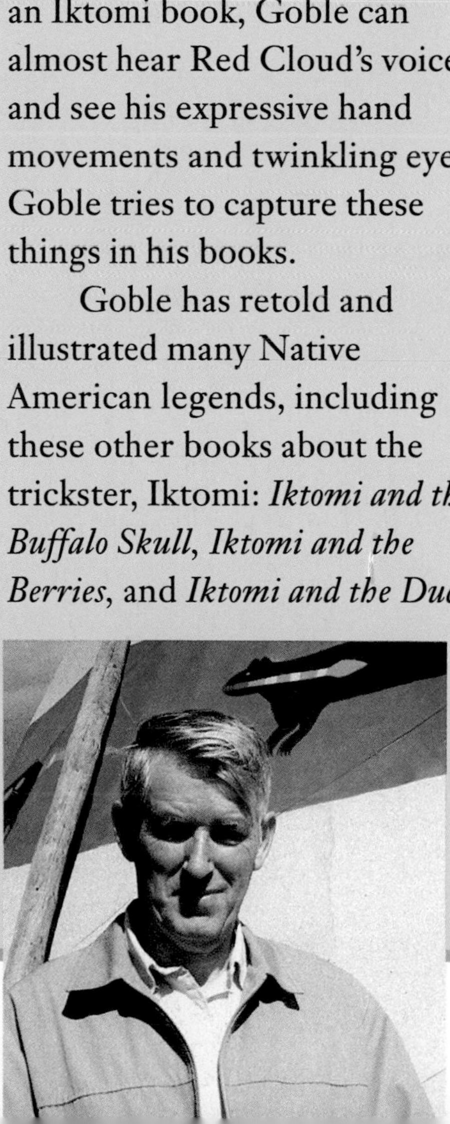

POOR OLD LION

Poor old lion,
Lyin' in his den.
Never goin' huntin'
In the jungle again.
Poor old lion,
Lyin' there sick.
If you want to see him,
Better see him quick.

Here come the animals,
Payin' a call.
How does he thank 'em?
By eatin' 'em all!

When he's finished,
What's he done?
Eaten his callers,
One by one.

Poor old lion,
Lyin' on some rocks.
Out in the sunlight
Stands Mister Fox.
"Hey, Mister Lion,
You're lookin' mighty thin."
"Yes, Mister Fox.
Won't you step right in?"

"No thanks, Mister Lion.
I'm stayin' right here.
You might feel ill,
But the message is clear.
That you're still a danger,
I have no doubt.
I see tracks goin' in,
But none comin' out!"

from Aesop's Fables
retold by Tom Paxton
illustrated by Robert Rayevsky

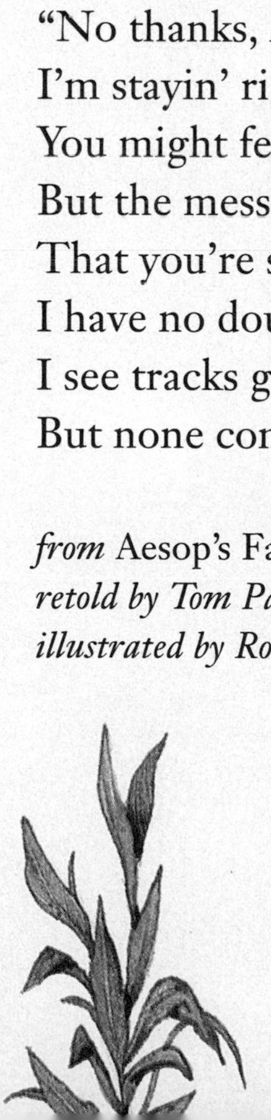

Award Winner

DONKEY

Oh, he likes us, he's our friend
that's why he lets us pretend
we're going for a donkey ride
but all the time he knows inside
that he's not going anywhere
he's just going to stand right there
he says as much in donkey talk,
"Hee-haw, when you get down, I'll walk.
I don't take passengers or freight,
I only carry my own weight."
Still we like to play this game
and we love him just the same
even though he'll stand right there
and never take us anywhere

written by Eloise Greenfield
illustrated by Amos Ferguson

PAINT BY MR AMOS 1969
FERGUSON

The Sign in Mendel's Window

by Mildred Phillips
illustrated by Margot Zemach

They called Kosnov a town. It was like calling a puddle a pond, a leaf a bush, a branch a tree. The whole town of Kosnov was no more than a dozen old wooden buildings huddled close, each leaning on its neighbor for support, just as the people who lived and worked in them did.

So when Mendel the butcher put the sign in the front window of his shop, the whole town came out to ask: Had Mendel and Molly struck it rich? Had fortune come knocking on their door? Why was the butcher shop FOR RENT? Goodness, could Mendel or Molly be sick?

"So many questions," Mendel said. "If only questions were zloty! Then we wouldn't have to rent out *half* the butcher shop!"

It wasn't a sudden gust of wind from the north that swept Mendel's hat off his head. It was the sigh of relief from his dear friends in Kosnov. Mendel and Molly were not leaving, and only half the shop would be rented.

Roshana the wigmaker kissed Tempkin the candlemaker, who hugged Simka the shoemaker, who hugged Mendel's wife, Molly, who, brushing away a joyful tear from her cheek, whispered to Mendel, "If only kisses and hugs could fatten the calf and buy feed for the chickens."

Mendel smiled. "Then, again, there'd be no need to rent, and we wouldn't be getting these kisses and hugs."

The new wall dividing the butcher shop was made by Molly from two old bed sheets sewn down the middle, bleached white until they dazzled and starched so stiff they stood straight up like a board. Tacked to the ceiling and tacked to the floor, the wall was better than perfect, Mendel said. It didn't even have to be painted.

For many weeks, the sign sat in the window. Then one day, late in the afternoon, a gentleman came into town and stopped in front of the butcher shop window. He was wearing a wide-brimmed black felt hat trimmed with fur and a fine cloth coat. Mendel went to the door.

"Mr. Butcher," said the stranger, tipping his hat, "you are looking at a very lucky man. After traveling so far, I was worried indeed that upon arriving I would find your shop already rented."

Not often, thought Mendel, did such an eloquent and prosperous-looking gentleman come to Kosnov. Mendel was impressed. "And who is to say which of us is the luckier, Mr. . . . ?"

"Tinker. Tinker is my name."

"Come in, Mr. Tinker. Put down your bag and rest your feet."

Tinker entered and sat down on a wooden stool. Stroking his thick, black beard, he spoke. "I heard by word of mouth from an old acquaintance of a distant cousin's uncle in the city — may

he rest in peace — that in this charming town there was a place for rent, a quiet room just right for my kind of work."

"Which is?" asked Mendel.

"I'm a thinker, Mr. Butcher. Tinker the thinker, a simple man with simple needs. For a humble meal and a place where I can think, I will gladly pay a week's rent in advance."

"Come take a look," Mendel said, leading the way out to a side door that opened directly into the new space. He stepped aside, saying, "Judge for yourself."

Moments later, Tinker returned. "It's a deal," he said as he paid the rent. Delighted, Mendel shook the gentleman's hand and wished him good night.

Soon it would be dark, for the sun was about to set. If only Molly weren't spending the night in Glitnik with her cousin. Mendel felt that if he didn't share the news, he would burst. He decided to drop in on Simka.

"Come in, landlord," Simka said jokingly.

"Already you know?" asked Mendel.

"Why else would a stranger stop right in front of the sign in your window? And why else would you be looking so pleased? So sit, Mendel, and tell me all about your new tenant."

While Simka worked on a pair of boots, Mendel gave an exact account of the meeting. "Imagine, Simka, so splendidly dressed and yet so humble, asking for nothing more than a place to work. Surely some divine providence has sent this great man to Molly and me."

Simka looked up. "Be careful," he warned. "Though it has only five letters, 'great' is a very big word. . . . You'll stay for supper? Don't worry, there's plenty."

Mendel felt very good.

What a busy week it was for Molly and Mendel in the shop. And with so many neighbors coming to welcome him, Tinker had little time in the day to do his work. But not once did he complain.

"A better tenant we couldn't have asked for," said Molly that Friday.

Late that day, as every Friday before the Sabbath began, Mendel was in his shop doing the books. It was his habit to count his weekly earnings aloud, dropping the coins one by one into a small wooden box that he kept on the shelf. So as not to disturb Tinker, he began in a whisper: "Five groszy, ten groszy, fifty groszy, one zloty, one zloty twenty, one zloty forty, two zloty — "

"Mendel, my friend," called Tinker, "you don't have to whisper. I enjoy the sound of your voice."

So Mendel counted louder: "Forty zloty seventy-one, forty zloty seventy-two, forty zloty and seventy-three groszy. That does it!"

"Your voice is like music to my ears," said Tinker. "Just once more!"

Flattered, Mendel counted again, this time chanting in his finest tenor voice. Still humming, he closed the box and put it on the shelf.

"I am thinking," called Tinker, "that I will go to the city for the weekend. May I borrow your horse?"

"Go in good health," said Mendel. "I will see you on Monday."

"First thing," answered Tinker. "First thing."

Just after sunrise on Monday morning, as Mendel was taking a few deep knee-bends in front of the window, he saw that his horse was back from the city, tied to the front post. But what were two other horses doing beside it?

Mendel dressed and went downstairs to his shop. Waiting for him there were not only Tinker but two uniformed policemen from the city, as well.

"Arrest that man!" shouted Tinker. "He is the man who stole my money, and the proof lies in that wooden box on the shelf. And in that wooden box are exactly forty zloty and seventy-three groszy. Count it, gentlemen. If it be so, then without a doubt the money is mine!"

Stunned and speechless, Mendel stared at a small hole in the partition, two inches from the floor. Not big enough for a mouse to get through, the hole was ample for a rat to get an eyeful.

Molly, awakened by all the commotion, rushed downstairs still in her nightgown. "Am I dreaming a nightmare?" she cried out. "What are you up to?"

"Forty zloty and seventy-three groszy," answered a policeman as he counted the last coin. "This proves without a doubt that your husband is a thief."

Molly laughed. "Mendel a thief? My Mendel is so honest that he wouldn't steal another man's joke. Mendel, darling, what happened?"

Mendel told her. "It hurts in my heart to know that I was fooled by fancy manners."

Just then, Simka's face appeared at the window. Molly rushed to open the door.

"I was worried that Mendel should go barefoot," said Simka, peering inside, "so I brought him his shoes, as good as new."

"In jail it doesn't matter," cried Molly. "Come in, Simka, and say good-bye."

"Are you going somewhere?"

"Not me, Simka. Him!"

Poor Mendel. A pair of handcuffs had been slapped on his wrists. "Mr. Policemen," cried Simka, "I am a senior citizen of Kosnov, and I demand to know what is going on!"

As the story unfolded, Simka nodded. "I'm a little deaf in my left ear," he said, "but from what I just heard it is perfectly clear that *Tinker* is the scoundrel."

"And where is your proof?" shouted Tinker.

Simka smiled. He whispered to the policemen, and one of them quickly left the shop.

Outside a crowd had gathered, as had dark clouds overhead. Simka paced the floor.

It felt like an hour, but it was only a matter of minutes before the policeman returned with his report. "How you knew about the money is a mystery," he said to Simka. "And, just as you said, everyone I questioned up and down the street also knew, exactly to the groszy, how much was in the wooden box. How is this possible?"

“I have the answer,” said Tinker abruptly. “If a man is a thief, then why not a braggart, too?”

“I am not a judge,” said the policeman. “We will have to take this case to the city!”

“Hold it!” Molly yelled. She flung open the door and called to her neighbors, “Get me a potful of scalding hot water!”

When this was done, Molly dumped all the coins from the wooden box into the water. Had Molly gone mad? What was she making?

Molly chuckled. "Groszy soup. And while it is cooking, I have three questions for Mr. Tinker.

"First," she began, "if you were a painter, what would be on your hands?"

"Paint, of course," answered Tinker.

"Second question. If you were a potter, would there be paint on your hands?"

"The answer to your foolish question is no! There'd be clay on my hands."

"Now let's say that you were a butcher. A customer just paid for his chicken. You took the coins and maybe put them in your pocket. My question is, would the coins be covered with clay?"

Tinker snickered. "If I were a butcher, the coins would be covered with — "

He looked into the pot. Skimming the surface, coating the water was a pale thin layer of fat. It had risen from the coins that lay on the bottom.

"A little fat?" Molly asked.

"A little fat," muttered Tinker.

As the handcuffs closed around his wrists, Tinker turned to Simka. "How *did* everyone know how much money was in the box?"

"Simple," said Simka. "Only a stranger like you wouldn't know that when our Mendel sings in his finest tenor voice, not only can everyone hear him, but we all stop to listen."

Tinker shrugged, and with a deep sigh he said, "I think I made a few mistakes. The biggest was coming to a little town like Kosnov."

At that, the whole town cheered. Yes, the whole town. Did you know that the town of Kosnov was so small that when Roshana the wigmaker sneezed, Mishkin the tailor said "God bless you" — though he lived a dozen doors away?

WELCOME TO KOSNOV

Where's the best place to spend your groszy in Kosnov? Kosnov may be a small town, but there's a lot to see and do there. Make a guidebook for people who want to visit Kosnov. Include places to shop, eat, and visit. Start with what you know from the story. You may want to draw a few pictures for your guidebook.

Author

Mildred Phillips

Phillips feeding lambs on her farm

Author Mildred Phillips is a busy woman. Writer, painter, sculptor, and even farmer, she has written a number of books for children, including *Maxie*, *I Wonder if Herbie's Home Yet*, and *Goodbye, Kitchen*. In college, she studied painting and sculpture. For a time she even put her artistic training to work at Macy's Department Store doing window displays.

Phillips lives in an 1820's farmhouse with "a big red barn and twenty-five acres, and lots of animals!"

Margot Zemach

Margot Zemach once thought she would be a "serious" artist. Maybe people would walk through museums where her paintings were hanging and say, "Hmmmmmmm" under their breath.

Yet no matter how hard Zemach tried to be serious, her work always made people smile. So she gave up trying to be serious.

"Humor is the most important thing to me — it's what I'm thinking about," she once said. "If I can make it beautiful too — so much the better."

Zemach earned many awards for her work, including the Caldecott Medal for *Duffy and the Devil* and Caldecott Honors for *The Judge* and *It Could Always Be Worse*.

An illustration from
Self Portrait: Margot Zemach

Match Wits

Flossie & the Fox
by Patricia C. McKissack
Flossie Finley has been warned to look out for that fast-talking slickster, Fox. Maybe Fox should have been warned to watch out for clever little Flossie instead.

The Gold Coin
by Alma Flor Ada
When a thief attempts to steal a gold coin from kindly Doña Josefa, he learns an invaluable lesson about the real treasures in life.

The Two Foolish Cats
by Yoshiko Uchida
Big Daizo and Little Suki are two silly cats. They're also greedy and stubborn. Mr. Monkey is sure going to have some fun with them.

with these Books

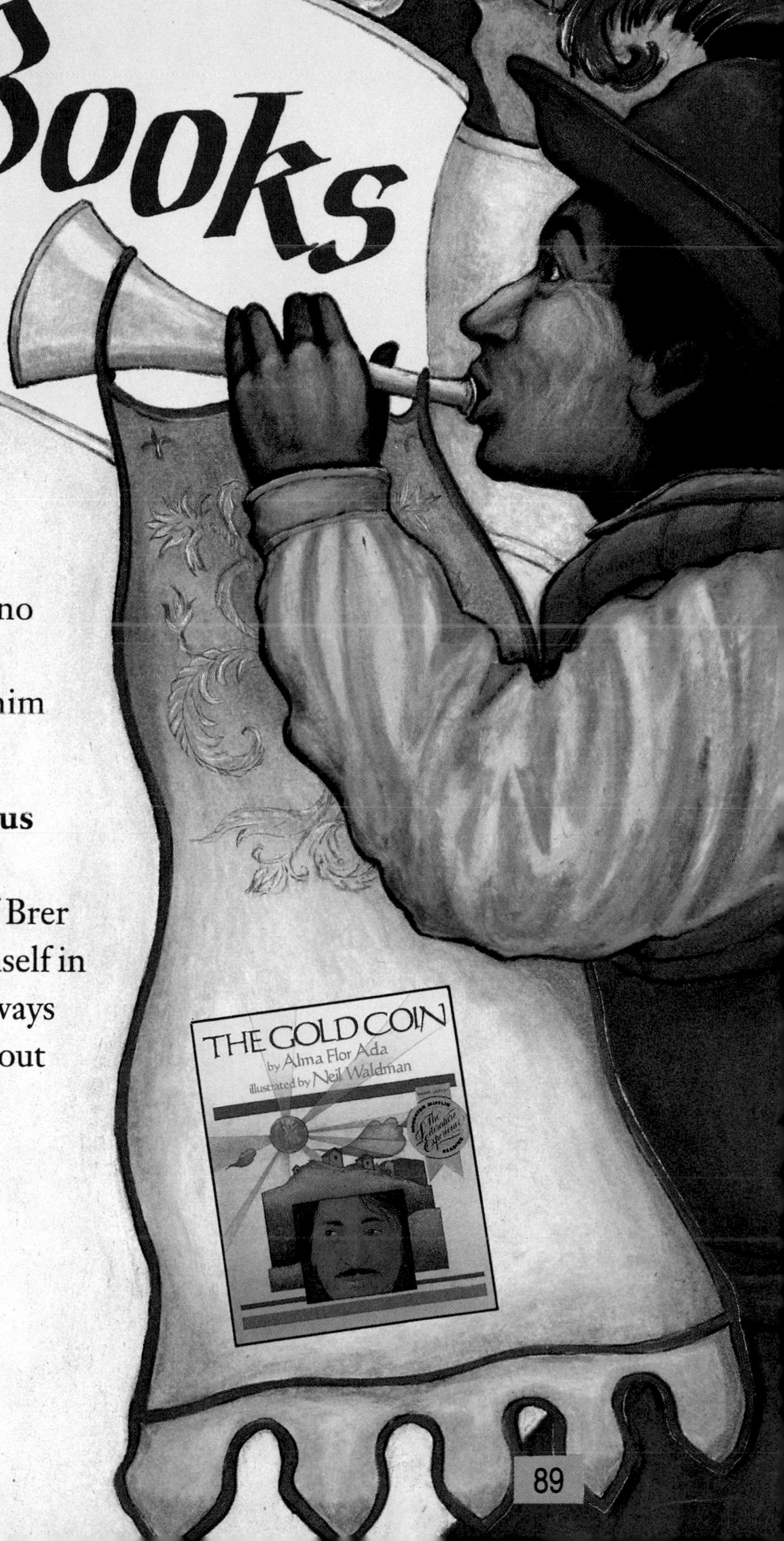

Brother Anansi and the Cattle Ranch
told by James de Sauza
Poor Brother Tiger. He's no match for Brother Anansi's grand schemes to swindle him out of his cattle.

The Tales of Uncle Remus
as told by Julius Lester
These are the adventures of Brer Rabbit, who often finds himself in sticky situations but who always manages to wriggle his way out of them.

NONFICTION

THEME 2

THEY WALKED THE EARTH

GASP...
AT
PREHISTORIC
ANIMALS
SO
ENORMOUS
you won't believe your
EYES
MARVEL...
at some of the
FIERCEST
MEANEST
STRANGEST
CREATURES
that ever lived!
SEE...
AMAZING
CREATURES
that actually
LIVED
millions of years ago!

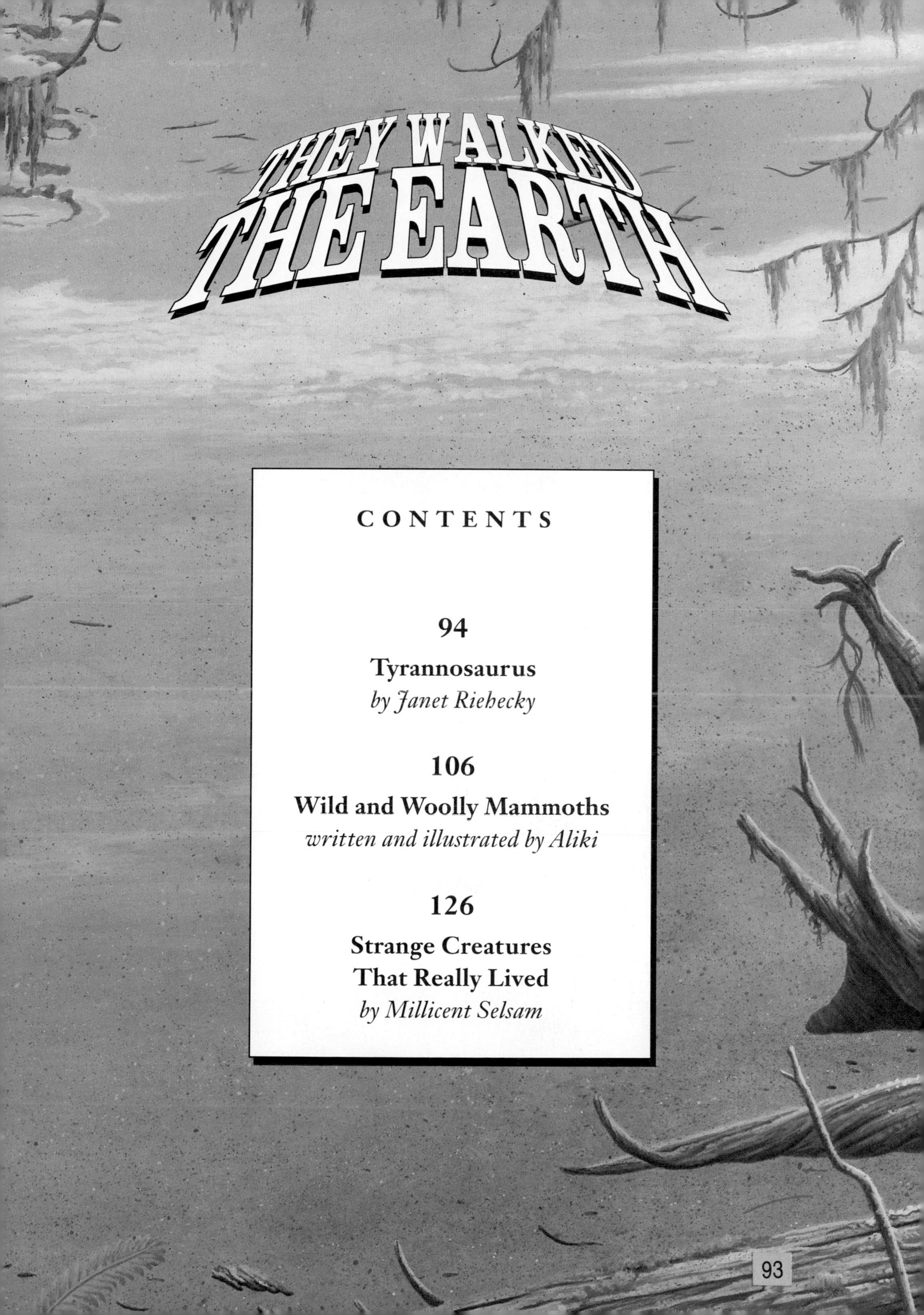

THEY WALKED THE EARTH

CONTENTS

TYRANNOSAURUS

BY JANET RIEHECKY

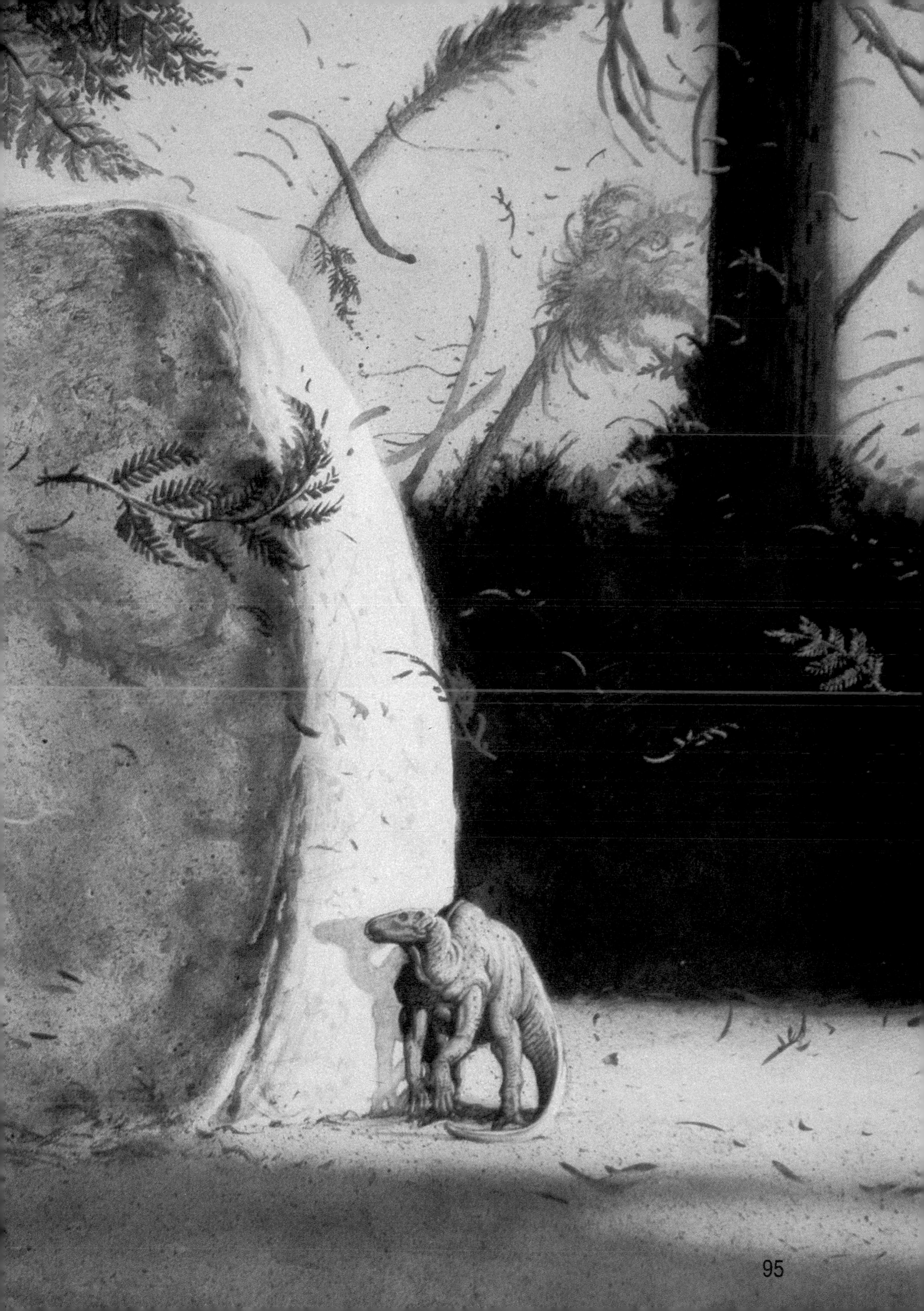

Before people lived on the earth, dinosaurs roamed the world.

It was a dangerous world then. But dinosaurs had many ways to protect themselves.

Some were small and fleet-footed. When trouble came, they just ran away.

Some were too big to be able to move quickly. When trouble came near them, they just moved together and formed a wall.

Others were protected by armor on their bodies. Animals that tried to bite an armored body might end up breaking their teeth.

Still others used parts of their bodies as weapons. They used the horns on their heads or clubs on their tails against enemies.

But there was one kind of dinosaur that didn't care what the other dinosaurs did to protect themselves — it would get them anyway! That dinosaur was the Tyrannosaurus!

The Tyrannosaurus (ti-ran-o-SAWR-us), whose name means "tyrant lizard," was the biggest meat eater ever to live on the earth. There were dinosaurs that grew bigger than the Tyrannosaurus, but they were gentle plant eaters. There was nothing gentle about Tyrannosaurus!

The Tyrannosaurus could grow twenty feet tall (that's more than three times as tall as your father), fifty feet long (that's longer than a city bus), and weighed more than seven tons (that's 14,000 pounds!). And every bit of the Tyrannosaurus was designed for hunting.

The Tyrannosaurus walked on its two back legs, towering over the countryside. Those legs were very strong. Some scientists think they were strong enough to let the Tyrannosaurus chase its prey at speeds as fast as 30 miles per hour — at least for a short distance. And then when Tyrannosaurus caught its prey, the three sharp claws on each foot became fearsome weapons!

Even more frightening, though, were the teeth of the Tyrannosaurus. They were three to six inches long with very sharp edges. Some scientists think the Tyrannosaurus killed its prey by just running at it with its mouth open and those awful teeth sticking out. This would save time. When the two would collide, the Tyrannosaurus would already have its first mouthful!

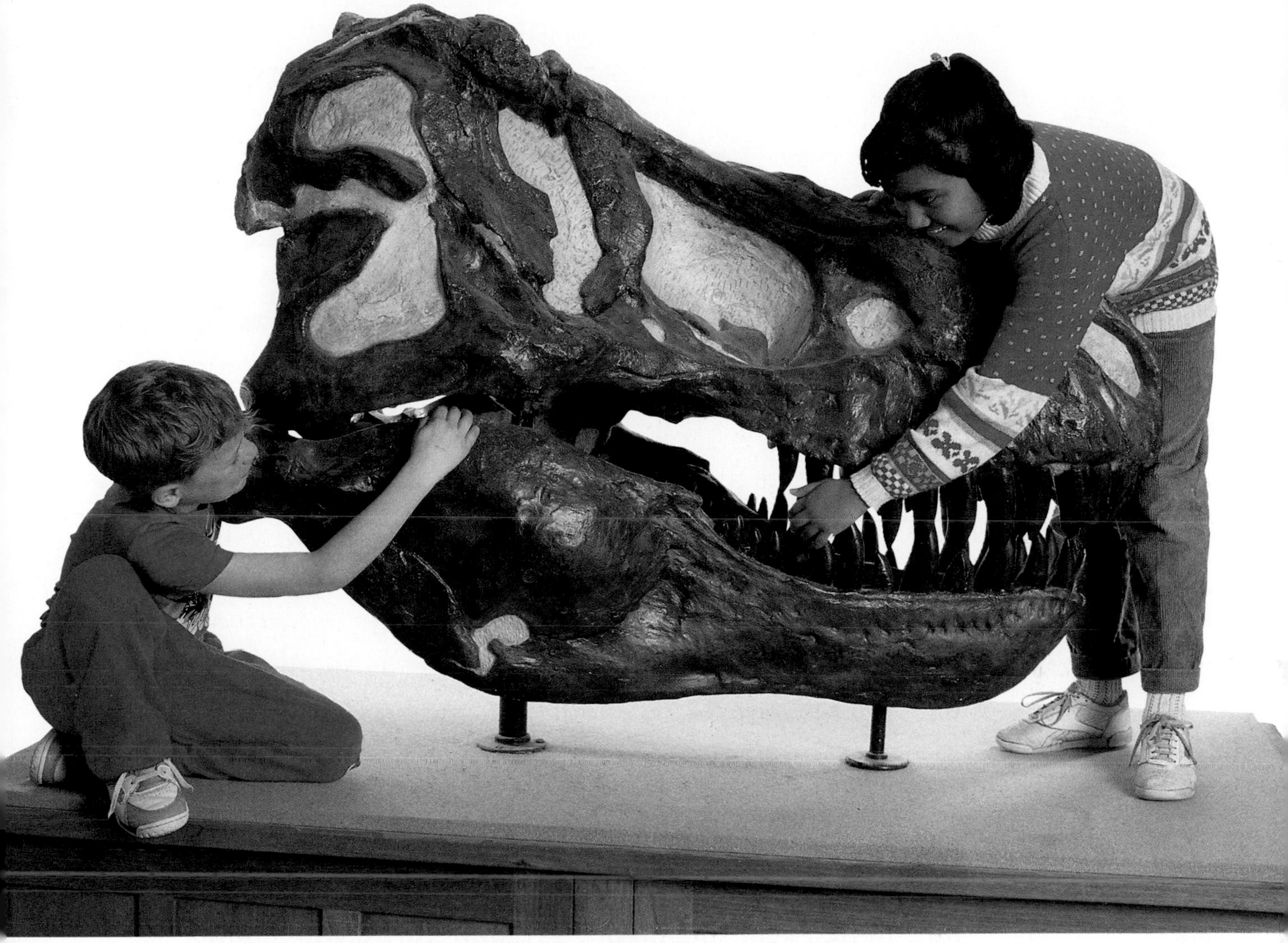

The Tyrannosaurus' big head also contained a fairly big brain — bigger than a human brain. But that didn't mean that the Tyrannosaurus was as smart as a person. Only a small part of that brain was for thinking (probably about its next meal). Most of the brain controlled how the Tyrannosaurus could see and smell (the better to track down its next meal!).

It would seem that a dinosaur like the Tyrannosaurus couldn't have a problem at all. But it did — a very strange problem. Scientists think that if the Tyrannosaurus lay down, it had trouble getting back up. And this was a dinosaur who couldn't wait to get up in the morning — for breakfast!

The Tyrannosaurus' arms were much too small and weak to push itself up. In fact, scientists wondered for years why the Tyrannosaurus even had those little-bitty arms — they weren't even long enough to reach the Tyrannosaurus' mouth.

Then one scientist suggested what those arms might have been used for. Each hand had two fingers with long claws. If the Tyrannosaurus dug those claws into the ground, they would keep it from slipping. Then it could use its strong back legs to lift its body.

We don't know if this is true or not, but it might be that those tiny arms were all that kept the mighty Tyrannosaurus from falling on its nose.

Not much is known about the family life of the Tyrannosaurus. The tracks that have been found suggest that most Tyrannosaurs traveled alone or in pairs. Apparently, they didn't like each other any more than the other dinosaurs liked them.

They probably laid eggs, but scientists don't know if the mothers took care of the babies when they hatched or just left the babies to take care of themselves.

Scientists continue to study the Tyrannosaurus, hoping to find the answers to these and other questions.

The Tyrannosaurus was one of the last of the dinosaurs to die, but it died out just as all the other dinosaurs did 65 million years ago.

Scientists don't know whether a sudden catastrophe killed all the dinosaurs, or whether they just gradually died off.

It could be that a terrible disease spread through the world. Or that the food supply disappeared. Or that the earth became too hot or too cold for dinosaurs to live. We may never know for sure.

But perhaps it's just as well the Tyrannosaurus isn't around today. It would make today's world a dangerous place for people.

A Day in the Life of Tyrannosaurus

Pretend you could go back in time to observe a Tyrannosaurus "in the wild" for one day. Write notes on everything you might observe. Use what you have learned from reading this selection to describe the creature's day.

In the distance, I see a large reptile.

TYRANNOSAURUS

Tyrannosaurus was a beast
that had no friends, to say the least.
It ruled the ancient out-of-doors,
and slaughtered other dinosaurs.

Jack Prelutsky

DINOSAURS LIVE *again*

If you ever visit the Smithsonian in Washington, D.C., be sure to go to the dinosaur hall in the National Museum of Natural History.

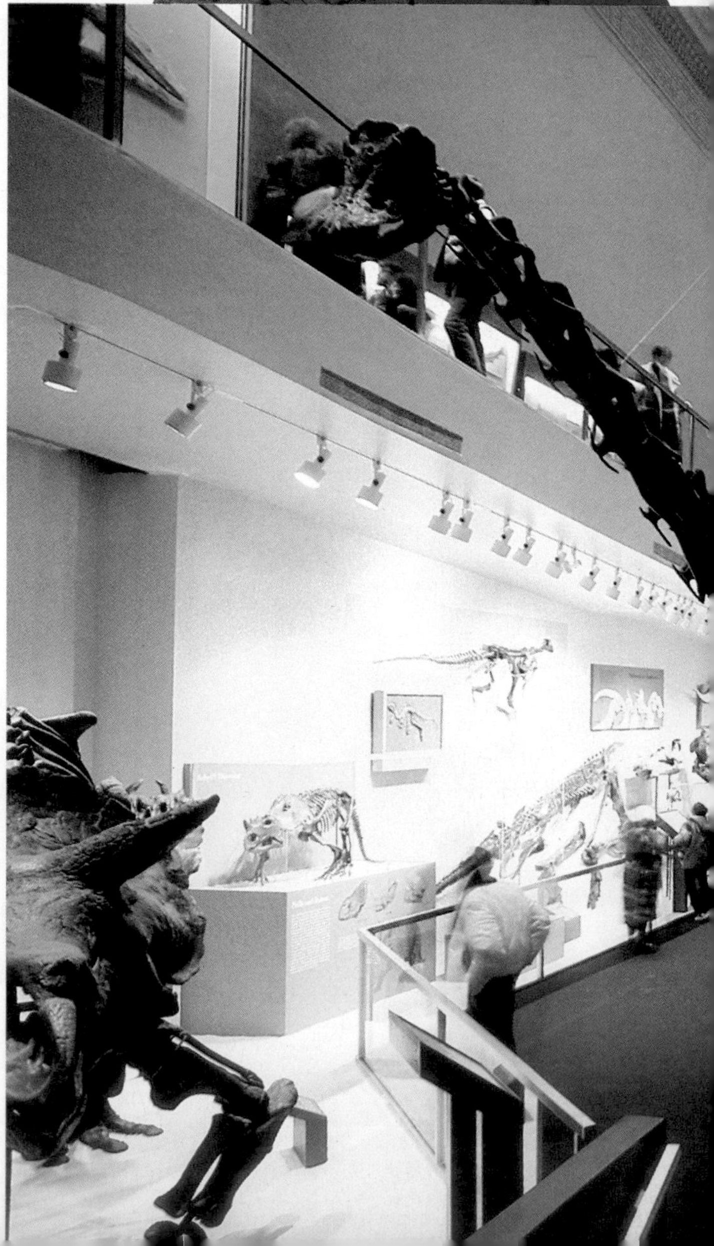

The hall has more than twenty dinosaur skeletons, as well as skeletons of other prehistoric reptiles. Most of the skeletons are built from real fossils, but some are made of plaster. You will see a giant pterosaur overhead, perhaps the largest animal that ever flew.

The skeletons look so real that one young visitor said, "I wonder if the dinosaurs come to life at night?"

skeleton of a Tyrannosaurus rex

Wild and Woolly Mammoths

written and illustrated by Aliki

Thousands of years ago, a wild and woolly beast roamed the northern part of the earth. It had two great, curved tusks and a long, hairy trunk. Its big bones were covered with tough skin and soft fur. The long hair on its humped back reached almost to the ground. It looked like an elephant, but it was not quite as big. It was a woolly mammoth.

Hundreds of woolly mammoths lived during the last Ice Age. Long before then, much of the earth was warm and partly swampy. That was when the dinosaurs lived.

Slowly, the earth grew cold. Some places in the north were so cold the snow never melted. It formed into great rivers of ice called glaciers.

Many animals died out because of the cold. That is probably what happened to the dinosaurs. Other animals did not die out, but went south, where it was warmer. Still others stayed in the cold north.

Some of the animals which lived during the Ice Age.

Many animals of the Ice Age grew heavy coats of hair. The hair protected them from the cold. The woolly mammoth was one of these. It lived in what is now Europe, and in China, Siberia, and Alaska.

The Columbian mammoth lived in a warmer climate, too. It traveled from Asia to Europe, and to parts of America.

Sometimes it is called the Jeffersonian mammoth. It was named after Thomas Jefferson, who was president when one was discovered in the United States. President Jefferson was interested in the past. He encouraged scientists to find out more about it.

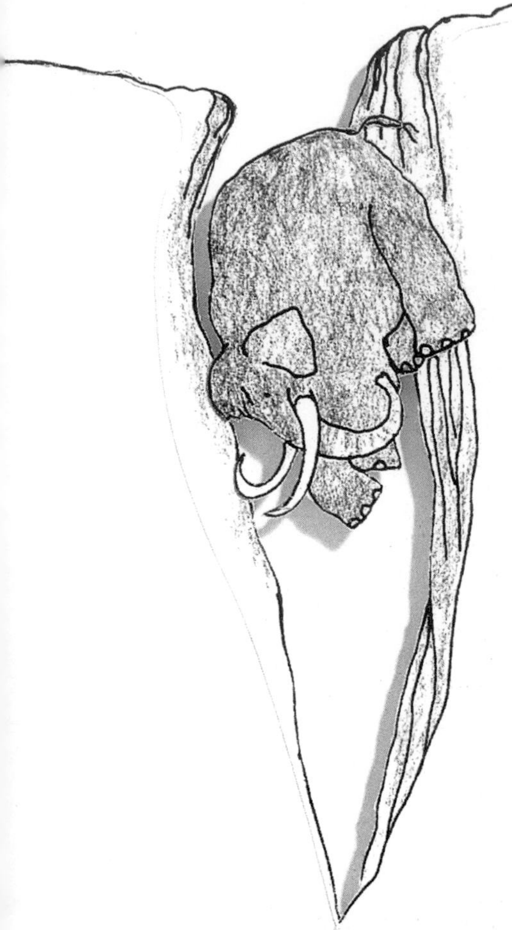

One day, a woolly mammoth fell into a deep crack in a glacier. It broke some bones and died. Snow and ice covered its body.

Thousands of years passed. Slowly the weather grew warmer again. The Ice Age ended. Ice began to melt.

In 1900, the mammoth's body was discovered in Siberia. Part of it was showing above the ice. Men passing by noticed their dogs sniffing the rotting flesh.

Scientists uncovered the body. Most of it was still frozen. That part was perfectly fresh. Dogs ate some of the meat, and liked it, even though it was more than 10,000 years old.

The food the mammoth had eaten before it died was still in its stomach. And what food! There were about thirty pounds of flowers, pine needles, moss, and pine cones.

Now scientists know a great deal about this ancient animal, even though the last one died thousands of years ago. Scientists found more frozen woolly mammoths. They found other kinds of mammoths, too.

The first Imperial mammoths lived 2 million years before the woolly mammoths. At first the Imperial mammoths were about the size of a pony. But by the time of the woolly mammoths they had become the biggest mammoths of all.

Imperial mammoths were not hairy. They didn't need to be. They lived in the warmest parts of the world. They lived in giant forests. Their teeth were flat, like those of the woolly mammoth — perfect to grind and crush leaves and twigs.

Mammoths were mammals. All mammals are warm-blooded. They usually have hair. They have milk to nurse their young. Mice, bats, monkeys, bears, and whales are mammals. So are human beings.

Mammoths were the giant land mammals of their time. They roamed quietly in groups. Mammoths were peaceful plant eaters. They did not have to hunt other animals for food. But they had enemies. One was the fierce saber-toothed tiger.

There were other enemies, too. Man was the mammoth's greatest enemy. Inside dark, damp caves scientists found out how important the mammoth was to early man. They discovered paintings of mammoths on cave walls.

These are some of the things found in caves in France.

Bone knife carved with bison and plants.

Woolly mammoth carved in stone

They found clay figures and bone carvings of mammoths and other animals. They knew no animal made them. They were made by early people who lived in the caves. They were made in the days of the mammoth hunters, more than 25,000 years ago. These hunters used tools made of stone, so we call their time the Stone Age.

A whole Stone Age village was found in Czechoslovakia and dug up. Archaeologists, who are scientists who study ancient ruins, learned a lot from this village and others like it. They learned more about mammoth hunters and how they lived.

This is what they found out. Mammoth hunters left the caves where they lived in the winter. In the spring they moved to river valleys where herds of mammoths roamed. They made tents in the valleys to be near the mammoths.

The mammoth hunters made knives and other tools of stone. They used wooden spears with sharp stone points to kill the mammoths. But first they had to trap them. Sometimes the hunters made fires around the herds. Then they forced the frightened mammoths down steep cliffs.

Other hunters waited at the bottom to kill the mammoths with their spears.

Sometimes the mammoth hunters dug deep pits. They covered the pits with branches and earth.

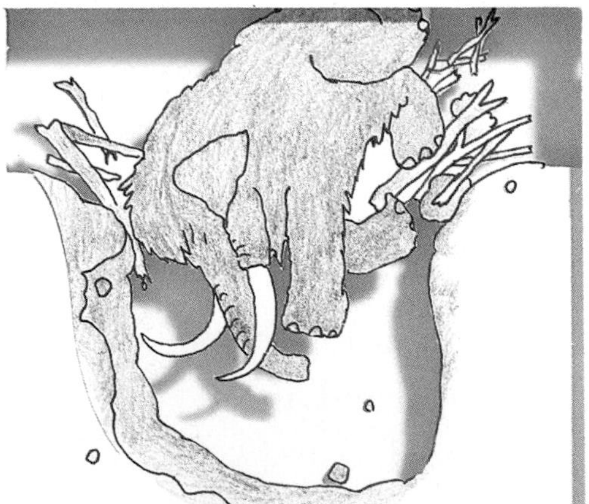

When a mammoth walked over the pit, the branches broke, and the mammoth fell in. It could not escape.

Hunters rolled heavy stones down on it and killed the trapped mammoth.

The hunters and their families ate the mammoth meat. They crushed the skulls and ate the brains. They used the bones to make tent frames. They used bones and tusks to make jewelry. They burned bones for fuel, too. But their skin was too tough for anything.

These people hunted other animals, too. The woolly rhinoceros and the giant sloth lived then. Today they are extinct. But bison, reindeer, horses, and foxes, which also lived then, have not died out.

Mammoths were hunted for a long time. There were plenty of them, and one mammoth was enough to feed many families.

Today there are no mammoths. Some people think it was the mammoth hunters who killed them all. Perhaps they died out when the climate grew too warm. No one knows. But not one live woolly mammoth has been seen for 11,000 years.

More Than One Way to Catch a Mammoth

There are more ways to catch a woolly mammoth than those in the selection. See if you can think of another way. Then draw a diagram that shows how your way works.

Digging In

A Contact Editor Joins a Fossil Hunt

By Curtis Slepian

KACHUNK! KACHUNK! As the sun beats down on the back of my neck, I slam my pick into the side of the hill. Kachunk! "There's gotta be a bone here somewhere," I think, wiping sweat out of my eyes. I slam the pick again. Kachunk! "When am I going to find some bones?"

I'm in Mexico digging for prehistoric fossils. I got the chance because of an organization called Earthwatch. They make it possible for ordinary people to help scientists do their work in the field. The field in this case is located in the central Mexican state of Guanajuato. And the people on the expedition are schoolteachers, a dental hygienist, and me, an editor from 3-2-1 CONTACT. What do we have in common? We want to find fossils but don't know how.

Luckily, two experts are in charge of our group: one is Oscar C. Castañeda, a researcher at the Autonomous University of Mexico. The other is Wade E. Miller, a professor at Brigham Young University in Utah.

Both men are paleontologists (say: pay-lee-on-TAL-o-jists). A paleontologist, says Castañeda, is a scientist who "looks for and describes the life of the past." The past life they study is so old, nothing remains of it except ancient bones — called fossils. Over millions of years, these bones have absorbed minerals in the ground and become hard.

With a sure touch, expedition leader Oscar Castañeda carefully unearths several bones.

A Painful Start

Our search for fossils begins with a ride to a ranch some four and a half hours north of Mexico City. Soon after arriving, Oscar sends us out to dig. On the walk to the dig area, I smell flowering cactus, hear the gobbling of wild turkeys, see red army ants — and twice step on mesquite needles so sharp they go right through my sneaker and into my foot. Not a great way to start.

The dig site is in a deep arroyo, a kind of dry river bed. With an icepick, I start to jab away at the steep side of the arroyo. Cutting away at the earth is easy because it is soft and crumbly. The fossils we are looking for are from mammals who lived four to five million years ago. If we had been looking for dinosaur bones, which are older, the ground would be more rocklike.

I dig for a while before it hits me — I don't really know what a fossil looks like. Before I started, I thought fossil-hunting would be a snap: After a little digging, I'd spot a bone sticking out of the ground — like the one a dog would bury in the yard, only bigger. I imagined that I'd make a major find in no time and everyone would pat me on the back.

But as I found out, it's a lot harder than that. For example, Peter, a science teacher from Massachusetts, spends a long time carefully digging what seems to be a giant white bone — maybe the leg bone of a mammoth, he hopes. Finally, Oscar comes over to see. "It's rock," he says, smashing into the "bone" with his pick. Oh, well.

And forget about pulling an entire skeleton out of the ground, or the head of a rhino, complete with horn. Actually, it's tough enough finding a single unbroken bone. Most of what we find are bone "fragments," which aren't very useful to scientists.

Paleontologists can't identify an animal from a fragment. But they can identify it from a single "complete" bone — a bone with at least one end intact. Oscar and Wade figure out an animal from one of its bones as easily as you can guess a soft drink brand from the shape of its bottle. But, says Wade, "It takes a long time to learn the skeletons of so many animals."

So in the hot afternoon sun, we Earthwatchers use picks, hammers and pickaxes to find complete bones. An hour later, I've found exactly . . . nothing. Ann, a retired schoolteacher from Chicago, is digging a few feet away. She's doing no better: "Where are the bones?" she cries in frustration.

Meanwhile, I believe I've made the discovery of the century. It's round and smooth and the size of my palm. To my inexpert eyes, it looks like the head of some ancient rabbit. "See," I tell Ann, "there's the rabbit's eye, and there's his nose, and there's his ear." I call over Gerardo, Oscar's assistant, to have a look. He just laughs. It's a rock, he says. So much for my major discovery of a prehistoric Bugs Bunny.

By the end of the first day, a few people have managed to get some small fossils. All I get is a bad case of sunburn.

That evening, after dinner (and after I've dumped a few tons of dirt from my sneakers), Oscar tells us that this part of Mexico is a great place to find fossils. Millions of years ago it had plenty of vegetation and water. Now-extinct bears, camels, saber-tooth tigers, lions, sloths and other animals made pit stops here while migrating between North and South America.

Since 1974, Oscar has been working these rich fossil deposits. He promises that we will find plenty of bones tomorrow. As I drift into sleep that night, I worry: What if I'm the only one who doesn't find a fossil?

The next day, we get up early and drive in two vans to another dig site, El Ocote. It is located in a high valley, an empty land where farmers use donkeys to plow corn fields.

Tools of the trade: Pick and brush expose a pink-colored fossil buried by time.

A Bone to Pick

Today I find my first fossil! Excitedly, I clear away about eight inches of the bone with my pick. But sometimes I dig too close to the bone, and part of it breaks off. And as I brush it to remove dust, the bone starts to flake apart.

I'm discovering something else about fossil-hunting: It's hard to find fossils, but once you do, it's easy to destroy them. The bones are very delicate. Often the slightest pressure will make them crumble to dust.

Oscar comes over and gives me a mini-lesson on how to properly uncover a fossil. "Dig above the fossil, not below," he says. "If you dig below, the ground holding the fossil might collapse, smashing the bone. Clear a layer so the bone sits on a 'flat table.'" Oscar takes a pick and like an artist digs around the edges of the fossil. "It's a rib," he finally decides, "but it's only a small piece of it. No good." At least I didn't ruin a good fossil.

Oscar gives me another spot. He points to the long tooth of an extinct horse sticking out of the ground. Because of the enamel in them, teeth are the best-preserved part of a skeleton. But this one isn't in top shape. So Oscar takes out a plastic container holding liquid glue and squirts the tooth. The glue should harden the bone. He tells me to "work all around the sides of the tooth, then get behind it and remove it."

Rubén, right, takes time off from goat-herding to go fossil hunting.

I guess I wouldn't make much of a dentist. When I pry out the tooth, it breaks into 20 parts. I'm glad to see that Oscar, working elsewhere, doesn't notice.

Late in the morning, the Earthwatchers find themselves surrounded by a dozen goats. The goatherd is a young boy named Rubén. He shyly watches us work. But his curiosity gets the better of him and he soon joins us. Sifting through earth broken from the sides of the gully, he helps find a huge mastodon tooth, a rhino tusk and the perfectly preserved molar of a peccary (a kind of pig). He's already done better than I have!

Fossils in a Jacket

After a lunch of cactus sandwiches (yes, cactus meat — it tastes great on a fresh tortilla), it's back to work. Gerardo uncovers a pretty big fossil — the jaws of a camel. He digs all around the bones, except under them. He is going to remove the fossil with a plaster "jacket." Delicate bones are usually taken out this way, so they won't break.

Much later, the plaster cast will be taken to a laboratory at Oscar's university. In the lab, the plaster and dirt are removed from the fossil. After the bones are hardened with resins and chemicals, they are catalogued and stored with fossils from the same area. Now Oscar and other scientists can study them whenever they wish.

Fossils like the ones we find allow scientists to figure out when these ancient animals lived. The fossils also help tell scientists what parts of the world the animals migrated to. Knowing all this, scientists can better figure out which prehistoric beasts are the ancestors of present-day animals.

Over the last few days, we haven't done badly: We've dug up a rare bird fossil, some camel jaws, a carnivore skull and assorted teeth. The next day we do even better. Well, Gerardo does.

He has discovered the tiny legs, hands and skull of some rodent. He isn't sure exactly what animal it is. Wade Miller looks at it for a while, then says: "It's a rabbit." A five-million-year-old rabbit! And unlike my rabbit-shaped rock, this ancient bunny is the real thing. It's an excellent find, says Dr. Miller, and we're all excited to have been part of it. In fact, we're pretty proud of the work we've done, considering we're just beginners.

I'm tired, dirty and sore from sunburn — but for the chance to know what a scientist goes through, for the thrill of discovery, it's all worth it. ◆

To make a fossil "jacket," Gerardo (top) first makes gooey plaster of Paris. Next, Oscar drenches burlap strips in the plaster, layering them over the fossil. He then coats them with more plaster. When the plaster dries, Oscar and Dr. Miller remove the cast from the earth. The many casts made during an expedition go to a university laboratory.

Award Winner

STRANGE CREATURES THAT REALLY LIVED

BY MILLICENT SELSAM

Strange animals have always lived on Earth. Some, like the dinosaurs, lived on land. Other queer animals lived in the sea. Some looked like fish, and some looked like lizards. Others looked like turtles with very long necks.

pteranodon

Strange-looking animals flew through the air, too. One of the largest of the flying animals was the *pteranodon* (ter-an-o-don). It looked like a huge bat with leathery wings. It could glide down from the sky and with its long bill snatch fish from the sea waves. It lived seventy million years ago.

Many other strange animals lived long ago. *Archelon* (ar-ka-lon) was the largest turtle that ever lived. It was twelve feet long — about the size of a car. It weighed six thousand pounds! It had a hooked beak and huge flippers. Its bones were found in South Dakota. Twenty-five million years ago, South Dakota was covered by water. Archelon lived in that inland sea.

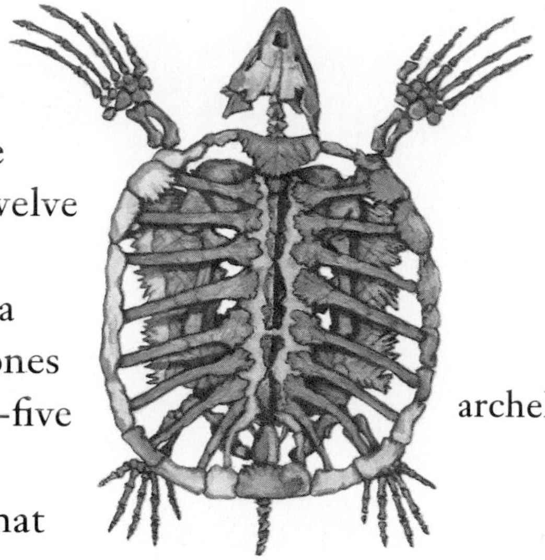

archelon

Here is another strange animal — a colossal crocodile (crok-o-dile) longer than a school bus! Two hundred million years ago, it roamed swamps and riverbanks all over the world. It snapped up any animal that came close to shore. The largest crocodiles today are dwarfs compared to the fifty-foot body of this animal.

crocodile

fossil of an
archaeopteryx

archaeopteryx

The *archaeopteryx* (ar-kay-op-ter-icks) looked like a small dinosaur with feathers. Scientists think it might have been the first bird ever to exist. It lived one hundred forty million years ago. It had a tail and rounded wings. It also had teeth in its jaws. No bird today has teeth. Did it fly? Did it glide from tree to tree? Scientists are not sure. Archaeopteryx may be the missing link between scaly reptiles and feathered birds.

Six horns on its head! Here is an animal as strange as any dinosaur. Its name was *uintatherium* (yoo-in-ta-ther-ee-um). It was about the size of an elephant. Its sharp teeth made it look scary, but scientists have discovered that it ate only plants. Sixty million years ago, it thundered over the plains of the American West.

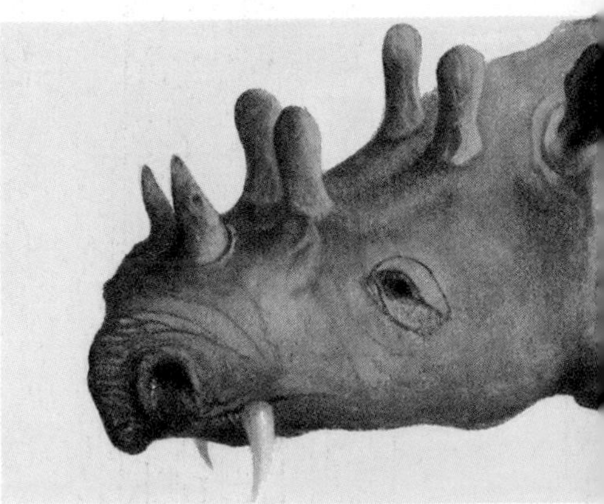

uintatherium

Huge animals once lived in South America. About one hundred years ago, a scientist named Charles Darwin found their bones. Other scientists put the bones together so they could see what these animals looked like.

One of these animals was a giant land *sloth* (slawth). It looked like a great hairy bear. It was as tall as a telephone pole. From its flat teeth, you can see that it ate plants. Scientists think it pushed over trees to get at the leaves in the upper branches. There are no such sloths alive in the world today. The last giant sloths died one million years ago. But we can find their relatives in Central and South America — the slow-moving sloths that hang upside down in the treetops there.

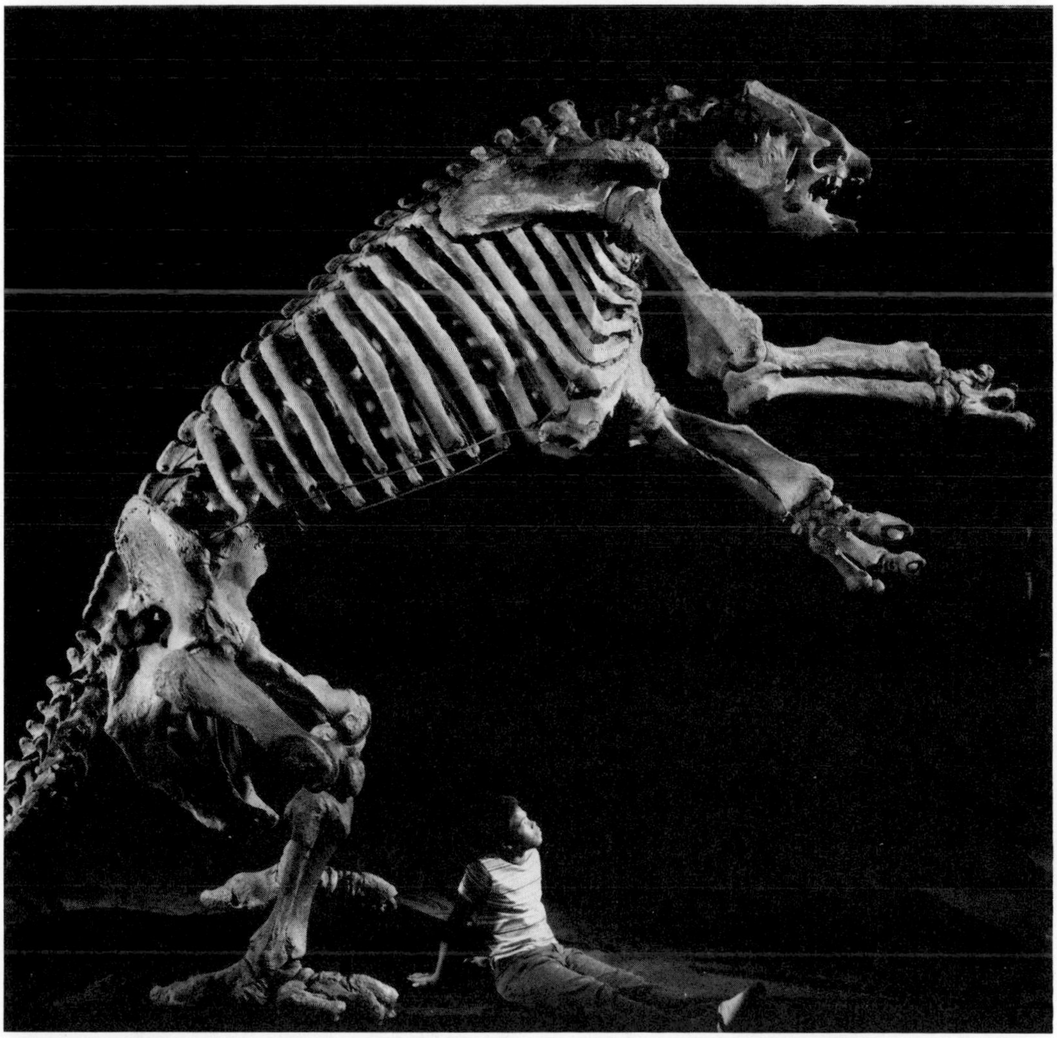

skeleton of a sloth

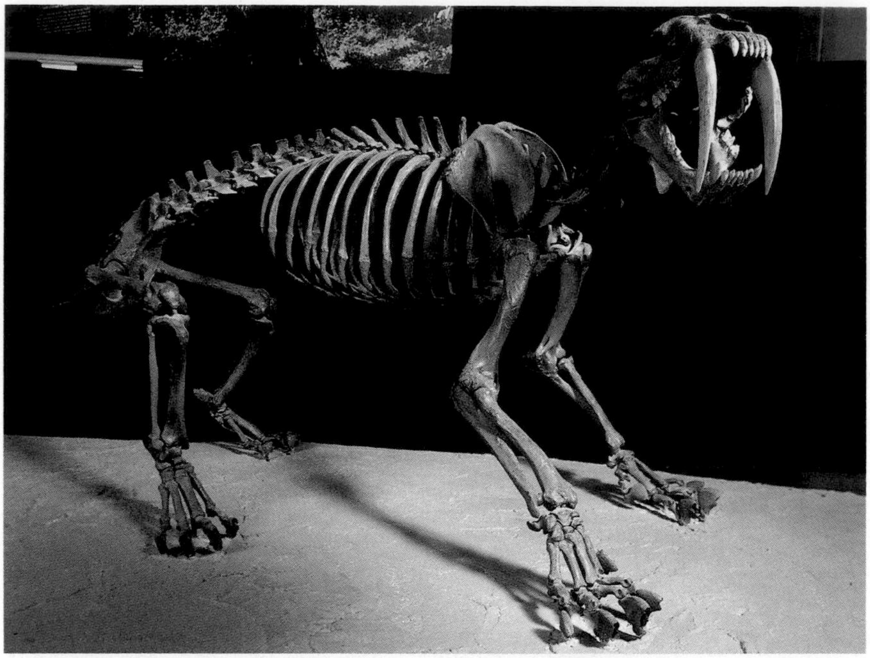

skeleton of a stabbing cat

This animal was called the "stabbing cat" because it had enormous teeth shaped like daggers. It used its teeth to stab and kill its prey. Fifty thousand years ago, many cats of this kind walked into tar pits and were trapped there. Their flesh decayed, but their bones remained. The bones of stabbing cats can still be seen in tar pits around the city of Los Angeles, California.

skull of a stabbing cat

aepycamelus

About twenty million years ago, there lived an animal called the *aepycamelus* (e-pe-ca-me-lus). It looked like a camel with a very long neck. No wonder it was called the "giraffe camel." Like the giraffe we know today, this camel fed on the leaves of trees. Did it have a hump? We don't know. Nothing is left that can give us an answer.

Three hundred million years ago, the land was covered with millions of insects. They lived in great swampy forests all over the earth. Some of them were no bigger than ants. But others were bigger than any insect that lives today. Huge roaches the size of a pencil ran on the forest floor. Giant-sized dragonflies flew overhead like kites.

In later times — forty to fifty million years ago — there were great pine forests. Sticky resin oozed from the cracks in the trees, and many small insects got caught in it. When the resin hardened, it turned into clear amber. When we look inside that amber today, the insects seem as though they might still be alive. But of course they are not.

gnat *preserved in clear amber*

In 1922, scientists went on an expedition to the Gobi Desert in Asia. There they found the bones of a giant animal that lived twenty to thirty million years ago. It looked like a rhinoceros without horns. Today all rhinoceroses have horns. It was called the *baluchitherium* (ba-loo-ki-ther-ee-um), or the "Beast of Baluchistan" (Ba-loo-ki-stan), because its bones were first found in Baluchistan, in what is now Pakistan.

It was the size of a small house. It measured thirty-four feet from nose to tail, and eighteen feet from the ground up. It traveled in herds across the plains of Asia. It was taller than a giraffe, but much heavier. Like a giraffe, it could reach the highest branches. It had only to stretch out its neck to eat twigs, leaves, and flowers twenty feet off the ground.

Just over three hundred years ago, there lived a funny-looking bird called the *dodo* (doh-doh). It was as big as a turkey. It waddled as it walked on short, stubby legs. Its curved beak was nine inches long. Its wings were so short that it could not fly. It lived on islands in the Indian Ocean. When ships stopped there, sailors killed the dodo for food. They left pigs, monkeys, and rats that ate up the dodo's eggs and their young. Now there are no dodos anywhere in the world.

dodo

All the animals in this book lived a long time ago. You cannot see them anywhere in the world today because they have died out. They are *extinct*. Right now, many kinds of animals are disappearing. Some of these animals may never be found again. They may also become extinct.

People spread over the land. They cut down forests. They build roads where only animals lived before. Soon there may be a time when we won't be able to see the animals we are looking at today. Only their skeletons will remain in museums. "What? No more elephants?" It may be, if we don't give them space to live alongside us.

Models of several extinct animals surround Iain Bishop at England's Tring Zoological Museum. He holds the one species still living — an endangered aye-aye from Madagascar.

1. Giant ground sloth 2. Aye–aye
3. Quagga 4. Moa 5. Passenger pigeon
6. Carolina parakeet 7. Tasmanian wolf
8. Toolach wallaby 9. Dodo
10. Great auk 11. Male heath hen
12. Female heath hen 13. Labrador duck

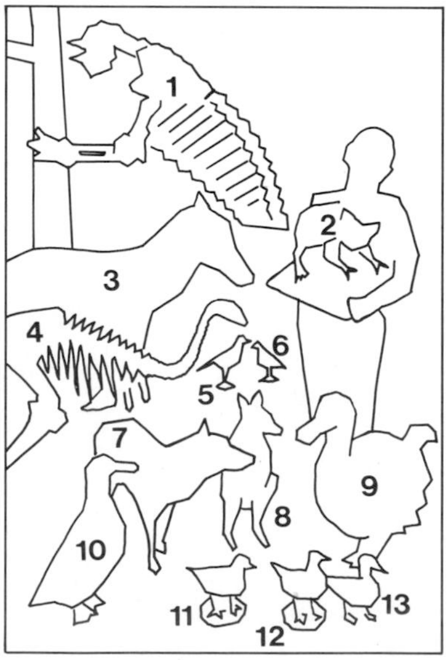

Save 'em, Trade 'em

The selection told you about strange animals. Choose five of them. With a partner, make up a set of Information Cards — one for each animal. Draw a picture of the animal on the front of the card and then write information about it on the back. Use the cards to test your knowledge.

Can you describe the creature?
Well... he looked like a huge leathery bat...

POEMS

The Mastodon

The mastodon
has traveled on
his only trace
a skeleton.

The north of Asia
his habitat;
then came the glacier
and that was that.

Michael Braude

Fossils

Older than
books,
than scrolls,

older
than the first
tales told

or the
first words
spoken

are the stories

in forests that
turned to
stone

in ice walls
that trapped the
mammoth

in the long
bones of
dinosaurs —

the fossil
stories that begin
Once upon a time

Lilian Moore

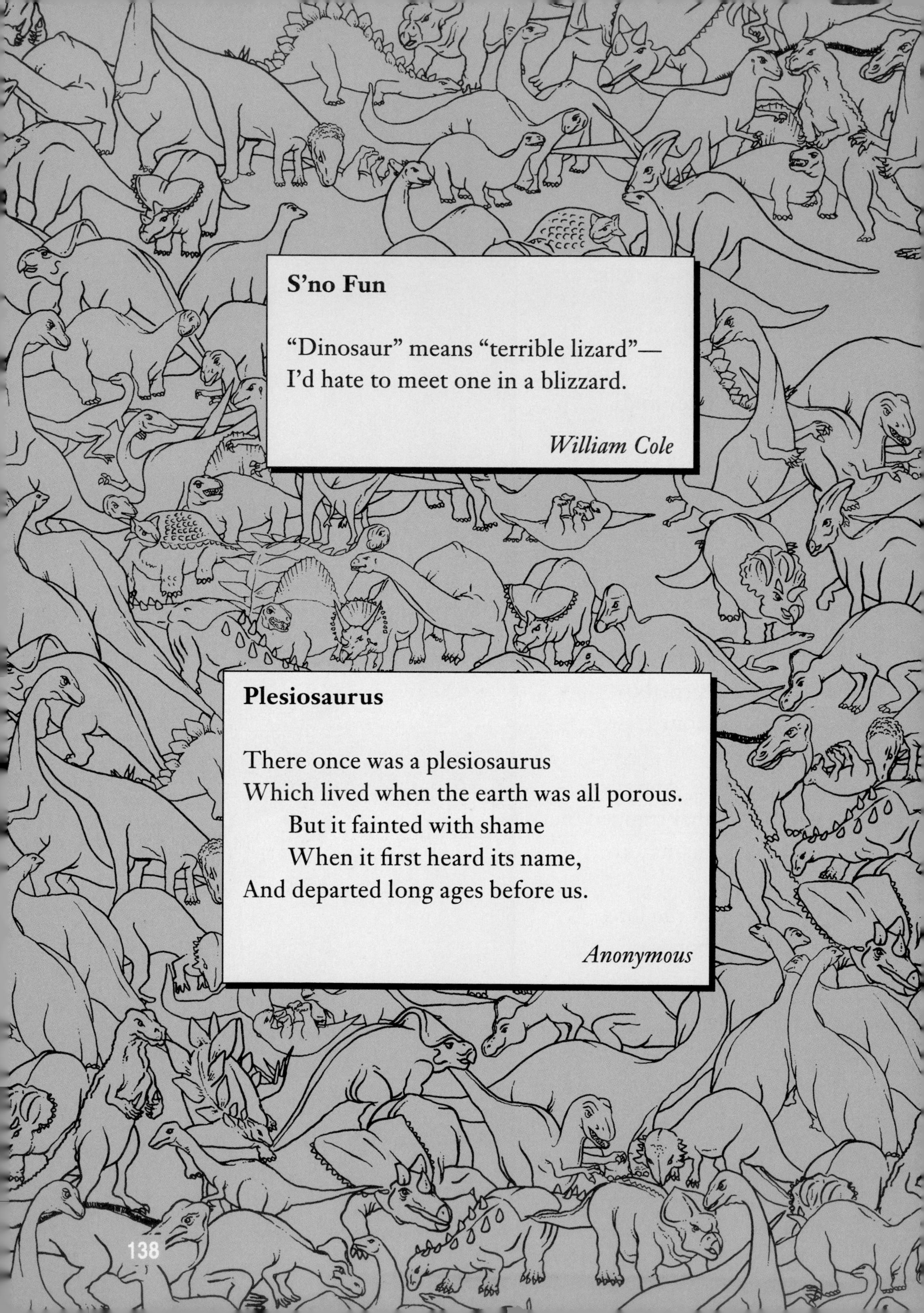

S'no Fun

"Dinosaur" means "terrible lizard"—
I'd hate to meet one in a blizzard.

William Cole

Plesiosaurus

There once was a plesiosaurus
Which lived when the earth was all porous.
    But it fainted with shame
    When it first heard its name,
And departed long ages before us.

Anonymous

What If . . .

What if . . .
You opened a book
About dinosaurs
And one stumbled out
And another and another
And more and more pour
Until the whole place
Is bumbling and rumbling
And groaning and moaning
And snoring and roaring
And dinosauring?

What if . . .
You tried to push them
Back inside
But they kept tromping
Off the pages instead?
Would you close the covers?

Isabel Joshlin Glaser

AUTHORS

Janet Riehecky

By age ten, Janet Riehecky had read all the children's books in her local library.

But reading is not her only interest. She has loved prehistoric animals since she saw museum exhibits of these giant, long-vanished animals when she was still a child. Riehecky decided then that someday she would write books about these creatures. Some of those books are *Ankylosaurus*, *Dinosaur Relatives*, and *Protoceratops*.

Aliki

When Aliki was five years old, one of her teachers predicted that she would become an artist. She did. She also became a writer. Aliki's full name is Aliki Brandenberg, but she uses only her first name when writing. Aliki's books are all about subjects that interest her very much. And, like many people, she is interested in dinosaurs. You might enjoy reading her books *Digging Up Dinosaurs* and *Fossils Tell of Long Ago*.

Millicent Selsam

Millicent Selsam's interest in biology and botany led her to begin writing science books for children. Her books encourage young readers to make their own observations and to trust those observations. "Children are excellent observers," she says. Millicent Selsam has written many science books for children. Two of her other books on prehistoric animals are *Sea Monsters of Long Ago* and *Tyrannosaurus Rex*.

THEY LIVE *in books*

The News About Dinosaurs

by Patricia Lauber

Believe it or not, scientists are still digging up new facts about dinosaurs. This book will update you on the latest discoveries, including why the Brontosaurus is no longer called Brontosaurus.

They Lived with the Dinosaurs

by Russell Freedman

Sharks, cockroaches, and turtles are just a few of the animals that lived when the Tyrannosaurus roamed the earth. If only they could talk, maybe they could tell us what happened to the dinosaurs.

The Fossil Factory

by Niles, Gregory, and Douglas Eldredge

So you want to be a paleontologist. This book provides the do's and don'ts of finding fossils, as well as enough fun experiments and projects to keep you busy until the next Ice Age.

Dinosaurs Down Under and Other Fossils from Australia

by Caroline Arnold

Since most people can't travel to Australia to see fossils, sometimes the fossils have to come here. Learn how a Kadimakaran fossil exhibit made the trip.

Dinosaur Dig

by Kathryn Lasky

Join the author and her family as they take a summer vacation to dig for fossils in the Badlands of Montana — where the bones of a Tyrannosaurus have been found.

Prehistoric Animals

by Daniel Cohen

This book takes another look at some prehistoric favorites. It also introduces creatures such as the moropus, which had the body of a horse and the feet of an anteater.

AUTHOR

THEME 3

Mildred Pitts Walter

Dear Houghton Mifflin Readers,

How pleased I am that you will be reading some of the books that I have written! You know, when I was your age, I never thought I would be a writer. I didn't know any writers, and I didn't have many books to read. I was born and brought up in Louisiana in a place where African Americans, at that time, were not permitted to go into public libraries. I always looked forward to school starting so that I would have books other than the Bible to read. I loved books and always wanted to be a teacher.

I did become a teacher, and I taught in Los Angeles, California. Most of my students were African Americans, and during that time there were few books about us written by African Americans. I met a book publisher and asked him to publish some books for the boys and girls I taught. He asked me to write some. I was not a writer and didn't think I could be one, so I said, "No. Find someone who writes." But he insisted I write a book, so I wrote ***Lillie of Watts: A Birthday Discovery***. He published my book and I became a writer.

I like to write for boys and girls your age and for those younger and older than you as well. In these pages, you are going to read a complete book that I wrote and get a taste of two of my other books.

Contents

Award Winner

I got the idea to write **Brother to the Wind** when I visited Nigeria, Ghana, and Cameroon, countries in West Africa. There I met people who told me about some beliefs from long ago. People believed that animals and people talked to each other and that animals were very helpful. There was another belief that snakes were special and that if a certain snake was found, it could make all wishes come true. I imagined that boys and girls like you might like a story that combined these African beliefs about nature with an American belief that technology and machines can make almost any wish come true. I also thought, what if I were a child again and could make a wish? What would that wish be? I would wish to fly.

A scene from

Brother to the Wind

by Mildred Pitts Walter
pictures by Diane and Leo Dillon

Emeke heard his grandmother say that Good Snake could make any wish come true. Emeke finds Good Snake and waits his turn to make a wish.

Finally Good Snake nodded at him. Emeke knew it was now his turn. "Oh, Good Snake, I would like to fly."

Good Snake uncurled his tail and brought forth a rock. "Are you sure you want to fly?"

"Oh, yes, Good Snake," Emeke whispered, hardly able to speak.

Good Snake held out the rock. "This is what you must do: Before the rains come, find the bark of a baobab tree and three large bamboo poles. Then make a kite exactly like the one on the back of this rock."

Emeke took the rock and placed it in his pouch. But what did a rock and a kite have to do with flying, Emeke wondered. He wanted to say, Why make a kite? All I want to do is fly like a bird. Instead he listened as Good Snake went on: "Before the feast of the harvest, you must find the right wind for the kite."

"Good Snake, how will I know the right wind?" Emeke asked.

Good Snake curled up his tail again and looked at Emeke. "The right wind will whisper words that will let you know for sure. Then, on the day of the feast, meet me high on the mountaintop. If you have done all the things that I have asked, then on that day you will fly. One other thing: Keep that rock with you always. It will help you."

Emeke was so happy and excited he almost forgot to thank Good Snake as he hurried back to his goats.

Good Snake called after him. "Be sure you find the bark and bamboo before the rains come."

Turtle laughed. "He, he, he. Beware! Things without wings don't fly."

Mariah Keeps Cool is a story about summertime and how a girl named Mariah fills her days during school vacation with swimming practice and family celebrations. When I was Mariah's age, I looked forward to church picnics, church fairs, and the holidays. For me, the best celebration of the summer was the June Nineteenth Celebration. On this day we celebrated the January 1, 1863, signing of the Emancipation Proclamation that freed slaves. You may wonder why we celebrated on June 19 instead of January 1. It was because June 19, 1865, was the date when slaves in Louisiana and Texas finally learned of the signing.

For this celebration, friends and families came from far and near to share food, tell stories, and dance. This special holiday in my life is just like the Juneteenth holiday in **Mariah Keeps Cool.**

A scene from

Mariah Keeps Cool

by Mildred Pitts Walter

illustrated by Pat Cummings

Mariah has been training all summer for her first diving competition. Now the day of the meet has arrived.

Mariah wished it were all over. If only she had chosen a more difficult program. But then she might be out of the competition: A tough dive not well-executed could be the kiss of death, bringing down the total score. Brandon and Mr. Lyons assured her she had done well and had a good chance to win.

Mariah paced back and forth, swinging her arms, breathing deeply, trying to relax. She heard the announcer call the final round. "Lorobeth Dillon will do a back dive with one somersault in the tuck position, degree of difficulty one point five."

"Oh, no," Mariah said. "That's my dive!"

Mariah's heart sank as she looked at Brandon. Brandon

smiled. "Don't worry about that. You're lucky you come second. You have time to really concentrate and see yourself doing your dive."

Mariah didn't want to concentrate. She wanted to see her competitor. Lorobeth had style and grace. She stood tall and straight, motionless as she planned every move. Now, in the final dive, Mariah felt that Lorobeth stood forever before she slowly raised her arms preparing for the back takeoff. Finally, Lorobeth somersaulted backward in a tuck position. She misjudged her timing and straightened her body, opening her dive too soon. She landed on her stomach, and the crowd groaned.

At first Mariah was elated. Then she felt an added tension. She must not open up too soon like Lorobeth did, but she couldn't be too late either. Too late would put her on her back. Her timing had to be just right.

"Mariah Metcalf will now do a back dive with one somersault in the tuck position, degree of difficulty one point five," the official announced.

Mariah stepped up on the board and glanced at the judges. Then she slowly walked to the end of the board, turned around, and carefully balanced herself with her head held high, eyes straight ahead, body erect, and arms straight at her sides. She stood motionless, concentrating on the dive. She waited, feeling the expectant silence. All eyes were on her.

Do you know anybody born on Christmas Day? Christopher Noel Dodd was and he agreed with his friends, Miles and Jamal, that being born on December 25 is not cool at all.

As you read ***Have a Happy . . .*** you will see how Chris celebrates his birthday and Christmas during a time of crisis in his family and how his uncle, aunts, grandmother, and friends make the holiday season a good one. You will also see how Chris's family and other African Americans celebrate a very special holiday called "Kwanzaa," which begins on December 26 and lasts through the first of January. I have celebrated this holiday with my family and friends since it began in this country in the 1960's. We gather in a large hall or in the homes of friends to talk, sing, tell stories, and share our experiences. We also exchange gifts that we have made with our own hands. I am glad I have books that I created to give as ***zawadi,*** or presents, to my family and friends.

Award Winner

Have A Happy...

by Mildred Pitts Walter

illustrated by Carole Byard

SWAHILI GLOSSARY

Swahili vowels are pronounced as follows:

a = like the *a* in car
e = like the *a* in play
i = like the *ee* in fee
o = like the *oe* in toe
u = like the *oo* in moo

The consonants are pronounced the same as they are in the English language. The *g* in *gele* is hard, like the *g* in go. The accent is almost always on the next-to-last syllable in the words used here.

harambee (ha-ram-be), a call to unity and collective struggle, pulling together.

karamu (ka-ra-mu), feast.

kwanza (kwan-za), first.

Kwanzaa (kwan-za), an African-American holiday celebration that begins on December 26 and ends January 1. Founded in 1966 by Dr. Maulana Karenga, the holiday is a time of ingathering of African-Americans to celebrate their history.

nguzo (n-gu-zo), principles.

saba (sa-ba), seven.

tambiko (tam-bi-ko), pouring drink for ancestors — a libation.

tamshi la tambiko (tam-shi la tam-bi-ko), statement made when pouring drink for ancestors.

tamshi la tutaonana (tam-shi la tu-ta-o-na-na), statement of farewell.

SEVEN PRINCIPLES OF KWANZAA

imani (i-ma-ni), faith.

kujichagulia (ku-ji-cha-gu-lia), self-determination.

kuumba (ku-um-ba), creativity.

nia (ni-a), purpose.

ujamaa (u-ja-ma), cooperative economics.

ujima (u-ji-ma), collective work and responsibility.

umoja (u-mo-ja), unity.

RITUAL SYMBOLS OF KWANZAA

bendera (ben-de-ra), flag.

kikombe (ki-kom-be), a cup.

kikombe cha umoja (ki-kom-be cha u-mo-ja), unity cup.

kinara (ki-na-ra), candle holder.

mazao (ma-za-o), crops.

mkeka (m-ke-ka), mat.

mishumaa (mi-shu-ma-a), candles.

mishumaa saba (mi-shu-ma-a sa-ba), seven candles.

vibunzi (vi-bun-zi), ears of corn.

zawadi (za-wa-di), gift or gifts.

SWAHILI GREETINGS

Habari gani (ha-ba-ri ga-ni), What's the news?

Kwanzaa yenu iwe heri (kwan-za ye-nu i-we he-ri), Happy Kwanzaa.

CLOTHING

buba (bu-ba), elegant robe or gown.

busuti (bu-su-ti), a robe with a scarf at the waist.

dashiki (da-shi-ki), a loosely fitting shirt for boys and men; a loosely fitting blouse for girls or women.

gele (ge-le), a head wrap.

kanzu (kan-zu), a robe for men.

CHAPTER

ONE

The long Christmas holiday had finally begun. Christopher, carrying gifts he had made for his family, walked hurriedly out of the school yard. Miles and Jamal raced by on their bicycles. Chris braced himself against the cold blasts of wind. He wished he had a bike, too.

He clasped the packages to his body and pulled his cap farther down over his ears. Several of his fingers were pushing through his well-worn gloves, and he blew on them to get them warm. Hurrying, he turned backward against the wind.

As he neared Miles's house, he saw that Jamal's bicycle was parked next to Miles's bike. The garage door opened and Miles called out, "Hey, Chris, come help me fold my papers."

"I've got to pick up my sister," Chris answered.

"Come on, Chris," Miles pleaded. "Just for a little while. I'll give you thirty-five cents."

"How much you giving *me*?" Jamal asked.

"Nothing," Miles answered. "You got more money than me."

Thirty-five cents, Chris thought, *that's a lot.* But he said, "I can't."

"Fifty cents."

"Okay." Then, not wanting them to know just how much he needed the fifty cents, he said, "I'll come for a little while, but I won't charge you."

In the closed garage, they folded and put rubber bands on newspapers that Miles would deliver that afternoon.

"What you getting for Christmas?" Jamal asked.

Miles answered first. "I don't think I'm getting much. I just got a lotta stuff for my birthday. This new bike, even. But I'll get something, what you bet?"

Chris kept on working as if he had not heard the question. He didn't want to talk about presents. His daddy hadn't worked steadily in eighteen months. His mama had said that this year Christmas might be like any other day for them.

Jamal went on, "My daddy sent my gifts already. Something big, but I don't know what."

"What I really want," Miles put in, "is a seat bag for my bike."

"Get one like mine," Jamal said. "Mine can hold my lunch, tire tubes, and tools. It's neat, man. Only cost about twenty bucks."

"Did your daddy send you that from Cleveland?" Chris asked without looking up.

"For my birthday," Jamal answered.

Chris remembered Jamal's birthday. *No party for me, ever. Everybody's too busy.*

They worked with only the crackling of paper and click of rubber bands. Finally Miles asked, "What you getting for Christmas, Chris?"

"I don't know." The answer came quickly.

"What you mean, don't know? What you want, man?" Jamal asked.

"Nothing for Christmas . . ."

"Nothing!" Miles interrupted.

"I want a bike for my birthday."

"Oh, that's right. You were born on Christmas Day. Christopher Noel Dodd. I always forget."

"That's all right. *Every*body forgets," Chris said sadly. "But I'll be eleven years old, just like you guys, this Christmas Day."

"It's uncool being born on Christmas Day," Jamal said, and laughed.

"Yeah, nothing cool about it at all." Chris didn't laugh. "Every present is a Christmas *and* birthday present."

All the papers folded, they began stuffing them into the double basket on the back of Miles's bike. Chris admired the sleek lines of the bicycle. Suddenly he thought about the time. "I forgot. I gotta go. Uncle Ronald is probably at my house right now. I'm making stuff for his Kwanzaa celebration."

"His what?" Jamal asked.

"Kwanzaa," Miles answered. "Don't you know what Kwanzaa is?"

"Never heard of it. What is it?"

"A celebration for us Black people," Miles said.

"Aw, man. That ain't telling me what it means."

"*Kwanzaa* means first fruit harvest," Chris said.

"Like Thanksgiving?"

"No-oo, no. Not like that," Chris replied.

"Then what is it?" Jamal persisted.

"It's a celebration. I gotta go." Chris grabbed his packages and started out.

"Hey, man, your money." Miles ran after him.

"No. It's okay." Chris waved him off. He still didn't want his friends to know he needed the fifty cents.

"But I promised. Here, and have a merry Christmas." Miles pressed the money into his hand.

"Don't wish me a merry Christmas. Wish me a happy birthday."

"I will — on your birthday."

Chris put the two quarters in his pocket and remembered the time when money hadn't seemed that important. He carried his gifts carefully, not wanting to crush the colorful wrappings. Everyone else in his fifth-grade class had made only one gift. But Mrs. Rush, his teacher, had let him make three: a towel rack for his mama, a tie rack for his daddy, and a small dollhouse for Beth, his five-year-old sister. Creating things with his hands was what he liked best.

The sun lowered, the wind blew colder. Chris hurried toward home. Trunks of tall trees wrapped with silver, red, and green foil made the walk a shiny lane. He passed brightly decorated houses. One had a Santa in a sleigh pulled by only one prancing reindeer. Chris knew that as soon as night fell his street would glow with lights, gold and white and all the colors of the rainbow.

In other years, a tree had stood in their big window, too, glittering a colorful greeting. *Maybe we won't be getting a Christmas tree*, he thought. *Probably not, with Daddy spending money looking for a job.* His daddy had been out of town a whole week trying to find work.

But it was not the tree that was troubling Chris. The haunting unhappiness that he often felt at this season came over him now. *December twenty-fifth should be my day, the way December third is Miles's and June twenty-eighth is Jamal's. But no, it's always merry Christmas, Chris!*

Chris knew he should have picked up Beth long ago. Remembering his uncle, he walked faster.

He didn't want Beth to see the gifts, so he went by home first. His uncle had not come. He quickly hid his packages in his room and ran to the baby-sitter's house.

Beth stood holding her wrapped packages, looking out the window, waiting impatiently. "You late," she scolded.

"How you know I'm late? You can't even tell time." Chris let the sitter know they were leaving. As they started home, he asked, "What's all that you got?"

"Presents I made."

"What'd you make?"

"It's a secret."

"Bet I can guess," Chris teased.

"Bet you can't."

"Let me hold them."

Reluctantly she handed him the packages. One felt thin as paper. The other, though smaller, felt heavy.

"I know I can guess," he said, "but I'll give you another chance to tell me."

"The little one is my hand for Daddy. The other is my picture for Mama."

"I knew all along that's what it was," Chris said smugly.

"You didn't."

Sensing she knew she had been tricked into telling, he dodged out of reach as she tried to shove him off the walk and escaped, laughing. "Every kindergartner makes a clay handprint and a paper silhouette for Christmas." The sad look on her face made him quickly add, "Mama and Daddy'll like them."

"How you know?"

"They liked mine. They still have them."

The house was cold and no aroma of good things cooking welcomed them. Before, when their daddy had a job, their mama was often home when they came in from school. A nurse, she had worked part-time. Now, not only was she on the job full-time, she often stayed overtime.

Chris turned on the heat. Then he went into the kitchen with Beth following. He looked into the refrigerator but found nothing tempting. "You hungry?"

"No," Beth answered. "I had some toast and milk. When is Daddy coming home?"

"Maybe Sunday." With their jackets still on, they sat in the kitchen, not talking.

CHAPTER TWO

"Hey, what's going on here?" Uncle Ronald walked into the kitchen loaded down with groceries. "You guys going someplace?"

"Hi, Uncle Ronald," Beth cried, happy to see him.

"Why you ask if we going someplace?" Chris wanted to know.

"You have your jackets on. Where's that sister of mine?"

"Mama hasn't come yet. She's late," Chris replied.

"Well, how about some help here, putting this stuff away?"

They scrambled out of their jackets and looked into the bags. "Is this fried chicken for us, too?" Beth asked.

"If you let me stay and have supper with you."

Beth set the table while Chris helped to slice the carrots, cucumbers, and celery his uncle had brought. When they took the chicken out of the box they discovered four biscuits with honey.

"How can we divide four biscuits among three people?" Uncle Ronald wanted to know.

"Give me two and you guys have one," Chris said.

"No, give me the two," Beth shouted.

"Wait, wait, just a minute. I think the person with the longest legs should decide," Uncle Ronald said.

Just then Mama came home.

"Mama, Mama," Beth shrieked. "Give it to Mama."

"I'll take it, whatever it is," Mama said, and they all laughed. Chris felt glad that she had come home.

After dinner, Uncle Ronald handed Chris a package. "Here's that stuff you asked me to get so you can finish up my animals."

In the package Chris found glue, some wood, and several packages of clothespins. "Want to see what I've done already?" he asked his uncle.

"Yeah, I'll come in a minute."

Chris went to his room and lined up all the finished animals. On smooth wood he had drawn ducks, rabbits, a mouse, reindeer, pigs, and birds. He had clamped the wood onto his workbench, then cut the animals out with his coping saw. His dad had given him a wood burner. With that he had made mouths, noses, ears, and eyes, and on some animals he had burned special designs.

Chris was excited about the job he had done. He hoped his uncle would like the animals, too. He waited impatiently, but Uncle Ronald didn't come. Finally he decided to return to the kitchen. He found Mama and Uncle Ronald huddled together, whispering.

"Are you coming?" Chris demanded.

"Christopher!" His mama called him that when she was not pleased with him. "You know better than to interrupt without saying excuse me."

"I'm coming, man." Uncle Ronald gave Chris a smile.

Back in his room, Chris wondered what they were whispering about. Had something happened to Daddy? Maybe he wasn't coming back at all, ever. *Surely Mama would tell me if that was so.*

Soon Uncle Ronald came bursting into the room. Chris was always amazed at how young his uncle looked and acted, for a high school teacher. Maybe it was because he was not a big, tall man. But to Chris he seemed to fill a room.

"Wow! These are great!" Uncle Ronald's pleasure warmed Chris. He picked up the animals and turned them about. "Let's see, now," he went on. "You have ten. Can you make ten more by Monday?"

"Why that many?" Chris asked.

"I need them for Kwanzaa, man."

"My daddy's coming Sunday. Monday's Christmas Eve. I might have something else to do."

"You can make them. Give it a try, anyway."

Still curious about the whispering he had heard in the kitchen, Chris said, "Uncle Ronald . . ." Then, remembering being embarrassed by his mama, he hesitated. "Oh, never mind."

"What is it, man?"

The way his uncle said "man" always put Chris at ease.

"What were you and Mama talking about?"

Uncle Ronald laughed. "That's between me and my sister." He was the youngest of four: two sisters and two brothers. Chris's mama was next to him, two years older. Uncle Ronald was already thirty.

He laughed. Couldn't be something bad. Then why can't they include me in the secret? Chris felt hurt.

His uncle was about to leave, but Chris wanted him to stay longer. "Uncle Ronald, what is Kwanzaa besides a celebration?"

"Isn't that enough?" Uncle Ronald asked, and laughed.

"Well, my friend Jamal wanted to know if it's like Thanksgiving."

"In a way, yes. *Kwanzaa* is taken from the African Swahili word *kwanza*, spelled with one *a*, which means 'first.' It is part of the phrase *matunda ya kwanza*, which means 'first fruit.' When I was in the Peace Corps in Ghana, I went to a celebration called *kwanza* for the harvest of the first fruit. That African celebration is somewhat like our Thanksgiving."

"Then what is our Kwanzaa?"

"Our Kwanzaa is spelled with two *a*'s but is pronounced the same. It is an African-American word. Now, know how we like to get together? Well, Kwanzaa is a get-together, or an ingathering, with a special purpose."

"Oh, I see. Like when we talk about the past and ancestors at the celebration. And when Grandma Ida and other older people talk about remembering, and stuff like that, huh?"

"Yes. Exactly. We celebrate ourselves as a people."

"Uncle Ronald, were you and Mama talking about Daddy?" Chris was still worried.

"Oh, no. Nothing like that." He drew Chris to him. "I can't tell you, but I promise, it's nothing to make you unhappy." He picked up a package of clothespins and asked, "Why did you have me buy these?"

"I can't tell you, but I promise it won't make you unhappy."

Uncle Ronald touched Chris's chin lightly with his fist, and they both laughed.

After saying goodbye to his uncle, Chris found Mama in the kitchen with Beth.

"Your sister said you were late today," Mama said sharply.

"I wasn't. Not *that* late." He glared at Beth, who stared at him wide-eyed. "Why'd you have to tell?" he snapped at her.

"You kept me waiting. A long time." Beth lowered her eyes.

"What happened, Chris?" Mama wanted to know.

"Mama, I helped Miles fold his papers. She doesn't know what late is."

"I depend on you to get home on time," Mama said.

"I do get home on time." He looked at Beth with a scowl.

"Mama, when will we get our Christmas tree?" Beth asked.

"I don't know," Mama said impatiently.

What's the matter with her, Chris wondered. He felt a lump rising in his throat. His mama was never like this before. He was sure there would be nothing for his birthday or Christmas. Suddenly he felt angry. "I don't care if we don't have a tree," he said.

"What's wrong with you, Chris?" Mama asked.

"Nothing. I just don't want a tree. I want a bicycle for my birthday."

"Let Santa bring you a bicycle. He brings things, huh, Mama?" Beth put in.

"Santa doesn't bring birthday presents," Chris retorted.

They were quiet. The silence was uncomfortable. Chris was glad when Beth said, "Well, Mama. Are we? Gonna get a tree?"

"Beth, we'll have to wait until your daddy comes."

"Is he still coming Sunday?" Chris wanted to know.

"Yes."

Chris sensed Mama's bad mood, but he asked anyway. "What were you and Uncle Ronald whispering about, Mama?"

She gave a little laugh. "None of your business."

The laugh encouraged him. "Aw, Mama, you can tell me."

"I can, but I won't."

"Will you tell me why we can't get our tree tomorrow?" Beth persisted.

"I have to work, for one thing." She picked up their jackets, which they had thrown over the kitchen stool.

"But tomorrow is Saturday," Chris blurted out. "When we going shopping?"

"There's no money for shopping. And I know tomorrow is Saturday, and I have to work. You can go over to your grandma's and help keep Beth."

"No, I can't." He shifted his weight and looked at Mama. She looked so tired and sad, he softened. "Do I have to?"

"Is there any good reason why you can't?"

"It's just that I have all those things to make for Uncle Ronald. I promised."

"Let me go to Grandma Ida's by myself," Beth pleaded.

"Your grandma might be busy tomorrow, and I don't want Chris here alone." Mama handed Beth the jackets. "Put these away, please."

Chris went to his room feeling angry and ashamed. Ashamed that he did not want to help take care of Beth. *But why can't she take off just one day?* As he worked, burning wings on birds, lines for a mouse's ear, and fat wrinkles on a pig, he wondered why he couldn't stay home alone. *Wish Daddy was here.*

CHAPTER THREE

Chris woke to the sound of laughter. *That could only be Grandma*, he thought. He bounded out of bed and dressed hurriedly. Maybe Grandma Ida would talk Mama into letting him stay home.

Mama had her coat on ready to leave for work. Grandma was at the kitchen counter dipping slices of bread into egg batter. Chris smiled and said a warm good morning.

"Come here and give me a hug," Grandma said, beaming.

Chris knew that was coming and wished she would learn that he was too big for that now. He shyly hesitated.

"C'mon," she said. "You never outgrow hugs, boy." She grabbed him.

He felt a flush of warmth around his head. He quickly hugged her back and escaped. Without looking at her he asked, "What you making?"

"Your favorite — French toast, and I brought over some sausages," his grandmother announced.

"Mama, why can't I stay home today?" Chris asked.

"Because I don't like you being here by yourself."

"But I'll be all right," Chris pleaded.

"I don't know that," Mama said.

"I won't let *anybody* in. I'll just do my work."

"I still don't like leaving you."

"Aw, Mama," Chris complained. "I'd be all right, huh, Grandma?"

"I don't see why not. Just this once," Grandma said.

"Well, all right. But I'm going to let Mr. Charles know you here and to keep an eye out. If you need anything, you call him."

Chris liked the next-door neighbors and was glad they were there if he needed them.

"Now listen," Mama said. "Let me find this house in one piece when I get back, you hear? And don't you go anyplace until I come home."

"Aw, Mama. I'm no baby."

"Oh, no?" Mama laughed. "That's news. Get Beth up. I gotta run. Be good, now, and remember what I told you. I have enough to worry about."

As he left the room, he heard his grandma say, "Myra, you should trust him. He's a good child."

When Grandma Ida and Beth finally left, the quiet in the house overwhelmed Chris. Feeling a little scared, he circled through the house, checking to see if all the doors were locked. In the living room, surrounded by familiar things, he felt big, proud to be alone. Then he went to his room, glad he had a lot of work to do.

Unwrapping a package of clothespins, he thought about the little chair, the bed, and the dresser he planned to make for Beth's dollhouse. He had seen his daddy make beautiful things with clothespins. Now he would try to make some furniture with them.

Chris discovered that the spring wires in clothespins come out more easily than they go in. As he removed them, he had an idea. Clothespins would make animals, too. He glued together legs, bodies, and other parts to make a giraffe, a horse, and a reindeer.

All morning he worked on the animals, remembering all the things his daddy had taught him. When he finished the giraffe, Chris was so pleased he wanted to run out and show it to somebody, just anybody, and say, "Look, *I* made this!" Instead he kept on working.

By the time he had finished three animals and started on the chair for Beth's dollhouse, he was hungry. He hurriedly stuffed down peanut butter and jelly sandwiches and leftover French toast, then went back to work on the chair.

Carefully he turned the pins so the indentations for the spring wires made interesting lines. He mixed and matched the varying shades of wood to make contrasts. When all the parts were glued, he had a real rocking chair.

He looked at it. Something was missing.

He figured out what to do. He took four pieces from two pins and placed them with the thinner part at the bottom, so the space that held the wire faced the back of the chair. He spread them to look like a Chinese fan, then glued them together. When the glue dried, he stuck them onto the back of the chair. It looked like a granny rocking chair. *Ah, my best piece ever.*

Now he was ready to make the bed. He looked around. Oh no, only one clothespin left. How could he make the bed and dresser for Beth's house? He tried to cut something from a piece of wood. That didn't work. Then he thought, *Toothpicks!*

In the kitchen he found two kinds: round thick picks and flat thin ones. *These will make a good bed and dresser,* he said to himself.

He had just finished them when the doorbell rang. *Who could that be?* he wondered. His first thought was not to answer. But maybe it was his neighbor.

At the door he heard Miles's voice. Should he open the door? When he opened it, he found Jamal there, too. They were on their bikes.

"We're going to the Toy-orama exhibit," said Miles. "Wanta come?"

"Can't."

"Ask your mama," Jamal said.

"My mama's working."

"Then come on, man," Jamal demanded.

He didn't want Jamal to think he was a baby. "How long you gonna be gone?"

"Not long," Miles said. "With us on our bikes, if you ride your skateboard, we'll be there in no time."

There wasn't much more work to do. He had finished the furniture and three animals. Maybe he could go. Chris rushed to his room to get his jacket. Then his grandmother's words rang in his mind: *Myra, you should trust him.*

He went back to the door. "I better not."

"Aw, come on." Miles acted disappointed.

"Yeah, man," Jamal pleaded.

"I can't, really. I'm still working on that stuff for Kwanzaa."

"Oh, yeah. Your uncle wants us to come over on Christmas Day for that."

"Aw, shut up, silly," Miles said, punching Jamal on the shoulder. "Kwanzaa's not on Christmas Day. It starts the day after."

"Oh, so you saw Uncle Ronald," Chris said, pleased.

"Yeah. I still don't understand what Kwanzaa's all about," Jamal complained.

If I tell him all about it, he might not come. "You'll have to see it. It's something you show, not tell," Chris said.

Finally they left. Chris went back to his work. He smiled. *So Uncle Ronald invited them to Kwanzaa. Silly Jamal, thinking it's on Christmas Day.* He thought about his daddy. *Be home tomorrow.* His heart leaped. *Maybe he got a job and I can have a bike for my birthday.*

By the time Mama came home, he had finished three clothespin animals and drawn seven more to make the ten Uncle Ronald wanted. He only had to cut them out. For that he had another whole day plus some. The house was all in one piece, and he had kept his promise.

CHAPTER FOUR

Sunday crawled along. After church and lunch at his grandma's house, Chris came home to work. But nothing went right. His mind was not on making animals. Finally, he gave up and lay on his bed thinking about Daddy coming home. *If only we could afford plane fare. He'd be home by now. A plane goes much faster than the bus. What if he missed the bus?* Chris didn't want to think about that.

The drawings of the seven animals lay on the board waiting. He got up and started working with his coping saw. After cutting only two, still bored, he went to find Mama and Beth. The house creaked in the quiet as he peeped in on Beth, fast asleep in her room. Mama, in the den with the TV on, was fast asleep, too. *How can they sleep when Daddy's coming home?*

He looked at the clock in the kitchen. Only three o'clock. He wished it were five. Then he wouldn't have to wait any longer. There was food, but he wasn't hungry. He felt full all the way up into his throat.

Back in his room he cut out three more animals. Only two more to go. He decided to put faces on the finished ones. He messed up two, one after the other. Disgusted, he fell on his bed.

A gentle shake and Mama's quiet voice awoke him. "Daddy's home."

At first he thought he was still asleep. He kept his eyes closed.

"Chris," his father said.

Chris sprang up. The look on Daddy's face was one of joy, yet Chris saw something else. Worry. Something almost like fear. Chris knew he hadn't gotten a job. He clung to Daddy's waist and buried his face in his father's firm stomach. With his eyes closed tight he hung on until the unshed tears passed away. Finally the words came. "I'm glad you home."

Later that evening, Beth asked if they could have a tree. "I think we can have a tree. What's Christmas without a tree?" Daddy said.

"See, Chris," Beth said. "He didn't want a tree, Daddy."

"You don't want a tree, Chris?" Daddy asked.

"Oh, she's just a tattletale. I said I'd rather have a birthday present."

"Beth, Chris, it's time for you guys to go to bed," Mama said.

"Since when do I have to go to bed when she goes?" Chris asked.

"Let Chris stay. He's old enough to know what we're up against."

After Beth was tucked in, his father talked about going to several towns, only to find there was no work. Many people were looking for jobs.

Chris knew Daddy had worked as an electronics assembler. He was part of a group that put together circuit boards for computer hardware. The company he worked for went out of business, leaving hundreds of people out of work. Now, as his father talked, Chris realized that eighteen months was almost two years. *That's a long time*, he thought.

"We might have to move out of this area," Daddy said. His voice had a strange sound.

Move. What would Chris do if he had to leave Grandma Ida, Uncle Ronald, all of his friends?

"I hope it won't come to that," Mama said.

"Hey, son." Daddy's voice startled Chris out of his thoughts. "I haven't forgotten. You want a bike for Christmas."

"No, for my birthday," Chris said.

"Oh, you make it tough for me." Daddy laughed. "If you wanted it for Christmas, I could easily say Santa can't come this year."

Mama said, "Yes, Chris knows Santa doesn't bring birthday presents."

"I don't see how we can manage a bike this year, Chris." His father did not look up.

"But Daddy, I need it. I'd like to deliver papers."

"Now, Chris . . ."

Before Mama could finish, Daddy said, "I'm glad you want to do that. Maybe, just maybe now, we can work something out."

"There's no sense in raising his hopes, Bruce," Mama said. "He needs other things more than he needs a bike. Shoes, for instance. He has to think of more than what he *wants*."

Chris wished Mama would see that he *was* thinking of more than just what he wanted. He could deliver papers and help out, too. He sat there hoping Daddy would say something to make her understand. But there was only silence between them.

Finally Daddy said, "How's your project for Ronald coming?"

"Want to see?"

In Chris's room, Daddy's face brightened. "You finished all of those while I was away? You're getting good. I better watch you. You'll outdo me, man."

Chris, pleased, showed him everything he had made except Beth's furniture. That had to remain a secret.

His father became serious. "Chris, your mama wants you to have a bike as much as I, but she's worried." He took Chris's chin in his hand and lifted Chris's face up toward his. "I don't want you to worry, though. We've had some good times in this house, haven't we?" His voice sounded as though he was about to cry.

Chris looked away. "Yes."

"We'll have good times again." Now Daddy sounded like himself. "Look at me, Chris. That I promise you." He pulled Chris to him briefly, then went back to the kitchen.

Alone, Chris sat on his bed thinking about this time last year. Even though his father had been out of work for six months, there had been hope. They'd all had a good time then.

He looked over into the corner of his room where last year's Christmas present, a train with a shiny black engine and silver, blue-streaked cars, stood on the track. He remembered how he and his daddy had put it all together. They had mounted the tracks on a board and built a tunnel and a small station.

We have *had good times*, he thought. He wanted to believe his father when he said they would have them again. But Chris was afraid.

Chris woke up in an unusually quiet house. There were no signs or sounds that today was the day before Christmas, the day before his birthday. *Where is everybody?* he wondered on his way to the kitchen.

Daddy was sitting at the table with his cup half full of coffee, looking at the want ads section of the newspaper. Chris knew from the burned bits of toast on the plate that his daddy had made breakfast. "Where's Mama?" he asked.

"She's working today."

"We not going shopping today?"

"We're going for a Christmas tree," Daddy answered.

"Is that all?" Disappointment sounded in Chris's voice. Mama had never worked on Christmas Eve before. Daddy was always home by noon on that day, and the family did special things together: last-minute shopping, visiting family and friends, and cooking special foods for Christmas Day.

"That's all the shopping." Daddy, annoyed, returned to his paper.

Chris felt closed out. Maybe he had asked the wrong question. Finally he said, "What's for breakfast?"

"Why don't I make you some hot cereal and cinnamon toast?"

Knowing his daddy's toast, Chris shook his head. "You make the cereal. I'll make the toast."

"That's a deal. Get Beth up."

While they had breakfast, the phone rang. "I'll get it," Chris said. It was Uncle Ronald.

"How you coming along, man?" Uncle Ronald wanted to know. "Can I pick up my stuff today?"

Chris tried to show some enthusiasm. "They're coming. I'll have them done."

The day went too fast for Chris. He worked hard, but he made mistakes. At almost five o'clock he was still trying to perfect animals. Beth was impatient to go for the Christmas tree, and kept bothering him. Finally he shouted, "Go on. I don't have to go."

"Daddy says you have to. So hurry up."

CHAPTER FIVE

Darkness had set in early. As they rode across town, Chris noticed people in hats and scarves loaded down with packages. *Why can't we be out shopping? No, we don't get anything this year.* He sank down in the seat, wishing he hadn't come.

Finally they came to the place near the railway yard where there were lots of Christmas trees. Some men were beginning to put them into boxcars to haul them away.

"You came just in time," one of the men said. "Business was terrible this year. We didn't sell many trees, so take your pick. Take two or three." He laughed.

Beth wanted a tree with heavy bushy branches. Chris found a tall silver-tip fir. Its cone shape was almost perfect. The branches formed circles. All of a sudden he realized he did want a Christmas tree after all. "This is it, Daddy," Chris called excitedly.

"Chris, you *would* choose that one. It's probably the most expensive tree on the lot."

"I got fifty cents," Chris said.

"That won't buy one branch of that tree," Daddy said.

"Aw, Daddy, let's ask."

They took it to the man directing the loading of the trees. "Make me an offer," the man said.

"Fifty cents," Chris answered eagerly.

"You don't really want *that* tree, do you?" the man said.

"Oh, yes we do." Beth spoke before Daddy or Chris had a chance.

"All right. You can have it for that."

Chris gave the man the fifty cents, glad now that Miles had insisted on paying him.

"Have a merry Christmas," the man said.

Chris and Beth shouted thanks and merry Christmas as they drove out of the lot.

As soon as they pulled into their driveway, Mama rushed outside. Without even noticing the tree, she called excitedly, "Come see, come on!"

They all rushed into the kitchen. Food covered the table and counter. There was a big turkey and a ham. Greens, sweet potatoes, yams, all kinds of fruits and vegetables, and many, many cans of food were spread about.

"Wow! Where'd all that come from, Mama?" Chris shouted. He glanced at Daddy, feeling how lucky they were. But what was that look on Daddy's face? Chris did not understand. Was his father feeling ashamed? Was he going to cry?

Then Daddy grinned. "Can't beat neighbors like ours," he said. "No, can't beat this with a switch."

"Now, Mama," Chris said, "you come see what we got."

Mama took one look and put her hand up to her face. "Oh," she said to Daddy, "why did you let them talk you into buying that tree? We can't afford a silver-tip."

Chris wanted to explain, but Beth, excited, took over and told what had happened. "And it didn't cost but fifty cents, huh, Daddy?"

"And our son paid for it." Daddy put a hand on Chris's shoulder.

"It's beautiful," Mama said. "That tree needs no decorations."

"Oh, yes it does. I'll get them," Beth said and ran inside with Chris right behind her. She rushed to the closet where year after year decorations were stored away until the next Christmas.

"Wait, Beth," Chris demanded. But Beth pulled at the nearest box, and all the boxes came tumbling down. Lights and

silver, blue, green, and red balls splattered over the floor. Many were in slivers.

"Beth!" Chris screamed. "Look what you've done!"

Mama and Daddy rushed into the room. "What's going on in here?" Mama asked, irritated.

Chris saw Beth's face scrunch up to cry, but he didn't care. "Miss Fast here has broken all the decorations," he said angrily.

"That's no reason for you to shout at her," Mama snapped at Chris.

"Don't get on me," Chris shouted back. "Get on Beth. She's the one. Now we have no decorations."

"All right!" Daddy exclaimed. "Stop this shouting, all of you. You don't talk to your mother and sister like that, Chris."

"What's wrong with him?" Mama asked. "He's been beside himself here lately."

"Now you apologize or go to your room," Daddy said.

Chris looked at his father. *I didn't do anything. Beth did. Mama screamed at me. Why do I have to apologize?* He folded his arms, brought them down hard on his chest. "I'm sorry," he muttered and ran to his room.

The animals were gone. Uncle Ronald must have come and taken them away. His room seemed empty now without them. Still smoldering, he wished his Uncle Ronald would take him, too.

He heard voices outside and knew his family was decorating the tree. *With what?* he wondered. He wanted to forget his anger and go help. *After all, it's my tree. I bought it.* But instead of helping, he stayed in his room, feeling worried. *Something is happening. We weren't like this before. Shouting at me and going on. Daddy better get a job.*

At bedtime he got under the covers and lay there trying hard to stay awake until the house became quiet. He wanted to see the tree and be the last person to put gifts under it. And he wanted to see if, just maybe, he might find a bicycle there.

He sang softly to himself. He recited nursery rhymes and counted backward from a hundred three times. Then he listened to see just how many sounds there were in the night. Dogs barked. Car horns honked and a lone siren screamed in the distance. The hum of the city reminded him of the sound in a seashell.

He dozed. Then he woke with a start and lay listening. All was still. He said a prayer for a bike and quietly got out of bed. He took his packages from their hiding place and, tiptoeing, made his way toward the living room.

Excitedly he looked all around the room. By the light that came in from outside, he could see that there was no bicycle. The tree stood in the window like one in a forest, blanketed with snow. The spotlight under it, covered with a blue sheet of cellophane, was now off. Beth's packages were there, the lighter one hanging from a branch. There were other packages, too. In the semidarkness he lifted them and felt their weight.

He turned on the spotlight. What was it that looked so much like glistening snow? The blue light on the snow gave it a cold feeling. The tree looks so alone, he thought. Suddenly Chris, too, felt alone and lonely.

CHAPTER SIX

Chris slept late the next morning. His family was up and about when Beth, already dressed, burst into his room.

"Get up, Chris. We wanta open our presents," she said.

Chris lay there, hating to move.

"Come on," Beth pleaded. "Get up. We gonna open them without you."

"I don't care, go on."

"Chris, come on," Mama called. "We're waiting for you."

Reluctantly he got up. When he walked into the living room, Beth, impatient, had already begun to open her presents. She liked her dollhouse, and when she opened the package with the furniture, she let out a squeal of joy. The chair was too big to go through the door or window, but the toothpick bed and dresser were just right.

"How'd you make this snow, Mama?" Chris wanted to know.

"That's a big secret," Mama said jokingly.

"She made it with hot water and soap flakes," Beth said. "She put it in the mixer, and me and Daddy plopped it on the branches with our hands."

"Looks real," Chris said. He opened presents to find shoes from Mama, a sweater from Grandma Ida, and a pair of gloves from Daddy. He tried to appear excited, but he felt disappointed.

Beth handed him her present. It was light like paper. Chris, excited now, opened it. Beth had drawn a big Santa saying, "Merry Christmas to my brother, Chris." He sighed. *Just another Christmas card. Why can't people take my birthday seriously?*

They could just say, Have a happy. Then I could add anything I want: happy birthday, happy Christmas, happy Kwanzaa, happy New Year. . . . Then he looked at Beth with a weak smile. "You made this. Thanks."

He began to feel better when Mama and Daddy made a big fuss over the things he had made for them and Beth. The chair was just the right size for Beth's small doll. Chris found some soft wire. He quickly made a pair of eyeglasses and put them on the doll. She became a granny for the rocking chair.

"Now, Chris," Mama said, "hurry up and get dressed. Ronald invited us over."

Chris played around, moving the furniture in and out of Beth's dollhouse and adjusting the doll's eyeglasses to make them fit better. He was not interested in getting dressed or in going anywhere. *What's the use*, he thought. It would be the same all day, nobody noticing that he had turned eleven.

"Chris, get up, right now, and get dressed," Mama demanded. "Put on something nice."

Reluctantly, he went to his room, taking his time even though he knew they were ready, waiting for him. *Why do we have to go to Uncle Ronald's so early?* He snatched socks out of his drawer. "Do I have to get dressed up?" he shouted.

"It's Christmas and your birthday, Chris. You should want to look nice," Mama called.

Finally, they were on their way. Chris sat in the backseat with Beth, frozen inside with unhappiness.

The blinds on his uncle's windows were closed when they arrived. "Looks like Uncle Ronald isn't even at home," Chris said sullenly.

"Well, he invited us," Mama said.

"Go ring the doorbell and see, Chris," his father suggested.

Chris unwillingly got out of the car, thinking of his warm bed. He leaned on the doorbell. The door opened and he was pulled inside. The sudden bedlam frightened Chris. Horns blew, floating streamers of paper wrapped around him. Lots of people shouted, "Happy birthday, Chris! Happy birthday!"

Overwhelmed, Chris could not move. He could not speak. He didn't know what to do.

Miles and Jamal were there looking at him, smiling. All of his family: uncles, aunts, cousins, and Grandma Ida. Everybody. Mama, Daddy, and Beth finally came in. Still he couldn't say a word.

Uncle Ronald said, "Here is the birthday boy at last. So, say something, Chris."

Chris tried to think of something to say. He looked at all of his friends. Only one thing came into his mind. "Have a happy . . . no, merry Christmas!"

After everyone had had their fill of small sandwiches, birthday cake, and ice cream, Uncle Ronald called for their attention. "First, let me invite all of you back here tomorrow for the Kwanzaa celebration. Tomorrow, December twenty-sixth, is the first day."

Then he looked at Chris and smiled. "Chris is now eleven, middle-aged." Everybody laughed. Uncle Ronald went on, "Today is Chris's day. So on *his* day, it is his turn to be important. And what does an important person do?" He paused. "What do you think, Chris?"

Chris glanced toward the table at gifts that weren't wrapped in Christmas paper. "Get presents?" he answered cautiously. He was unable to hide his excitement. *Maybe now I'll get that bicycle*, he thought.

"Have you thought that sometimes important people *give* gifts?" his uncle asked.

"But that's *very* important people," Chris said. There was soft laughter.

"Well, that's exactly what you're going to be today. A very important person. You're going to give gifts." His uncle brought out packages wrapped in colorful paper.

Chris gave everyone a package, thinking, *I must be jinxed. Whoever heard of the birthday person giving gifts?*

"Oo-ooo-o, look at this," Grandma Ida said. "A giraffe!"

"Chris made those with his own hands!" Uncle Ronald exclaimed.

"I don't believe you made this," Jamal said happily. He had one of the animals made of clothespins.

"He made them. Chris makes real nice things," Miles said.

Chris listened to their praises, and satisfaction warmed him.

"Now," Uncle Ronald said, "here are your presents, Chris." He led Chris to the table.

Right then, Chris knew there would be no bicycle. He opened his presents: a game from Jamal, puzzles from Miles. Uncle Ronald gave him blades for his coping saw. He also received paints and paintbrushes. His excitement showed when he thanked everyone.

As Miles and Jamal were leaving, Jamal asked, "Did you get a bicycle?"

Chris's face felt hot, but before he could answer, Miles said, "His birthday isn't over yet."

When everyone had left, Chris said to Uncle Ronald, "So that's what all the whispering was about, huh? And ten more animals for Kwanzaa!"

His uncle grinned. Chris knew this was the happiest day of his life and the best birthday he had ever had. But he was not so sure that giving was better than getting gifts. He still longed for a bike.

CHAPTER SEVEN

The day after his birthday, Chris's parents asked him to stay home just in case his daddy had to go out. Daddy did have to go out, and now Chris sat in his room waiting for Beth to wake up from her nap. He'd gotten tired of her chattering and had told her if she didn't go to sleep, she couldn't go to Kwanzaa. The first celebration started at six that evening. Only three hours away. Bored, he checked the wheel bearings on his skateboard. The wheels turned fast and smoothly. He took care of his board, his means of getting around. But it wasn't a bicycle.

Bet my friends are all out now. Riding. Any other holiday he'd be with them, Mama at home taking care of Beth.

He wandered into the kitchen, wishing Daddy would come home. *Maybe he got a job.* His heart beat faster. *Probably not.* He sank into a chair.

Beth found him with his head down on the table. "Chris, what's the matter?"

He started up. "Nothing."

She sat at the table looking at him. "You worried?" she asked.

"Why should I be worried?" he answered, annoyed.

"Because we here by ourselves," she said.

"Naw." But he did feel worried. Frightened about a lot of things that he didn't understand. Couldn't talk about. He felt that lump rising in his throat.

"Well, you worried about something else?" she persisted.

"Why you asking all these questions?"

"*I'm* worried," she said, and started to cry. "I want Mama to come home."

"She'll be here," he said, trying to make Beth feel better. "It's already three o'clock."

Just then Daddy walked into the kitchen. "Did you get a job?" Chris asked before Daddy spoke.

"Nothing." Daddy sat down without taking off his coat.

Unable to stand the sad, worried look on his father's face, Chris turned away and got up from the table. "Can I ride my skateboard for a while?"

"Don't be long. We go to your uncle's, you know."

"I won't be long," Chris said and went to get his elbow and knee pads.

The sun was shining brightly, but it did not warm the afternoon. With his helmet securely fastened, Chris pushed off on his way. The cold wind stung his face as he moved against it. He swallowed hard, trying to remove the lump in his throat. But tears he could not hold back smarted on his cheeks. He felt stupid, crying. Glad that he had to be aware of every crack and crease in the pavement, of every tree, person, and place he passed, he propelled himself, stopping only for curbs. *Why can't Daddy find a job? He might have to go away again. No, no, not that.*

At a distance he saw Miles and Jamal resting on their bikes, talking to some girls. Chris turned quickly and started home, but not before they had seen him.

They raced after him, shouting his name. He quickly wiped his face with the back of his hand. He braced himself, hoping they would not notice his pain.

"Hey, birthday boy," Jamal shouted. "You were some surprised." Jamal and Miles sat on their bikes while Chris rested on the curb. "You should've seen your face when you came through your uncle's door, man." Jamal bent over with laughter.

"And you almost messed it up, Jamal," Miles scolded.

"When?" Chris asked.

"Remember when we talked about Kwanzaa and he said that was why your uncle had asked us to come to his house on Christmas Day?" Miles answered.

"You looked funny, man. That was good." Jamal couldn't stop laughing.

Chris slipped off his helmet. "You really gonna come to Kwanzaa, huh?"

"I want to. But I don't know if I'll like it, man," Jamal said.

"I like it," Miles responded. "But we don't do it at our house. We always go to your uncle's, huh, Chris? And to the community center."

"Yeah. We all go over to my uncle's every year, too. Uncle Ronald's into that kinda stuff."

"You'll like it, Jamal." Miles grinned. "It's fun, huh, Chris?"

"And it's serious, too," Chris said.

"I don't like serious stuff, man," Jamal muttered. "Like school and church."

"Not that kind of serious, huh, Chris?" Miles asked.

"Some of it's fun. You make things and listen to people tell stories. Older people talk about what they remember, stuff like that. I like it, especially the drums and music." Chris's enthusiasm came through.

"My whole family goes," Miles said.

"My family's just me and my mama," Jamal said softly.

"Not at Kwanzaa," Chris said. "Everybody is your family at Kwanzaa, right, Miles?"

"Yeah, that's Kwanzaa. But you have to go to know. We going tonight," Miles said.

Chris put on his helmet and pushed off on his skateboard. Miles and Jamal rode their bikes alongside him near the walk.

"If we come to your uncle's, do we have to get dressed up?" Jamal asked.

"Not unless you want to," Chris answered. "Wear anything you want. Just come, okay?"

"And no giggling at the Swahili words," Miles demanded.

"Aw, you intelligent, huh, Jamal?" Chris asked.

"I hope so." Jamal gave a little laugh. "I've heard Swahili before. *Habari gani.* That means, What's the news? Like we say, What's happening?"

"All right!" Chris exclaimed. He stepped off his board to slap Jamal's palms. "My uncle starts things on time. You guys don't be late, now."

CHAPTER EIGHT

That evening Chris's uncle greeted his guests standing by his door in a long white *kanzu*. The living room had a festive air. Black, red, and green balloons floated among paper streamers. The black, red, and green *bendera*, the flag, stood out. Chris, in his colorful *dashiki*, felt a pulse of quiet excitement.

Many of the women had on dresses in African styles. Chris thought that his mother's pale blue *busuti* was especially beautiful. On her head she wore a *gele*, of the same material as her *busuti*. Chris watched as she talked with Jamal's mother, and he felt pleased that she looked so pretty.

Grandma Ida, round and plump, looked regal in a plum-colored high-crowned *gele* the same color as her loosely fitting *buba*. She laughed and talked with the people near her.

Voices quieted when Uncle Ronald moved toward the center of the room. People took seats in a circle with the table in the middle. The elderly sat closest, with the children on the floor at their feet. Feeling the warm friendliness in the room, Chris smiled at Miles and Jamal. Then he took hold of Beth's hand and waited.

Uncle Ronald's deep, strong voice filled the room. "Welcome to our first day of Kwanzaa celebration. You are going to hear a lot of Swahili tonight."

"Why Swahili?" one of the children whispered.

"It's African. We African-Americans." The response was whispered, also.

"Now," Uncle Ronald went on, "this is the first day of our celebration of togetherness. A time for remembering our past and looking at where we are today. It is a time for us to make promises for a better life for ourselves and for our children. Everybody can take part, especially the young people here.

"Chris, Miles, and Beth, y'all come on up and help me. Some of us here are new and don't know what all these things are on the table."

The table was covered with a cotton cloth tie-dyed in black, green, and red. All the symbols of Kwanzaa were on the table. Chris knew that Uncle Ronald had brought many of those things home from Kenya when he returned from the Peace Corps.

Uncle Ronald continued, "The children will give us the Swahili words for the symbols and tell us what they mean. You will repeat after them so we'll all learn together, okay? Beth, you go first."

On the table were apples, oranges, and bananas in a large, hand-carved wooden bowl, surrounded by greens, carrots, yams, squash, coconuts, and many ears of corn. "This is *mazao*, which means crops," Beth said. "All the food stands for rewards for our work. Like farmers have to work, watering plants and pulling weeds, we have to work hard for prizes and awards." Beth smiled as everyone applauded.

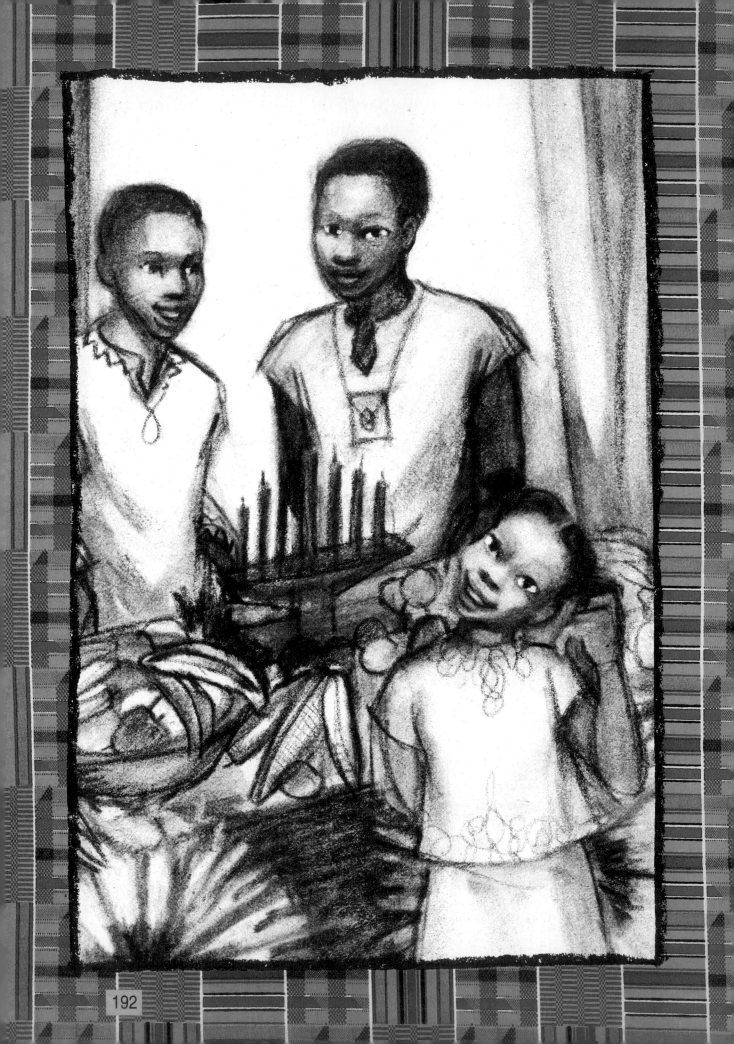

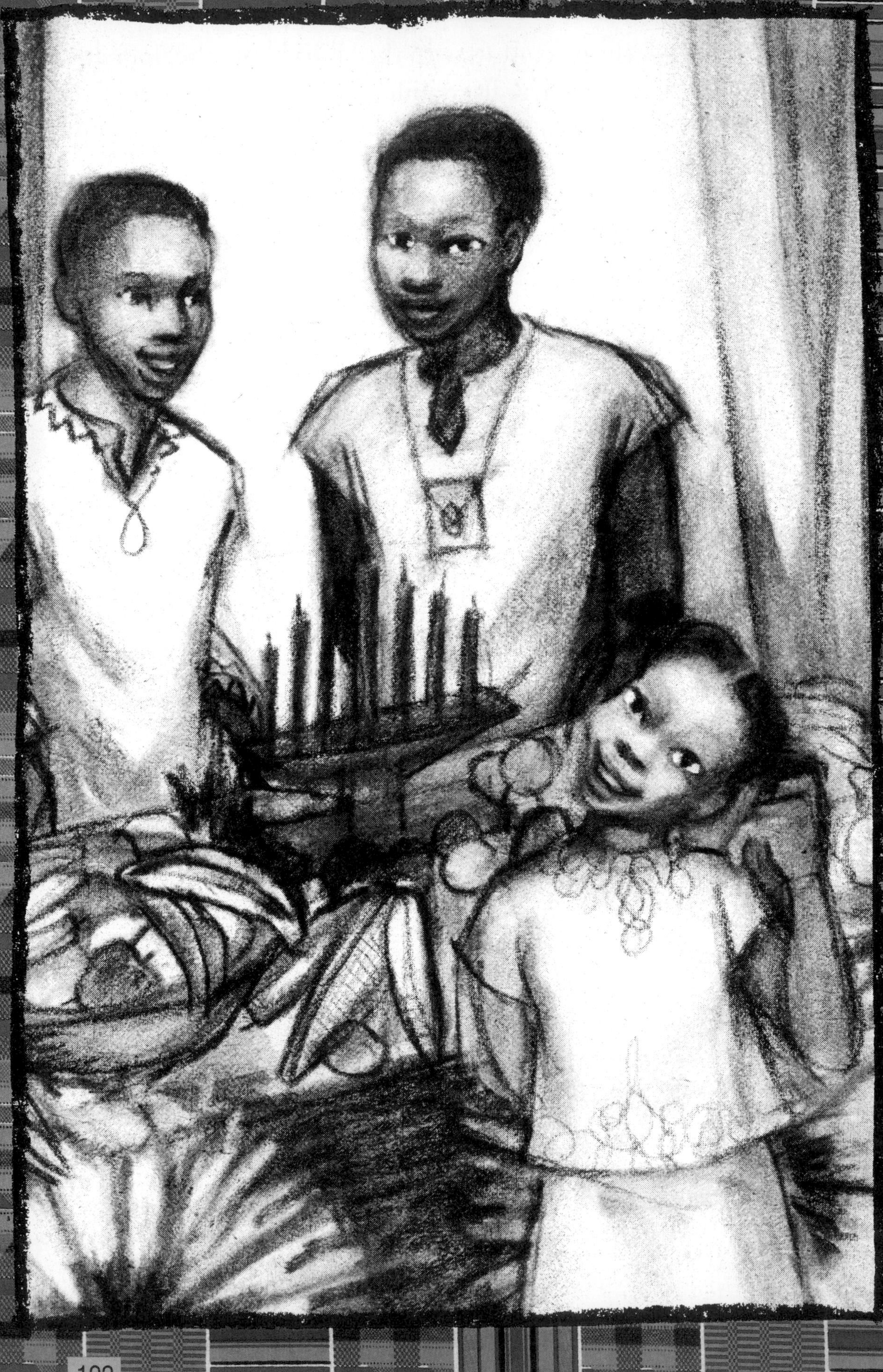

Miles had a turn defining the *mkeka*, a mat woven from palm leaves. "The mat and fruit bowl came from Africa," he said. "In Africa people make a lot of things by hand. That is an old custom. This *mkeka* stands for our history."

Then Miles explained that the candle holder, or *kinara*, stands for ancestors, parents, and all Black people. "The *kinara* holds the flame," Miles said. "And the corn, the *vibunzi*, stands for children, an ear for each child."

"That was a great job, Miles," Uncle Ronald said. "Let's give Miles a big hand." Everybody applauded.

Chris felt nervous at his turn, but relaxed as he got going. He told about the gaily wrapped gifts on the table. "These *zawadi* stand for all the things children have said they would do and have done. They also represent things parents have done for children."

He placed his hand on a cup made from a gourd. "This is a *kikombe cha umoja*, the unity cup. This cup is used for drinks in honor of our ancestors," Chris said. "The seven candles here in the *kinara* are called *mishumaa saba*. They represent the seven principles of Kwanzaa, what we believe in."

Chris then explained that the colors of the candles also had meaning. "The black one stands for our people, the three green ones on the right are for youth and hope for the future, and the red ones on the left stand for struggle that goes on and on."

Chris got a big hand, too. When he sat down he smiled at Miles and Jamal. His heart beat faster when they smiled back.

"*Habari gani*," Uncle Ronald cried. "*Kwanzaa yenu iwe heri!*"

"*Umoja!*" everyone responded.

The ritual for the first day of Kwanzaa began. Beth lighted the first candle. As she held the match to the black candle in the center of the *kinara*, she said, "We begin this first day of Kwanzaa, *umoja*, which means unity."

Everyone remained quiet as small cups of grape juice were passed around. By the light of the candle, Uncle Ronald poured some juice into the *kikombe*. Then he set a small flowerpot filled with earth on the floor. "This earth is a mixture from Kenya, an East African country in our native land, and from America, our new land." He lifted the cup. "For all of our mothers and fathers unknown to us in our native land of Africa, we make this *tambiko*, or libation." He poured the drink into the pot of earth.

He refilled the cup and lifted it. Chris raised his cup with all the others in the room.

Uncle Ronald then began the *tamshi la tambiko*. "For all of our people known everywhere who struggled for freedom; for our brothers, Malcolm, Martin, and Medgar; for our sisters, Mary Church, Fannie Lou, and Ida B. May they live in the hearts of freedom-loving people as long as the earth turns warmed by the sun." He drank from the cup as all the people in the room drank from theirs.

Then people were invited to stand and talk about *umoja* in their lives, or in the lives and history of Black people. Chris listened with interest when one woman talked about Harriet Tubman and how Harriet practiced the unity principle when she helped slaves follow the North Star and run away to freedom. Then his father stood to speak. Chris felt an uneasy surprise.

"So far, all the things talked about tonight have been happenings in the past. I can speak of *umoja* in the present, today," he said. "As most of you know, I'm out of work."

Chris could not look at his father. He felt a heaviness in his chest.

His father went on. "I can say there has been unity in my family and among my friends. You have shared food and other goods. You have given your support and understanding, too. I want to thank all of you. I think I can speak for Myra, a good wife and mother, and for Chris and Beth, too, when I say we are proud to be a part of you. But we might have to leave here. . . ."

Chris, still feeling uneasy, glanced at Mama. She held her head down and Chris sensed that she was close to tears. *Oh, no. Don't let her cry.* The heavy lump in his chest spread as he fought back his tears. He'd just die if Miles and Jamal saw *him* crying.

His father sat down and there was silence. Then Uncle Ronald stood and said, "Come on, everybody. It's time for some food. Time for fun! Let's begin the *karamu*."

There were baskets of bread, bowls of fruit punch, platters of meat and vegetables, and pans of pies and cobblers. All the children were served first. Then the elderly helped themselves. Chris's mama and daddy and the other people in between served themselves last.

After the feast, some of Uncle Ronald's friends beat drums. Music, dancing, and laughter went on into the night. But in spite of all the good food and entertainment, Chris was glad when the celebration ended. He went home feeling more worried and afraid than ever.

CHAPTER NINE

The shrill ringing of the telephone brought Chris out of deep sleep. Then he heard his daddy's voice. The search for a job went on. *How do people find work?* he wondered.

"Chris," Daddy called.

Chris hurriedly put on his robe and met his daddy in the hallway. "You got a job?" His voice cracked with excitement.

"Well, something. You take over until your mama comes, okay?"

If Daddy had a job, why didn't he look happy? Chris wanted to ask some questions. But he decided not to.

"Oh," Daddy said. "I almost forgot. This is where I'll be." Chris took the small piece of paper and looked at it. "The phone number is there, but you're not to call . . ."

". . . unless there's an emergency," Chris finished the sentence. They both laughed.

As he followed his daddy through the house toward the garage, Chris noticed a neatly wrapped package on the table. "What's that?" he asked.

"Your uncle brought that for Kwanzaa. Yours and Beth's. Don't open it now. Not until Beth is up," Daddy said. "Bye now."

Alone, Chris toyed with the ribbons. Tempted, he pulled the attached cluster of ribbons off the top. *Beth won't know the difference*, he thought. Then he decided to get her up. He stuck the ribbon back in place.

He didn't have to get Beth up. Right then she stumbled into the room like someone walking in her sleep. But when she saw the package, she became wide awake. "We got a present," she cried.

They wasted no time unwrapping the box. Inside were three things: a magic slate for Beth, a booklet neatly done in Uncle Ronald's handwriting, and a small *kinara* with the black, green, and red *mishumaa saba*.

"Let's light the candles," Beth said.

"No. We have to wait until Mama and Daddy get home. We'll do it together." He began to read a note he had found with the booklet.

Dear Chris,

This ***kinara*** is for you to use to observe the remaining six days and principles of Kwanzaa listed for you in this booklet. Each day, light a candle. Then remind your family of the principle for that day and for what that principle stands. We have celebrated ***umoja***. Today, you will celebrate ***kujichagulia,*** which means self-determination.

The other five principles are: ***ujima,*** collective work and responsibility; ***ujamaa,*** cooperative economics; ***nia,*** purpose; ***kuumba,*** creativity; and ***imani,*** faith.

"What you reading?" Beth wanted to know. "What does it say?"

"It's for me. Uncle Ronald is putting me in charge. I'll do the Kwanzaa for us this year." He looked at her and grinned proudly.

"But what does it say?" she persisted.

Chris continued reading aloud: "'All of this may seem hard at first . . .'" He stopped and looked at Beth. "The principles of Kwanzaa, you know."

"Yeah. Like *umoja*," she said.

Chris read on: "'But you will learn all the seven principles —the *nguzo* — and when you're older, you'll understand exactly what they mean.'"

He looked at Beth and knew she was not listening. She was scribbling letters and numbers on her magic slate.

Chris wondered what Miles and Jamal were doing. They're probably together right now, he thought. If only Mama would let them come over when he had to stay in to take care of Beth.

Beth opened the blinds and shouted, "Ooo, look!"

Chris joined her at the window. Snow falling thick and fast blanketed the walk and street. Wind pushed and shoved the silent snow hurling down, sticking, growing. Steam flowed from vents and dark smoke curled from chimneys, white against the lead-colored sky. A lone car moved cautiously in the street, its wheels making a muffled sluicing. Chris sensed an inner hum in the silence. A peaceful satisfaction.

All too soon he was brought back to the present with Beth's cry, "I'm hungry. Let's eat."

Reluctantly he moved with her toward the kitchen, wishing he could go back to bed.

By the time Mama came home, he and Beth had tired of one another. Breakfast, lunch, a little talk, reading aloud, and lots of unanswerable questions from a five-year-old left him feeling restless and bored.

He greeted Mama with the news that Daddy had found a job. *Was it a good job?* he wondered now. *Or just a few days of work?* He didn't want the family to have to move.

Mama was pleased to hear about the job. Things were different at home when she was happy. Soon the house had an aroma of corn bread cooking and meat and vegetables warming. Her good feelings spread to Chris and Beth. They set the table, laughing and teasing as they put the small *kinara* on the buffet and placed fruit festively around it. Beth stuck the matches under the edge of her plate, claiming the right to light the candle.

When Daddy came home they all rushed to him. "How is the new job?" Mama asked.

"I don't want to talk about it." Daddy walked through to the bedroom and closed the door.

In silence they put food on the table. Soon the family was seated for dinner. Daddy looked tense, tired. Chris announced that he and Beth would do the Kwanzaa ritual. With the booklet turned to pages about the second day, he asked Beth if she was ready. She nodded and came to stand on the other side of the *kinara*.

Chris felt the uneasiness that had begun when Daddy arrived. At first he didn't know how to begin. Then, remembering his

uncle's approach, he stood tall and straightened his shoulders. *"Habari gani!"*

"Kujichagulia!" they all responded.

Beth relit the black candle for *umoja*, then lighted a red one. "For *kujichagulia*, the second day of Kwanzaa," she said.

Chris saw a smile spread over his father's face and gathered courage to go on. He read the principle of *kujichagulia*. "Self-determination is deciding things, speaking up for ourselves, and doing things the way we feel they should be done."

In the glow of the candles they ate. Chris still felt underlying tension and knew why Mama cautiously chose words, trying to prevent silence from settling around them. Unpleasant things were not allowed to surface at the table while they were eating.

"Well, Bruce, do you want to tell us about the job now?" Mama asked as soon as they had finished dinner.

"There is no job." Daddy spoke with some sharpness. "It was a day's work with little pay."

"What was it?" Chris asked timidly.

"I don't want to talk about it."

"Why? Why can't you talk about it?" Mama was less cautious.

"I'm getting tired of going on these little penny-paying jobs thinking they're going to turn into something and it's always the same — nothing."

There was silence. Chris didn't remember ever hearing such bitterness in his daddy's voice. He kept his eyes on his plate as Daddy went on. "I feel like giving up and never going out there again."

"Now certainly is not the time to think of giving up," Mama said.

"You think I'm not even trying. I know you think I'm no longer the man of this house with you taking care of us," Daddy said angrily.

"How can you say that?" She tried to take the edge off of his anger. "That's not what I think at all, Bruce. I still think there is something out there for you."

"I'm glad you think so. There may be jobs, but not for me. I file an application and I'm told I'm overqualified. If I get to an interview, one look at me and I'm just not what they're looking for."

One look at me rang in Chris's mind. *This is happening because we're Black.*

"You'll find something." Mama sounded as if she were pleading for Daddy to hang in there.

"I've found nothing all this time. I'm beginning to think I'll never find anything again. I can't go on like this."

Chris looked up and caught Mama's eye. She turned to Daddy and said, "I wish you wouldn't talk like this in front of the children."

"I said I didn't want to talk about it. You insisted. They need to know the truth. A man can't determine what he's going to do with his life if he has no job." He left the table, put on his coat, and said, "I'll be back."

They waited and waited. Beth and Mama went to bed. Chris waited some more. Finally he went to his room. He lay in his bed. *What is Daddy doing out there in the cold night? What will happen to us if he never comes back?* He tried to recall the feeling he'd had while looking at the snow that morning. The sleep he had longed for then would not come now. Every sound alerted him. Not until he heard the car in the driveway and the door to his parents' bedroom close did he fall asleep.

CHAPTER

TEN

Another day went by; the weather warmed. Sun and snow made the sky unbelievably blue. The city sparkled, but Chris's mood did not reflect the change. With Beth taking a nap, bored, he paced from room to room, restless. *The holiday almost gone and I've had no fun. Stuck in this house with Beth, can't even see my friends.*

The night before, they had lighted the candle for *ujima*, collective work and responsibility. The worried look on Mama's face had kept him from saying much about *ujima*. Now, Chris felt ashamed of his restlessness. He knew he was with Beth because they had no money for the sitter. He wanted to be cooperative, responsible. He could really help if he had a bicycle, but that couldn't even be mentioned without a hassle.

Later, he and Beth had just popped some corn when the doorbell rang. Beth ran ahead of him to the door.

"Wait," he said. "Let me see who's there."

"It's me. Your favorite uncle," said a voice from outside.

Laughing, they opened the door to let Uncle Ronald in.

"That popcorn sure smells good."

"Come on, you can have some," Beth said.

"Later. I came to celebrate *ujamaa* with you guys. Let's do the ritual and you can do it again with your mom and dad tonight."

Beth and Chris took turns relighting the three candles. Then Beth lighted a red one, the fourth, for *ujamaa*.

"Cooperative economics," Uncle Ronald said. "That principle has to do with making money by working together."

Chris thought about Daddy and said nothing.

"Mama makes the money in this house now," Beth said.

"Aw, shut up," Chris muttered angrily.

"Let her talk, Chris. Your mama does make money. Your daddy, too. He'll be working steadily again, soon. But I was thinking we should start a business. Work for ourselves. Wait a minute."

Uncle Ronald went out and came back into the house rolling a red bicycle with streaks of black and green. A streamlined one.

"Uncle Ronald!" Chris screamed. "Is that for me?"

"For *ujamaa*. All of us, everybody in our family, got together and bought you this bicycle. That's one means of cooperative economics. You can start your paper route business."

"Oh, I can't believe this," Chris cried. "How'd you know I wanted to deliver papers?"

"Your mama told me."

"Now I can deliver them."

"While Beth and I find something to do, why don't you go out and visit your friends?" Uncle Ronald suggested.

Trembling with joy, Chris booted the kickstand, making sure it was in place. He wheeled the bike out to the sidewalk. Then, swinging his leg over the top tube, he pumped down and broke free. He raced away, not noticing the coldest wind, everything whirring by, blurred. He felt weightless. There was only one thing in his mind: *It's mine, it's mine*, he said over and over to himself.

Miles came out of his back door just as Chris rode into his open garage and braked his bike.

"I saw you coming," Miles said. "Is that yours?"

"It's mine. Got it for *ujamaa*, cooperative economics day."

"All right!" Miles smiled.

"Now I can deliver papers, too." Chris breathed hard with excitement.

"You're just in time. I'm waiting for Mr. Moore right now. He's bringing my papers. He's the district manager."

"Think he'll hire me?"

"He might. Wait and ask him."

Soon a truck loaded with newspapers drove up. A stocky man jumped out and grabbed a stack of papers. "I can always depend on you, Miles," he said, dropping the bundle.

Miles introduced Chris to Mr. Moore and told him Chris wanted to deliver papers.

"What kind of work is your dad doing?" Mr. Moore asked.

"He's not working now," Chris said with his head lowered.

"Oh, too bad. You need somebody with a steady job to vouch for you. You know, back you up. You have to be responsible."

"Oh, Chris is responsible," Miles said.

Chris looked at Mr. Moore and said eagerly, "And my mama works. She's a nurse. And my uncle. They'll vouch for me."

"You'll have to be bonded," Mr. Moore said. "That's a kind of insurance."

"How much a bond cost?" Chris asked.

"Three hundred dollars."

"Three hundred dollars!" Chris screamed.

"Oh, don't get excited now." Mr. Moore laughed. "You'll have to pay it, but not all at once. Now, if you were eighteen or older, you'd have to pay it before you went to work."

"I paid mine a little at a time, till I paid it all, huh, Mr. Moore?" Miles said.

"Yeah. That's right. Only grown-ups have to pay up front."

"Whew!" Chris shook his head rapidly. "Then you'll hire me?"

"I guess I can use a boy like you. You ten?"

"Just made eleven, huh, Miles?" Chris beamed.

"Fine. You can start in right after the holiday." Mr. Moore straightened papers around in his truck. He turned to Chris. "Oh, yeah, I won't be your manager. Somebody else will train you."

"How come you won't do it, Mr. Moore?" Miles wanted to know.

"Miles, didn't I tell you? I got promoted. I thought I had told you I'm going to be a supervisor." Mr. Moore grinned and went on his way.

"He's real nice," Miles said. "Wish he wasn't leaving."

Suddenly Chris had an idea. "You think my dad could get *his* job?"

"Sure," Miles answered excitedly, "if he's got three hundred dollars."

You don't have to come up with that kind of money. Only grown-ups do, flashed into Chris's mind. *Where will we get three hundred dollars right away?*

Chris rode home worried. He had thought getting a bicycle and a job delivering papers would make him the happiest person in the world. But instead, he was more anxious than ever about his father getting a job.

That night he tossed and turned. He hadn't told his family about Mr. Moore and the jobs. How could Mama and Uncle Ronald get three hundred dollars for Daddy? *My bike. I could give it back. That would bring some money. Maybe two hundred dollars. Oh no, never. Not that. I want my bike.* He tossed and turned some more, and finally fell into troubled sleep.

The next morning Chris woke feeling tired. He couldn't figure out a way to tell his parents about the job openings without offering to give up his bike.

All day he moped around, irritable. He was short-tempered with Beth. Though the weather had warmed even more and the sun shone brightly, he refused to let her go outside. He wouldn't even let her open the blinds.

"You're a mean brother," Beth accused him with tears in her voice.

Chris moved restlessly about the sunless rooms, feeling miserable. Why was he being so mean? He didn't want to be. He wanted to go find Beth, open the blinds, and play with her outside. But he just couldn't bring himself to do it.

His parents came home together that evening. When Beth saw them she burst into tears, trying to tell them how mean Chris had been.

Chris stood under their glares wishing they could understand what he was feeling.

"It's all right, Beth," Mama said. "We're home now, and guess what? Daddy and I brought us all some pizza for supper. Come on. Wanta help me get it ready?"

Chris and his father sat together, waiting, in that dreadful silence that had crept into their house and that no one seemed able to shatter. The quiet increased Chris's uneasiness. *Why doesn't Daddy say something? Why doesn't he wanta know why I've been so mean? Say something! Anything, but something.*

Before eating, Chris lit the candle for *nia*, the fifth principle, which stresses purpose. He had a purpose: to deliver papers and help his family. But he didn't want to talk about that.

They ate pizza and salad by candlelight. He could tell that Beth had a hand in the salad. It was loaded with sunflower seeds. Even though it was a delicious supper, no one savored the food. The meal ended quickly.

"May I be excused?" Chris asked, getting up from the table.

"In just a minute," Daddy said.

Chris sat down, sensing something important about to happen. Maybe Daddy had found a job at last. *But that should make them happy.* He waited. Nothing but that awful silence.

Finally Daddy spoke softly. "Well, your mama and I have decided that we will have to leave this place."

"You mean move to another town?" Chris cried.

"Yes." Mama did not look up.

"Oh, no, I can't leave here. Not now. What about Grandma Ida, Uncle Ronald, the family?"

"Why do you always have to think of just yourself?" Mama scolded.

Chris felt stung. He looked at Daddy, pained.

"She didn't mean it the way it sounds, son. She's trying to tell you we're all hurting. It's our family, too, you know."

"But you can find work here," Chris cried.

"Now, Chris, I've looked. You know that. Every single day for almost two years."

Feeling desperate, Chris blurted out, "There is a job. At the newspaper. A manager's job." He told what he knew about Mr. Moore's promotion. He wanted to tell them about his job, too. But he thought about the bond for him and his daddy, six hundred dollars. He would surely have to give up the bicycle. He decided not to mention his own job at all.

CHAPTER ELEVEN

On the morning of New Year's Eve, Chris's house crackled with excitement and anticipation. Mama had a day off, and Daddy had an appointment with Mr. Moore to see about the job. The appointment was for that afternoon. Even though it was New Year's Eve, the job had to be filled right away.

"How would you and Beth like to get out of the house to do

something today?" Mama asked.

Chris, still worried about the bond money, was not sure. He only wanted to stay in his room away from everybody and everything. "Like what?"

"Like going to the community center. A lot of your friends will be there doing creative things today." Today was the sixth day of Kwanzaa, *kuumba,* based on the principle of creativity.

"I wanta go." Beth liked the idea.

"I don't know," Chris said.

"Chris, you need to get out of this house. I want you to go," Mama pleaded.

"Well, all right. I'll go."

Mama dropped them off at the center just in time for the lighting of the sixth candle. Miles and Jamal were there, happy to see Chris.

"We know you're going to woodwork," Jamal announced to Chris.

"Yeah. Where y'all going?"

"I'm going to essay writing," Miles said.

"I'm going to poetry," Jamal said.

"You, poetry? I don't believe it," Chris said.

"Me," Jamal said, beating his chest. "Believe it. I'm gonna surprise you."

"Well, I can hardly wait. Roses are red, violets, blue . . ." Chris laughed.

"I'll laugh last, man, what you bet?" Jamal bragged.

Chris took Beth to the paper arts section and hurried to woodwork. He had decided to make a big *kinara* for his family to have for next year's Kwanzaa. He explained to the instructor, Mr. Pierce, that he wanted the *kinara* in the shape of the African continent. Immediately they got busy drawing the design: three candle holders on the east side of Africa, three on the west, and one at the southern tip.

He watched as the wood took shape under the zing of the electric saw. Soon he had sanded and smoothed the form and painted it black.

"What you using for candle holders on that wood?" Mr. Pierce asked.

"You think it'll burn, huh?"

"Not likely, but I'd make sure."

Chris had been thinking about making this *kinara* for a long time. Why hadn't he thought of safe holders? *The holders should be metal!*

Looking around the place, he finally found what he needed: a long, thin strip of tin. While measuring the tin he hit upon an idea for a special design. With a hammer and small nail, he pounded little holes all over the tin. As he worked, his mind wandered to his daddy. *What if he gets that job? I'll have to give up my bicycle for his bond. I don't wanta give it up. If only we weren't Black.*

His thoughts flashed to his family, to Uncle Ronald, and he felt ashamed and guilty. *What would Uncle Ronald say if he knew I wished we weren't Black?* He pushed that painful thought out of his mind by pounding the tin harder.

Time seemed to fly, and Chris wondered if he'd have time to finish before Mama came to take them home. He carefully used the heavy scissors to cut seven pieces of tin four inches long. Then he clipped each around the bottom and folded it, making holders that could be glued upright on the board.

"Gosh, it's not dry," he said aloud to the room. He waited. Again his mind wandered to Daddy. Trying to forget that, he focused on the noise about him. People hammered and sawed. From the other rooms came the sound of music and feet moving in dance.

He decided to make gifts for Miles and Jamal while he waited. He drew profiles of Malcolm X and Martin Luther King on pieces of wood. When Mr. Pierce had cut them on the saw, Chris sanded them and painted them with black watercolor. That would dry fast.

Finally the form was dry and ready for the candle holders. The silver color on the black wood looked amazingly attractive. The pounding had created raised designs of small people, birds, and animals. Mr. Pierce invited the other people working in the shop to stop and look at the *kinara*. Chris felt pride and satisfaction.

When Chris and Beth came outside looking for Mama, Miles and Jamal were waiting. The three friends exchanged gifts with a promise not to open them until they got home. Miles and Jamal took off on their bikes.

Soon Mama came. Before getting into the car, Chris cried, "Did Daddy get the job?"

"I don't know yet. I've been so busy. Your grandma called. The family wants to celebrate the New Year at our house. We're going to have a party."

"Can I come?" Beth cried.

"Can't you hear? It's at our house, silly," Chris told her. "Anyway, you'll probably be asleep before it starts."

"Aw, Chris, please," Mama scolded. "Sure, Beth, you can come."

Chris sighed and sank back into the seat. Since he had first heard about the jobs and bonds he had not had a moment of peace. "You know, Mama, I don't think Daddy'll git that job."

"Why you say a thing like that?"

"He'll need three hundred dollars." Chris then told her about his job. "I'll have to pay three hundred dollars, too, but I can pay mine out of what I earn delivering papers. We don't have that kind of money, do we?"

"No, we don't."

"I could take my bike back."

"You don't like your bike?" Beth asked.

"Yeah, but . . ."

"You will not give up your bike," said Mama. "No, no indeed, Chris. That's awfully nice of you to offer, but you are not responsible for getting your daddy a job. Your daddy and I will handle that."

"But you don't have the money. You didn't have any for Christmas and my birthday."

Mama gave a little laugh. "That's different, Chris. Of course we wouldn't borrow money for gifts, but for a job we would. Please don't worry."

Chris did worry. He could hardly wait to get home to see if things had gone well for Daddy.

Daddy was not there when they arrived. Grandma Ida, Uncle Ronald, and the aunts were there, and the house was full of hustle and bustle. *Daddy's got to get that job. We can't leave our family. Where will we go?* He hurried to his room and closed the door.

He sat on his bed and tried to control the fear. Noise and laughter resounded throughout the house. Chris didn't want to feel so all alone. He hurried from his room.

Uncle Ronald had everything ready for the last ritual of Kwanzaa. There was a delicious aroma of food cooking, and Grandma Ida's voice rang from the kitchen. "What's New Year's without black-eyed peas and collard greens? Peas for good luck and collards for the greenback all year long! No house should be without them on New Year's Day."

"Cook, Mama," one of Chris's aunts said. "We need some luck, *and* we sure need some greenback."

"What's greenback, Grandma?" Beth wanted to know.

"Money, honey," Grandma exclaimed. Everybody laughed.

Chris listened to the laughter and fun and some of his sadness disappeared. But why didn't Daddy come home?

It was now almost ten o'clock. People were coming in and out, but still Daddy hadn't come. Chris finally asked, "Where's

Daddy?"

"He'll be here," Mama said. "Stop worrying, Chris. C'mon, have some fun."

"Yeah," Grandma Ida put in. "We don't like long faces in this family. I'm getting old, and you're gonna have to take my place, Chris, keeping the laughter alive. Don't ever forget how to laugh, boy."

That kind of talk made Chris even more sad. He wandered back to his room and decided to open his gifts from Miles and Jamal. Miles had prepared a booklet on three African-American scientists. Chris glanced through paragraphs about a famous biologist, Ernest E. Just. He had heard about George Washington Carver and Charles Drew, but never of Ernest E. Just.

When he opened Jamal's gift, he smiled. There was the promised poem.

Drums! Drums! Drumming!
To the beat moving feet
Making tracks, shaping roads
In the drumming voices humming
Your turn, your turn, your turn.

Chris read the poem thinking about what his grandma had said about laughing. *And maybe it's my turn to stop worrying so much. Even if I have to give my bike up, I'll give it up!* He read Jamal's poem again. "All right!" he said aloud to the room. "I'll give you the last laugh!"

Just then Chris heard the sound of the car in the driveway. Daddy was home. He ran to the front of the house. The pleased look on his father's face let Chris know that he had the job.

"What kept you so long?" Mama asked.

"I had to see the territory. Mr. Moore took me around tonight." He turned to Chris. "Why didn't you tell me? I was surprised to learn that my very own son will be my first trainee." He grabbed Chris and hugged him.

"But what about the bond?" Chris asked worriedly.

"Mr. Moore was very impressed. He said you let him know right away that our family is behind you."

"No. *Your* bond," Mama said.

"District managers don't put up bonds. Only the carriers do that," Daddy answered.

"What?" Chris cried. "After all of that! And I thought I'd have to . . . whew!" Relieved, Chris was ready to get on with the party. When twelve o'clock arrived he joined in blowing whistles, tossing streamers, and hugging and kissing everybody to bring in the New Year.

Right after midnight, they woke Beth to join them for the last ritual of Kwanzaa. Chris relit the six candles and Beth, still not wide awake, said, "I light the seventh candle for *imani*, the principle of faith."

After drinking *tambiko* from the *kikombe cha umoja*, Grandma Ida talked about faith. "Black people through ups and downs have practiced *imani*. When our rights were denied, we kept the faith. When we were bitten by dogs and bombed with water, we kept the faith. And as a family we practice *imani*. We keep the faith. We stand together, and tonight we celebrate that unity and faith without fear that Bruce, Myra, Chris, and Beth will be separated from us. So come, let's rejoice."

They celebrated with a feast of black-eyed peas and rice, mustard and collard greens, yams, okra, and much more, by the light of seven candles. When they opened their gifts for the end of Kwanzaa and the beginning of the New Year, Chris had a great surprise. Grandma Ida gave him a seat bag for his bicycle that she had made with her very own hands.

Chris presented his *kinara* to his parents. "I made this for our family so we can celebrate Kwanzaa in our house every year from now on." They all touched the *kinara*, amazed at its beauty.

"That boy is sure good with his hands," Grandma Ida said.

"Yes, he is," Mama agreed. "But he's not only clever with his hands, he has a big heart, too."

Chris knew she was talking about his offer to give up his bicycle. He beamed with pride. *Maybe Uncle Ronald was right, after all, when he said that important people give.*

In the wee hours of the morning, the family made a circle around Grandma Ida, Beth, and Chris. Grandma Ida gave the *tamshi la tutaonana:* "In this new year let us continue to practice *umoja*, *kujichagulia*, *ujima*, *ujamaa*, *nia*, *kuumba*, and *imani*. Let us strive to do something that will last as long as the earth turns and water flows."

"Now," Uncle Ronald said, "let's leave this house with the word *harambee*. In Swahili that means pulling together."

"*Harambee!*" they all shouted. They repeated it seven times, with Chris's voice the loudest of them all.

KWANZAA

Unity, self-determination, collective work and responsibility, cooperative economics, purpose, creativity, and faith. These are the seven principles of Kwanzaa.

With a group, discuss how these principles were important to Chris and his family in the story. Then choose one or more of the principles and discuss how they might be important in your life.

In all of these books, the characters make choices. They have the courage to stick to their choices and change. I hope as you see them in action you will become thoughtful and aware of yourselves and others. I hope you will come to understand that we are all very much alike even though we may speak different languages, eat different foods, and have different beliefs.

Within a few years you and young people everywhere will inherit the earth. The earth is your home and you are all brothers and sisters even though you may never meet. Is it too much to hope that you will work to find ways to make your home safe, clean, and not infested with greed, bigotry, poverty, and war? Is it too much to hope that you will work together to use technology and all the resources of the earth to find a way to peace? I think not.

I embrace all of you and wish I could see each of you face to face. That is impossible. But I shall keep writing, believing that you will enjoy reading my stories as much as I enjoy writing them for you.

Stay young at heart always,

Mildred Pitts Walter

More Books by

Mildred Pitts Walter

Justin and the Best Biscuits in the World
Just about everything Justin does at home is wrong. That's why he's eager to visit his grandfather, the only person who seems to understand a nine-year-old boy with two older sisters.

Ty's One-man Band
Ty meets a one-legged man who claims he can make music with a washboard, two wooden spoons, a tin pail, and a comb. No one in town believes this man can make music, but the one-legged man shows up and surprises everyone.

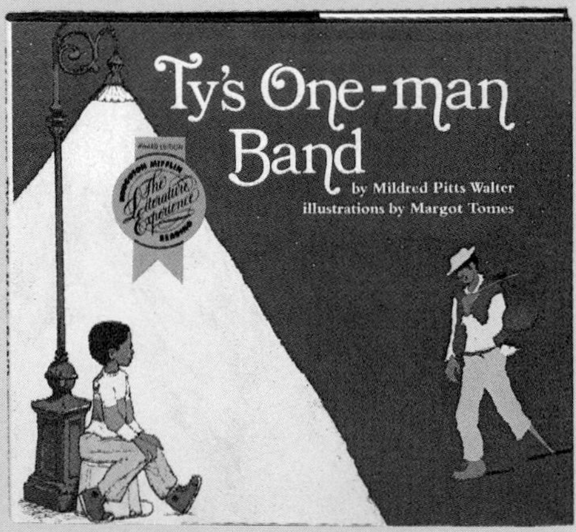

MEET ANOTHER AUTHOR:

Johanna Hurwitz

Unlike Mildred Pitts Walter, Johanna Hurwitz always knew she wanted to be a writer. "When I was twelve I received a check for fifty cents for my first published work. It was a poem that said: 'For me to read a book is still/And always will be quite a thrill.' It concluded, 'And what is more, I'll read until I'm grown/And then I'll write books of my own.'

"I was right!" says Hurwitz.

Johanna Hurwitz has written a great many books of her own and has created characters that you may enjoy getting to know.

ALDO PEANUT BUTTER

Aldo wants a puppy for his birthday and — to his surprise — he gets five. Although he keeps just two, he finds out that keeping himself and two dogs out of trouble is a full-time job.

THE COLD & HOT WINTER

Rory and Derek's friend Bolivia is back for a Christmas vacation visit. Everyone is happy and excited until some of their prized possessions disappear. Could one of these best friends be a thief?

HURRAY FOR ALI BABA BERNSTEIN

Ali Baba Bernstein still hasn't changed his name back to David. He thinks that having a special name will lead to exciting adventures — and he's right. Join Ali Baba as he meets a "king" and solves two mysteries.

Award Winner

Meet John Ciardi

Some of poet John Ciardi's earliest memories were of his childhood home in Medford, Massachusetts. "Our house was on the Mystic River, an ancient Indian fishing stream," Ciardi recalled. "We gardened for food in the beginning and kept chickens, and I often wandered the neighborhood selling vegetables from a cart."

Though Ciardi had a head start as a vegetable vendor, his ambition was to become a poet. He began writing poetry for young people as a way to entertain his children and his nephews. *I Met a Man* is a collection of poems Ciardi wrote for his daughter, Myra. "The Cat Heard the Cat-Bird" is a poem from this collection.

Once Ciardi's children were grown-up, he said he could no longer pretend that he wrote poetry just for them. "I write because I was once a child and mean never to lose the remembrance," Ciardi said. In *Fast and Slow: Poems for Advanced Children and Beginning Parents*, Ciardi wrote about everything from Noah and the ark to the warning about sharks that you'll read on page 222.

THE CAT HEARD THE CAT-BIRD

One day, a fine day, a high-flying-sky day,
A cat-bird, a fat bird, a fine fat cat-bird
Was sitting and singing on a stump by the highway.
Just sitting. And singing. Just that. But a cat heard.

A thin cat, a grin-cat, a long thin grin-cat
Came creeping the sly way by the highway to the stump.
"O cat-bird, the cat heard! O cat-bird scat!
The grin-cat is creeping! He's going to jump!"

– One day, a fine day, a high-flying-sky day
A fat cat, yes, that cat we met as a thin cat
Was napping, cat-napping, on a stump by the highway,
And even in his sleep you could see he was a grin-cat.

Why was he grinning? – He must have had a dream.
What made him fat? – A pan full of cream.
What about the cat-bird? – What bird, dear?
I don't see any cat-bird here.

THE SHARK

My dear, let me tell you about the shark.
Though his eyes are bright, his thought is dark.
He's quiet — that speaks well of him.
So does the fact that he can swim.
But though he swims without a sound,
Wherever he swims he looks around
With those two bright eyes and that one dark thought.
He has only one but he thinks it a lot.
And the thought he thinks but can never complete
Is his long dark thought of something to eat.
Most anything does. And I have to add
That when he eats his manners are bad.
He's a gulper, a ripper, a snatcher, a grabber.
Yes, his manners are drab. But his thought is drabber.
That one dark thought he can never complete
Of something — anything — somehow to eat.

Be careful where you swim, my sweet.

When Ciardi died in 1986 he left cabinets, desks, and boxes full of unpublished poems. Some of these poems were found folded in books. Others were found scribbled on the backs of old letters. Thirty-one of these poems were published for the first time in a book titled *Mummy Took Cooking Lessons and Other Poems.* "The Early Bird" and "How to Assemble a Toy" are two poems from the collection.

THE EARLY BIRD

The early bird – so I have read –
Gets the worm. I stay in bed
And put myself in the worm's shoes.
Had it stayed in for one more snooze
And then a second, then a third,
By then, would not the early bird
Have gone to feed the early cat?
I take a worm's eye view of that.
Why get up early just to start
The day as bird food? Call that smart?
Ask any worm and it will say,
"Being eaten spoils my day!"
Getting out of bed too soon
Spoils mine. Call me at noon.

HOW TO ASSEMBLE A TOY

This is the whatsit that fits on the knob
Of the gadget that turns the thingamabob.
This is the dingus that fits in place
With the doodad next to the whosiface.
This is the jigger that goes in the hole
Where the gizmo turns the rigamarole.
Now slip the ding-dang into the slot
Of the jugamalug, and what have you got?

It's a genuine neverwas such a not!

FANTASY

THEME 4

Fantasy Close to Home

A brother and a sister find a board game with strange instructions. *As they start to play the game . . .*

A boy receives a present from his favorite uncle. He opens the small box *and all of a sudden . . .*

A girl follows a little dog into a mysterious thicket. *Unexpectedly, she finds herself transported to . . .*

The characters in **Fantasy Close to Home** learn that an ordinary day isn't always what it seems to be. Sometimes, without warning, an ordinary day can become *an adventure in fantasy!*

CONTENTS

Award Winner

JUMANJI

written and illustrated by Chris Van Allsburg

"Now remember," Mother said, "your father and I are bringing some guests by after the opera, so please keep the house neat."

"Quite so," added Father, tucking his scarf inside his coat.

Mother peered into the hall mirror and carefully pinned her hat in place, then knelt and kissed both children good-bye.

When the front door closed, Judy and Peter giggled with delight. They took all the toys out of their toy chest and made a terrible mess. But their laughter slowly turned to silence till finally Peter slouched into a chair.

"You know what?" he said. "I'm really bored."

"Me too," sighed Judy. "Why don't we go outside and play?"

Peter agreed, so they set off across the street to the park. It was cold for November. The children could see their breath like steam. They rolled in the leaves and when Judy tried to stuff some leaves down Peter's sweater he jumped up and ran behind a tree. When his sister caught up with him, he was kneeling at the foot of the tree, looking at a long thin box.

"What's that?" Judy asked.

"It's a game," said Peter, handing her the box.

" 'JUMANJI,' " Judy read from the box, " 'A JUNGLE ADVENTURE GAME.' "

"Look," said Peter, pointing to a note taped to the bottom of the box. In a childlike handwriting were the words "Free game, fun for some but not for all. P.S. Read instructions carefully."

"Want to take it home?" Judy asked.

"Not really," said Peter. "I'm sure somebody left it here because it's so boring."

"Oh, come on," protested Judy. "Let's give it a try. Race you home!" And off she ran with Peter at her heels.

At home, the children spread the game out on a card table. It looked very much like the games they already had. There was a board that unfolded, revealing a path of colored squares. The squares had messages written on them. The path started in the deepest jungle and ended up in Jumanji, a city of golden buildings and towers. Peter began to shake the dice and play with the other pieces that were in the box.

"Put those down and listen," said Judy. "I'm going to read the instructions: 'Jumanji, a young people's jungle adventure especially designed for the bored and restless.

> " 'A. Player selects piece and places it in deepest jungle. B. Player rolls dice and moves piece along path through the dangers of the jungle. C. First player to reach Jumanji and yell the city's name aloud is the winner.' "

"Is that all?" asked Peter, sounding disappointed.

"No," said Judy, "there's one more thing, and this is in capital letters: 'D. VERY IMPORTANT: ONCE A GAME OF JUMANJI IS STARTED IT WILL NOT BE OVER UNTIL ONE PLAYER REACHES THE GOLDEN CITY.' "

BALDWAY

"Oh, big deal," said Peter, who gave a bored yawn.

"Here," said Judy, handing her brother the dice, "you go first."

Peter casually dropped the dice from his hand.

"Seven," said Judy.

Peter moved his piece to the seventh square.

" 'Lion attacks, move back two spaces,' " read Judy.

"Gosh, how exciting," said Peter, in a very unexcited voice. As he reached for his piece he looked up at his sister. She had a look of absolute horror on her face.

"Peter," she whispered, "turn around very, very slowly."

The boy turned in his chair. He couldn't believe his eyes. Lying on the piano was a lion, staring at Peter and licking his lips.

The lion roared so loud it knocked Peter right off his chair. The big cat jumped to the floor. Peter was up on his feet, running through the house with the lion a whisker's length behind. He ran upstairs and dove under a bed. The lion tried to squeeze under, but got his head stuck. Peter scrambled out, ran from the bedroom, and slammed the door behind him. He stood in the hall with Judy, gasping for breath.

"I don't think," said Peter in between gasps of air, "that I want . . . to play . . . this game . . . anymore."

"But we have to," said Judy as she helped Peter back downstairs. "I'm sure that's what the instructions mean. That lion won't go away until one of us wins the game."

Peter stood next to the card table. "Can't we just call the zoo and have him taken away?" From upstairs came the sounds of growling and clawing at the bedroom door. "Or maybe we could wait till Father comes home."

"No one would come from the zoo because they wouldn't believe us," said Judy. "And you know how upset Mother would be if there was a lion in the bedroom. We started this game, and now we have to finish it."

Peter looked down at the game board. What if Judy rolled a seven? Then there'd be two lions. For an instant Peter thought he was going to cry. Then he sat firmly in his chair and said, "Let's play."

Judy picked up the dice, rolled eight, and moved her piece. " 'Monkeys steal food, miss one turn,' " she read. From the kitchen came the sounds of banging pots and falling jars. The children ran in to see a dozen monkeys tearing the room apart.

"Oh boy," said Peter, "this would upset Mother even more than the lion."

"Quick," said Judy, "back to the game."

Peter took his turn. Thank heavens, he landed on a blank space. He rolled again. " 'Monsoon season begins, lose one turn.' " Little raindrops began to fall in the living room. Then a roll of thunder shook the walls and scared the monkeys out of the kitchen. The rain began to fall in buckets as Judy took the dice. " 'Guide gets lost, lose one turn.' " The rain suddenly stopped. The children turned to see a man hunched over a map.

"Oh dear, I say, spot of bad luck now," he mumbled. "Perhaps a left turn here then . . . No, no . . . a right turn here . . . Yes, absolutely, I think, a right turn . . . or maybe . . ."

"Excuse me," said Judy, but the guide just ignored her.

". . . around here, then over . . . No, no . . . over here and around this . . . Yes, good . . . but, then . . . Hm . . ."

Judy shrugged her shoulders and handed the dice to Peter.

". . . four, five, six," he counted. " 'Bitten by tsetse fly, contract sleeping sickness, lose one turn.' "

Judy heard a faint buzzing noise and watched a small insect land on Peter's nose. Peter lifted his hand to brush the bug away, but then stopped, gave a tremendous yawn, and fell sound asleep, his head on the table.

"Peter, Peter, wake up!" cried Judy. But it was no use. She grabbed the dice and moved to a blank. She rolled again and waited in amazement. " 'Rhinoceros stampede, go back two spaces.' "

As fast as he had fallen asleep, Peter awoke. Together they listened to a rumble in the hallway. It grew louder and louder. Suddenly a herd of rhinos charged through the living room and into the dining room, crushing all the furniture in their path. Peter and Judy covered their ears as sounds of splintering wood and breaking china filled the house.

Peter gave the dice a quick tumble. " 'Python sneaks into camp, go back one space.' "

Judy shrieked and jumped up on her chair.

"Over the fireplace," said Peter. Judy sat down again, nervously eyeing the eight-foot snake that was wrapping itself around the mantel clock. The guide looked up from his map, took one look at the snake, and moved to the far corner of the room, joining the monkeys on the couch.

Judy took her turn and landed on a blank space. Her brother took the dice and rolled a three.

"Oh, no," he moaned. " 'Volcano erupts, go back three spaces.' " The room became warm and started to shake a little. Molten lava poured from the fireplace opening. It hit the water on the floor and the room filled with steam. Judy rolled the dice and moved ahead.

" 'Discover shortcut, roll again.' Oh dear!" she cried. Judy saw the snake unwrapping himself from the clock.

"If you roll a twelve you can get out of the jungle," said Peter.

"Please, please," Judy begged as she shook the dice. The snake was wriggling his way to the floor. She dropped the dice from her hand. One six, then another. Judy grabbed her piece and slammed it to the board. "**JUMANJI**," she yelled, as loud as she could.

The steam in the room became thicker and thicker. Judy could not even see Peter across the table. Then, as if all the doors and windows had been opened, a cool breeze cleared the steam from the room. Everything was just as it had been before the game. No monkeys, no guide, no water, no broken furniture, no snake, no lion roaring upstairs, no rhinos. Without saying a word to each other, Peter and Judy threw the game into its box. They bolted out the door, ran across the street to the park, and dropped the game under a tree. Back home, they quickly put all their toys away. But both children were too excited to sit quietly, so Peter took out a picture puzzle. As they fit the pieces together, their excitement slowly turned to relief, and then exhaustion. With the puzzle half done Peter and Judy fell sound asleep on the sofa.

"**W**ake up, dears," Mother's voice called.

Judy opened her eyes. Mother and Father had returned and their guests were arriving. Judy gave Peter a nudge to wake him. Yawning and stretching, they got to their feet.

Mother introduced them to some of the guests, then asked, "Did you have an exciting afternoon?"

"Oh yes," said Peter. "We had a flood, a stampede, a volcano, I got sleeping sickness, and —" Peter was interrupted by the adults' laughter.

"Well," said Mother, "I think you both got sleeping sickness. Why don't you go upstairs and put your

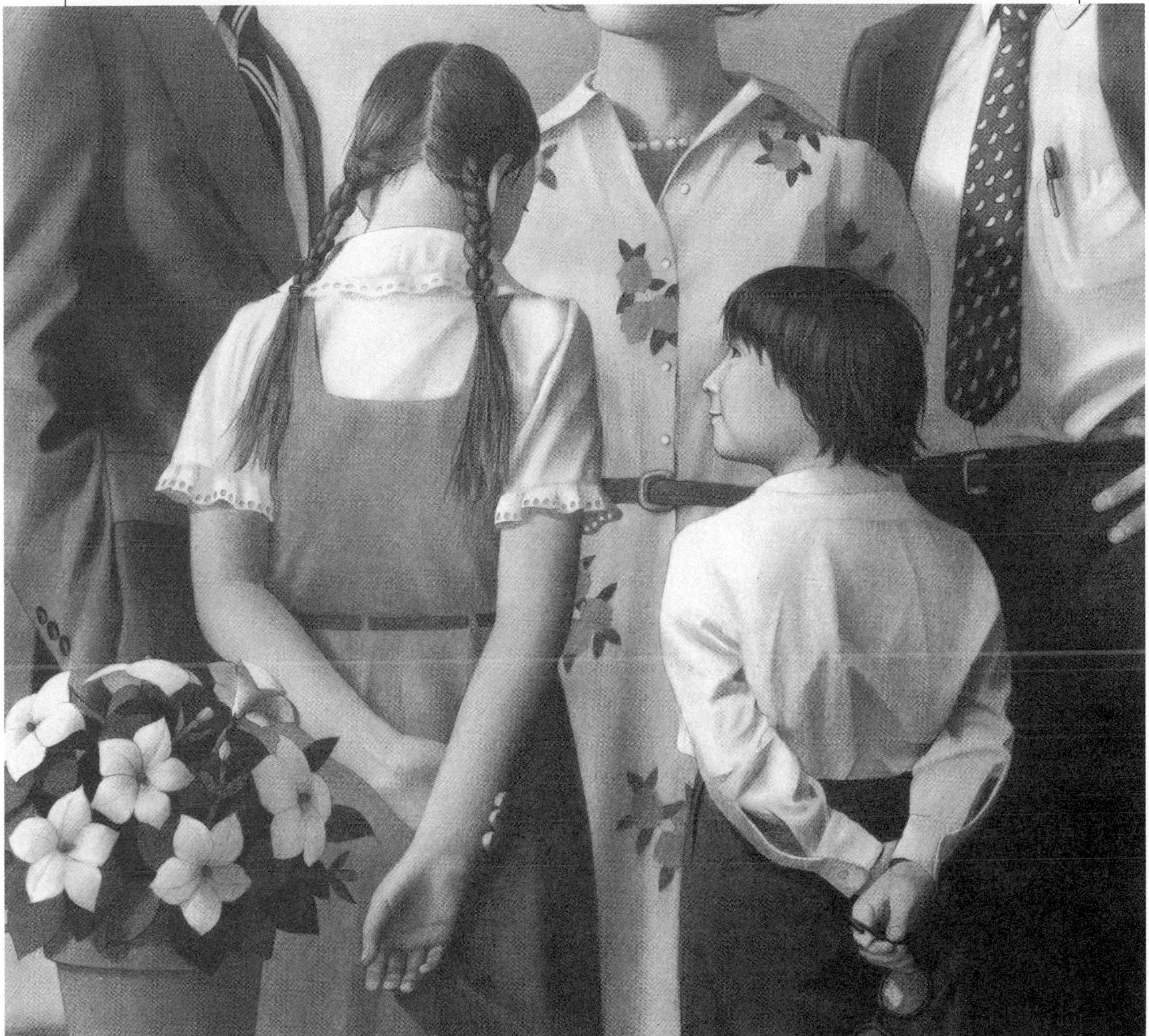

pajamas on? Then you can finish your puzzle and have some dinner."

When Peter and Judy came back downstairs they found that Father had moved the puzzle into the den. While the children were working on it, one of the guests, Mrs. Budwing, brought them a tray of food.

"Such a hard puzzle," she said to the children. "Daniel and Walter are always starting puzzles and never finishing them." Daniel and Walter were Mrs. Budwing's sons. "They never read instructions either. Oh well," said Mrs. Budwing, turning to rejoin the guests, "I guess they'll learn."

Both children answered, "I hope so," but they weren't looking at Mrs. Budwing. They were looking out the window. Two boys were running through the park. It was Danny and Walter Budwing, and Danny had a long thin box under his arm.

WARNING! THIS IS NO ORDINARY GAME!

You're playing your favorite board game with a friend. All of a sudden, the game comes to life! Write a fantasy story about your adventure playing this game.

Assignment: Imagination

If Chris Van Allsburg were your art teacher, he might ask you to draw some very unusual things.

In his classes at the Rhode Island School of Design, Van Allsburg asked his students to make up their own country. They had to name their imaginary country, draw postage stamps and travel posters, and even write a national anthem, or song, for it.

Chris Van Allsburg

When Chris Van Allsburg was a boy, playing ordinary board games bored him. They never seemed real enough to him. It was this memory that inspired Van Allsburg to write *Jumanji.*

Van Allsburg has written and illustrated many other books. All of them include a strange mix of mystery and fantasy, and most of them have a surprise twist at the end. You never know what's going to happen next if you're reading a book by Chris Van Allsburg.

Other Van Allsburg books you may enjoy are *The Mysteries of Harris Burdick, The Stranger,* and *The Wreck of the* Zephyr.

Dog Watch

Did you notice the little white dog with the black patch over his eye on page 231 of *Jumanji*? That's Fritz. He first appeared in *The Garden of Abdul Gasazi,* Chris Van Allsburg's first book. Since then, Van Allsburg has included Fritz in each of his books. As you read other books by Van Allsburg, keep an eye out for Fritz. But look carefully — sometimes he's hiding in odd places.

From *The Garden of Abdul Gasazi*

Award Winner

A River Dream

written and illustrated by Allen Say

The week that Mark had a high fever, Uncle Scott sent him a small metal box for trout flies. Mark was thrilled to have his uncle's favorite fly box. And what's more, it brought back memories of his first fishing trip.

Last summer, Uncle Scott had taken him to a secret place on a sparkling river, and Mark had hooked a rainbow trout with a fly. How the little fish had jumped! More than anything else, Mark wanted to show his catch to his mother and father, but the fish got away and he never caught another.

"Better luck next time," Uncle Scott had said.

When Mark opened the box, he was startled by a cloud of mayflies that rose up from it. As the flies fluttered out the window, he looked outside and rubbed his eyes in wonder.

The whole neighborhood had disappeared! A river flowed where the street had been, and a forest spread out as far as he could see. Then he noticed the mayflies hovering over the water, and shiny fish began to leap up after them. Mark rushed outside.

He saw a rowboat bobbing in the shallow water.

"I wonder whose it is," he whispered. He looked all around but saw no one. But the mayflies had moved down the river, with the leaping fish after them.

"Well, I'm going to borrow this, just for a little while," he said and got into the boat.

As Mark drifted around the first bend in the river, he saw a lone fisherman below him.

Then, quite near Mark, a fish leapt out of the water, almost splashing him. It was the largest trout he had ever seen. It had a hook in its mouth.

"How about that, Mark!" shouted the fisherman.

"Uncle Scott!" Mark cried. "What are you doing here?"

"Funny you should ask," said Uncle, reeling in the fish. "I was about to ask what you were doing in my boat."

"This is your boat?" said Mark.

Uncle nodded. "Well, I'm glad to see you're feeling better. So, did you like the box I sent you?"

"Oh, yes, thank you very much. But you know what? All the flies flew away. I mean, they were real flies!"

"What magic!" Uncle laughed. "This fellow certainly thought my fly was real."

Uncle Scott netted the fish, removed the fly from its mouth, and let it swim away. Mark was amazed.

"Why did you do that?" asked Mark.

"Why didn't I kill the fish?" said Uncle. "I like to leave the river the way I found it. It's like cutting trees, Mark. You keep cutting trees and soon you're going to have bald mountains."

"Then why do you fish?"

"Just for the fun of it," Uncle replied. "Besides, maybe one day I will catch a mermaid. A wise old fisherman said that."

"But mermaids aren't real," said Mark.

"Aren't they?" Uncle smiled.

Mayflies began to flit all around them, and rising trout made rings on the water.

"The magic hour, my boy," said Uncle, climbing into the boat. "Do you remember your roll cast?"

"Yes, like this." Mark nodded, swinging his hand back and forth.

"Well, this may be your lucky night." Uncle handed Mark the rod.

Mark flushed with excitement. He raised the rod tip high, until the line hung behind his shoulder — just as his uncle had taught him. Then, with a quick, chopping stroke, he whipped the rod downward. The line shot out, and the cream-colored fly drifted down on the slick water like a snowflake. Mark took a deep breath.

"Fine cast!" Uncle exclaimed. "Now keep your eye on the fly. Remember, you're not going to feel the strike. You're going to see it. When you see a fish take your fly, raise your rod. Easy does it, my boy, you don't want to break your line."

Mark kept his eye on the fly, and suddenly the water swelled under it. Then a gaping mouth broke the surface and the fly was gone!

"Set the hook!" Uncle shouted.

Mark raised the rod, and the rod bent over from some heavy weight. The reel screeched as the line ran out. A large trout leapt in the air.

"It's bigger than the one you caught!" yelled Mark.

"Some rainbow!" Uncle agreed. "Let him run! Keep the rod up!"

The great trout put up a mighty fight, running again and again, leaping and twisting, but it could not break the line. When it could fight no more, Mark reeled it in. It barely fitted in Uncle's net.

"He's beautiful!" said Mark.

"Magnificent!" said Uncle. "And you're some fisherman!"

Mark sat down to admire his prize.

"Can I keep it?" he asked finally.

"Kill it, you mean?" said Uncle.

"Well . . . I want to show it to Mom and Dad. . . . It's my fish."

"That it is," said his uncle. "You must kill it quickly." He opened his knife and gave it to his nephew.

"I have to do it?" asked Mark.

"It's your fish," said Uncle.

"How?" The boy waved the knife.

"Give it a quick stab there." Uncle Scott pointed at the rainbow's head. "Mind your hand, it's very sharp."

Mark stared at the gasping fish, then at the gleaming blade.

The knife dropped from Mark's hand with a loud clatter.

Then he lifted his catch with both hands and lowered it into the river. The limp fish did not move.

"Is it dead?" asked Mark.

"It'll be all right," said his uncle. "Rock it back and forth and let water go through the gills."

So Mark rocked the fish, back and forth, back and forth — until the fins began to wave. Then the sleek fish stirred, as though waking from a long sleep. With a flick of its tail the rainbow slipped out of the boy's hands, and the boy watched his trout swim away.

"That was fun," he whispered.

"So what's the use in fishing if you don't keep any fish?" Uncle Scott asked.

"Oh, it's good to leave the river the way I found it," said Mark. "Besides, I might catch a mermaid some day."

"That's my man," Uncle said, laughing. "Just for that I'm going to build you a rod."

"A rod like yours?" shouted Mark.

"Exactly like mine, with your name on it," said Uncle.

Just then they heard someone talking quite nearby.

"Sounds like a woman," said Uncle Scott. "Maybe that *was* your mermaid."

They looked upstream and saw a house. All the windows were lit except for Mark's. It was still open, and his mother's voice drifted out of it.

"I've kept you out long enough," Uncle Scott said and took the oars.

Mark said good night to his uncle and climbed into his room through the window. A short while later, when his parents opened the door, Mark pretended to be fast asleep.

"Leave it to my brother," Mother whispered. "Sending fishing lures to a sick child. Why, they're all over the bed. He could have hurt himself!"

"Look," said his father. "His temperature seems almost normal."

"Thank goodness," said his mother.

And Mark fell asleep.

Look Again!

When Mark looked out his bedroom window, he saw that his neighborhood had vanished and there was a river where the street used to be.

Draw two pictures. First draw the ordinary view from your window. Then draw the scene you might see if fantasy hit close to your home.

Show your classmates the two pictures and describe what might happen to you in the second picture.

illustration by Shennen Bersani

Allen Say

Allen Say grew up in Yokohama, Japan, and from the age of six he knew he wanted to be an artist. When he was twelve, Say became an apprentice to his favorite Japanese cartoonist, Noro Shinpei. For four years he worked with Noro Shinpei, learning his craft.

To continue his art studies, Say later moved to California, where he still lives today. Say has written and illustrated many books, including *El Chino, The Lost Lake,* and *Tree of Cranes,* which he dedicated to Master Noro Shinpei.

When he's not at the drawing board working on another book, Say can usually be found in a river enjoying one of his favorite hobbies, fly-fishing.

The Mysterious Girl in the Garden

from the book by Judith St. George

illustrated by Alexander Farquarson

CHAPTER 1

"Mom, we're not going to Kew Gardens again today, are we?" Terrie poured more milk on her cereal than she needed and it splashed on the table.

"Please don't start that again, Terrie. You know I'll be working at Kew Gardens all summer," her mother answered. She seemed annoyed about the milk, but she mopped it up without a word.

Terrie Wright and her parents were spending the summer in Chiswick, England, just outside of London. Mr. Wright had to be in England on business and Mrs. Wright had decided to take courses at the Kew Botanic Gardens nearby. That meant Terrie had to hang around the Gardens every day with nothing to do. The worst part was she could have spent the summer with her grandmother on Cape Cod. Granny had a house right on the beach and she had invited not only Terrie but her dog, Wags, too. Terrie had begged and nagged and pleaded with her parents to let her go. But they had said no, she had to come to England with them. So here she was, having the most boring, awful summer an almost-eleven-year-old American girl ever had.

"I'll tell you what, Terrie. On Saturday we'll go to the London Zoo and have a Chinese dinner afterwards. How does that sound?" Dad reached across the table and squeezed Terrie's hand.

"Okay, I guess," Terrie mumbled. That still left almost the whole week to get through.

"When we're in London, let's get your hair cut, Terrie," Mom suggested. "It's much too long."

"I like it long."

Mrs. Wright didn't answer. Terrie figured she probably didn't want to argue. Mom must know what a terrible summer she was having, when she could have been swimming and sailing every day on Cape Cod.

Tuesday was Mrs. Wright's day to work in the Bamboo Garden out by the Queen's Cottage. Kew Botanic Gardens covered three hundred acres and it was a long walk. Neither Terrie nor her mother said much the whole way. Mrs. Wright was glancing through her notes and Terrie was wondering what she would do all day. When they arrived at the Queen's Cottage, Terrie flopped down on a park bench. She had already been through the Cottage and it was a big nothing, just a house with a thatched roof that some queen had built two hundred years ago.

"I've packed us a nice picnic lunch," Mrs. Wright said. "I'll come back at noon and we can eat in the rose garden."

"Mmm."

Mrs. Wright had already started to leave, but now she turned back. "Really, Terrie, I wish you weren't so negative. I know this summer isn't very exciting for you, but you've closed your mind to enjoying yourself in any way. I saw a whole group of children sailing boats on the pond yesterday. Your father and I would be happy to buy you a boat so you can join them."

"Babies sail boats, Mom. I'm not a baby."

"Well, sometimes you act like one." Mom handed Terrie her tote bag. "There's plenty in here to keep you busy. Good-bye, dear." She gave Terrie a worried kind of kiss and left.

Terrie didn't even open her tote bag. She already knew what was in it — books to read, her flute to

practice, playing cards and writing paper. Boring, boring, boring. Terrie watched two old ladies feeding pigeons. They looked bored too. Finally, clucking and cooing like pigeons themselves, they got up and walked away.

Terrie was still slumped on the bench doing nothing when she saw the dog. He was a small, white dog with long hair that covered his eyes. He was chasing a red ball that rolled over the grass. A little bell around his neck tinkled. He picked up the ball in his mouth, then trotted into an enormous stand of rhododendron bushes. Because Terrie knew dogs weren't allowed in Kew Gardens, she tried to watch where he went. But she couldn't see into the dense rhododendrons, which were at least twice as high as a tall man. The ball flew out again. It bounced over the grass and stopped by her foot. A moment later, the little dog ran out after it.

Terrie had never liked long-haired dogs much, but she missed Wags terribly. And this dog was cute. He had a prancing kind of walk as if he were on the most important errand in the world. Without even looking at Terrie, he picked up the ball and strutted back into the bushes with it.

Terrie stood up, walked over to the rhododendrons, and peered in. But she couldn't see anything more than twisted roots, thick branches and big shiny leaves.

Swish, out came the ball again, followed by the white dog with his jingling bell. He brushed so close Terrie could have touched him. This time she went after him. She stooped under a low hanging branch and entered the shadowy thicket. Two steps farther in and the leaves became a dark roof. Even the air seemed cooler and damper. Ahead of her, Terrie saw the flash of a white tail. She stumbled after it in the dim light.

"For pity's sake, can't I be left alone for five minutes? Truly, I shall expire of impatience."

Terrie was so surprised she jumped back, cracking her shoulder on a branch. She rubbed her shoulder where it hurt and looked in the direction of the voice. A girl about her age sat on a dusty root, her feet tucked up under her long skirts. The little dog played with his ball nearby.

The girl seemed furious as she glared at Terrie. "What do they want of me this time?" she demanded. "I promised I wouldn't stray. Still, they send their spies to snoop on me. Give me your message, girl, and begone."

Terrie cleared her throat to answer, but nothing came out. She could only stare.

CHAPTER 2

"Must I repeat myself? What do they want of me now?" the girl asked even more crossly than before.

Terrie was getting cross herself. "No one wants you for anything. I saw your dog and followed him in here, that's all."

The girl reached down and rubbed her dog's ears. "Lioni is my dog. He does anything I tell him. He will even attack you if I give the order." The girl stuck her chin up in the air.

Lioni didn't look like he would attack anyone. Besides, Terrie had always gotten along well with dogs. She crouched down and whistled. "Here, Lioni, here, boy."

The dog got up and padded right over. Terrie scratched his throat as he wagged his tail with pleasure.

The girl jammed her hands on her hips. "I don't believe it. Lioni is my dog and mine alone. He hates everyone else."

Terrie had to laugh as Lioni nuzzled into her lap. "He doesn't hate me." Never in her life had she met such an impossible girl. And her outfit was unbelievable. She wore earrings, a necklace, bracelets, and a long dress that looked like a nightgown. Maybe it *was* a nightgown and she was sleepwalking.

"Humph." The girl scowled, her hands still on her hips. "This is my private place. You have no right to be here. I order you to leave."

Terrie smiled, hoping it would annoy her. "I have as much right to be here as you do."

"You certainly do not. My grandfather owns all this land. I shall call for my guards if you don't leave."

"Will they attack me like your dog did?"

The girl sputtered. "How dare you be flippant with me, Princess Charlotte Augusta of Windsor Castle, Carlton House and Kew Palace, future queen of England?"

Terrie stood up and curtsied. "Pardon me for not introducing myself, Your Majesty. I am Princess Terrie Ann Wright of Stilton, Massachusetts, future president of the United States."

"United States!" the girl cried. "I should have guessed from your horrid accent that you were American. Who would expect anything more from an American female than to have a man's name and to appear before me in trousers?"

"Now just a minute . . ."

The girl Charlotte made a big show of looking at the watch pinned to her dress as if the conversation bored her. "Personally I never believed that losing the American colonies was the tragedy that Grandpapa thought it was. A country full of ragtag failures never was worth fighting a war over."

That was too much. Terrie leaped up, ready to take Charlotte on. But a yelp of pain stopped her. She had jumped on Lioni's foot. He whimpered and hobbled back to his mistress.

The girl hugged her injured dog. "Did that dreadful person harm you, my precious?"

Terrie patted him too. "I'm sorry. I didn't mean to hurt him."

"Princess Charlotte, where are you? Are you sulking in those bushes again?"

It was a woman's shrill voice right outside the rhododendron bushes. Charlotte put her finger to her lips for Terrie to be still. "I'm here, Miss Hayman," she called back, all nicey-nice. She shook Lioni's bell so it jingled.

"Hear? Lioni's with me. He hurt his paw and I am comforting him."

"You mustn't frighten me. I feared something had happened to you."

"Who . . . ?" Terrie started to ask, but Charlotte shook her head for silence.

"That was Miss Hayman, my great goose of a governess," Charlotte whispered after a few minutes. "She never lets me be. If she doesn't see Lioni or hear his bell, she pursues me."

Terrie stared at Charlotte. What was going on? Charlotte had said she was a princess and that woman had called her princess too. They must both be crazy. Terrie jumped up and brushed off her jeans. "I'd better go," she announced.

"No, please don't." All of a sudden, Charlotte didn't sound so uppity. "I mean, I have nothing to entertain me. I haven't seen anyone my own age since I arrived here at Kew Palace in June to spend the summer with my grandparents."

Terrie could understand that. She hadn't had anything to do since she arrived in June either. Besides, Charlotte didn't really seem dangerous and her dog Lioni was adorable. He had dropped his ball in Terrie's lap for her to play with him. "I'll stay only if you stop ordering me around," Terrie agreed.

"I order anyone around I please." Charlotte's chin went up in the air again. Then she seemed to wilt. "At least I order my guards around. Otherwise, everyone orders me about, Papa and Grandmama and Grandpapa and all my aunts and uncles. I'm like a piece of taffy pulled first in one direction, then in another."

For some reason, Terrie felt sorry for her. "I get ordered around too," she said. "I wanted to stay with my grandmother this summer, but my mother and father ordered me to come here to England with them. It's been the worst summer I ever had." Terrie picked up the ball and threw it out of the bushes. Lioni took off after it. His injured paw seemed all better.

"If my parents did anything together, I would be pleased beyond measure." Charlotte scratched lines in the hard dirt with the toe of her black slipper. "Mama and Papa have been separated since seventeen ninety-six. They have hardly spoken to each other since the year I was born."

Seventeen ninety-six! Charlotte *was* crazy. "Are your parents divorced?" Maybe that was why Charlotte was so weird.

"Naturally not. My father is the Prince of Wales and royalty never divorce. But Mama and Papa detest each other and it has caused great gossip and scandal."

Lioni had already returned, and without thinking, Terrie took the ball from his mouth and tossed it out of the bushes again.

"Because Papa won't let me live with Mama, I had nowhere to go this summer," Charlotte went on. "That's why I'm here at Kew Palace with my grandparents, King George III and Queen Charlotte. It's been

horrid. My parents have always fought over me, but now my grandparents have joined in the bickering. And Grandpapa's court is dull beyond words. Even his subjects call him 'Farmer George.' When I become queen, my court will sparkle with wit and gay music and interesting people."

Wow, it was time to get off the subject of parents, Terrie decided. She pointed to a big hatbox half-hidden behind a root. "What's that?" she asked.

"It's my playbox." Charlotte pulled out the box. It was covered with colored, varnished paper with "Royal Playthings" stenciled on the top. She lifted the cover. Inside were two packs of playing cards, a tiny chess set, a backgammon board and a set of dominoes.

"I always win at dominoes," Charlotte declared. "Are you willing to risk a game with me?"

Royal Playthings

Terrie had never met anyone in her life who could be pathetic one minute and completely obnoxious the next. "You bet I am," Terrie answered, "and you'd better watch out. I'm the best domino player in Stilton, Massachusetts."

CHAPTER 3

Terrie had a surprisingly good time with Charlotte. They each won two games of dominoes and Terrie was all set for a rematch the next day. But when she woke up, she saw it was raining. It wasn't just raining, it was pouring. There would be no finding Charlotte in the park today. And rainy days in Kew Gardens were deadly. Mrs. Wright always worked in the greenhouse, which Terrie hated because it was so hot and steamy.

But as Terrie and her mother hurried through the rain from the main gate to the greenhouse, Terrie noticed the Kew Palace building set back a way from the path. She remembered that was where Charlotte had said she was spending her summer. Terrie knew that was impossible because Kew Palace was a museum, but all of a sudden, taking a tour through the palace seemed like a good idea. Mrs. Wright, delighted at Terrie's new interest in history, was happy to buy her a ticket.

Terrie took her time walking through the building. It wasn't big, more of a house than a palace, but every room had a fireplace and great high windows that let in lots of light. Deep window seats in the King's Breakfast Room were perfect for snuggling up with a book. Terrie looked out one of the rear windows. A lovely formal garden bloomed out back, all soft heathery blues and silvers and purples in the rain. The highest point in the garden was a gazebo that overlooked the River Thames as it slowly flowed toward London.

The museum display was in the last room of the palace. Terrie and a guard sitting on a stool reading his newspaper were the only ones in the room. Terrie strolled around looking at everything and reading her booklet. King George III and Queen Charlotte had first stayed at Kew Palace in 1760 and lived here on and off for fifty years. There were portraits of them both, as well as pictures of their fifteen children. Fifteen children. It seemed like an awful lot. As Terrie studied the portraits, the words "Farmer George" caught her eye. Wasn't that what Charlotte had called her grandfather?

From then on, Terrie paid closer attention to the displays and the descriptions that went with them. Then unexpectedly, she found herself reading about Princess Charlotte Augusta. As the only child of King George III's oldest son, she was the future queen of England. Princess Charlotte's parents separated soon after her birth and for years Charlotte was shuttled back and forth between her parents and grandparents.

It was just the way Charlotte had described herself. But that was ridiculous. That girl in the rhododendron bushes couldn't be Princess Charlotte Augusta. Then Terrie almost laughed out loud. Charlotte must have toured Kew Palace too, read all this history and made up a big fat story. And it had been a pretty good story, Terrie had to admit.

The glass case of toys was the last display in the room. Terrie glanced at it in passing, then stopped short. A colored, varnished hatbox with "Royal Playthings" lettered across the top sat in the middle of the case. Surrounding it were two packs of faded playing cards, a tiny chess set, a backgammon game and a yellowed set of ivory dominoes.

As Terrie raised her eyes to a picture above the case, little mice feet scampered up her back. She was looking at a portrait of a young girl about her own age with short blonde hair. The girl wore a necklace, bracelets, earrings and a dress that looked like a nightgown with a tiny watch pinned to it. And in her lap was a little dog with long white hair. Terrie stared at the girl's bright blue eyes set in a mischievous face, and the bright blue eyes seemed to stare back at her. "Princess Charlotte Augusta and her Maltese terrier, Lioni. 1805," stated the label.

Terrie jumped as a loud harrumph sounded behind her. It was only the guard clearing his throat and rattling his newspaper. Before Terrie's heart had been ready to burst through her shirt, now it didn't seem to be beating at all. Terrie turned back to the portrait. Princess Charlotte Augusta was the same in every way as the girl Terrie had met, and there was the toybox . . . and Lioni . . . and Charlotte's story about her parents . . .

Stop it, Terrie told herself, it can't be. It's just an English girl playing dress-up to fool a dumb American. Yes, it was only a joke. Nevertheless, Terrie stood looking at Princess Charlotte's portrait for a long, long time.

Back in Time

You are sitting on a park bench
and you are bored, bored, bored. You
walk through the rhododendron
bushes and find . . . who?
Is there someone from long ago
you'd like to meet? A president?
A famous explorer?
Your great-great-grandparents?
With a partner, write a scene in which
you meet someone from the past.
Then act out the scene for your class.

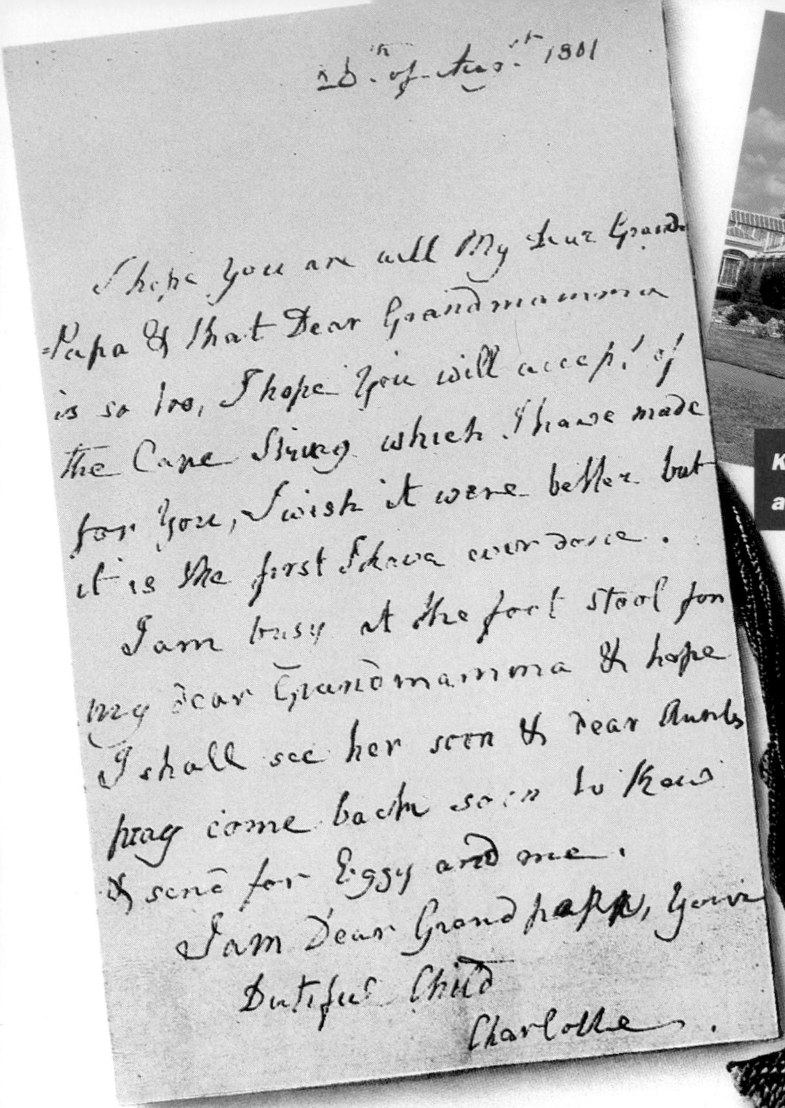

26th of Augst 1801

I hope you are well My dear Grand Papa & that Dear Grandmamma is so too, I hope You will accept of the Cape String which I have made for You, I wish it were better but it is the first I have ever done.

I am busy at the foot stool for my dear Grandmamma & hope I shall see her soon & dear Aunts may come back soon to Kew & send for Eggy and me.

I am Dear Grandpapa, Your Dutiful Child

Charlotte.

Kew Botanic Gardens as it looks today

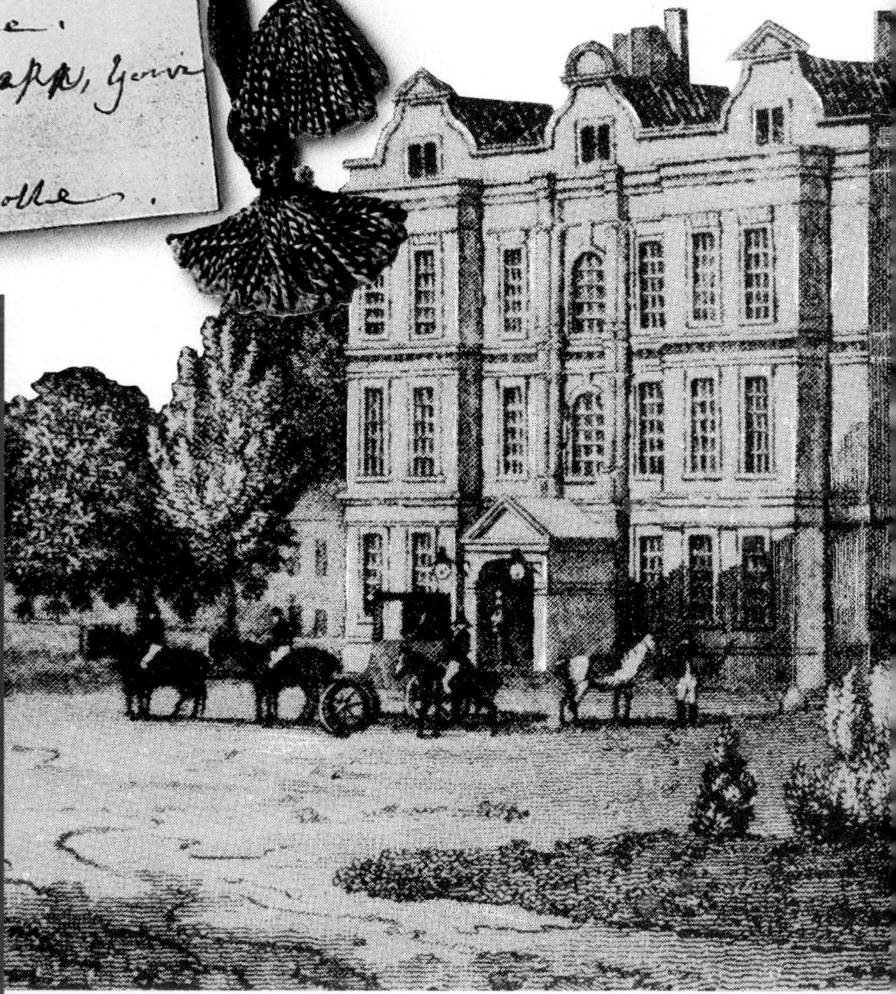

Who Is That Girl?

Princess Charlotte Augusta, the mysterious girl in the garden, was a *real* princess who lived from 1796 to 1817. She spent many summers at Kew Palace, just like the character did in the story.

The photo above shows a letter Charlotte wrote to her "grandpapa," King George III of England. The tassel on the letter is a cape string she made for him. She sent the letter from Kew Palace.

Princess Charlotte Augusta, age nine

Judith St. George

One Sunday afternoon, while living in London for the summer, Judith St. George and her family visited Kew Botanic Gardens. It was there, in Kew Palace, that St. George first saw a portrait of Princess Charlotte Augusta. Back home in New Jersey, St. George began to do research to learn more about the mysterious princess. She decided Princess Charlotte would make an interesting character in a book, and that is how *The Mysterious Girl in the Garden* came to be.

St. George has written a number of books with historical settings, including *The Shad Are Running* and *The Amazing Voyage of the* New Orleans.

Judith St. George, age nine . . . and today

ESCAPE FROM THE LAND OF BOREDOM

Flat Stanley
by Jeff Brown

Stanley Lambchop is a perfectly ordinary boy — until the night a bulletin board falls on him and flattens him like a pancake.

The Wonderful Wizard of Oz
by L. Frank Baum

When a cyclone strikes her uncle's Kansas farm, Dorothy finds herself and her little dog magically transported to the Land of Oz.

The Black Snowman
by Phil Mendez

Jacob and Peewee don't realize that the old piece of cloth they find in the trash is really a magic *kente* from Africa.

Time Out
by Helen Cresswell

It's 1887 and the Wilkses are planning a family vacation. What they don't plan on is traveling one hundred years into the future.

The Pigs Are Flying!
by Emily Rodda

Being sick in bed is no fun, Rachel complains. But when she wakes up the next morning, she's in a world where pigs can fly.

The Castle in the Attic
by Elizabeth Winthrop

William is thrilled to receive a model castle as a gift and even more surprised when a toy knight comes to life.

FLAT
STANLEY
by Jeff Brown

MYSTERY

THEME 5

The Mystery Hour

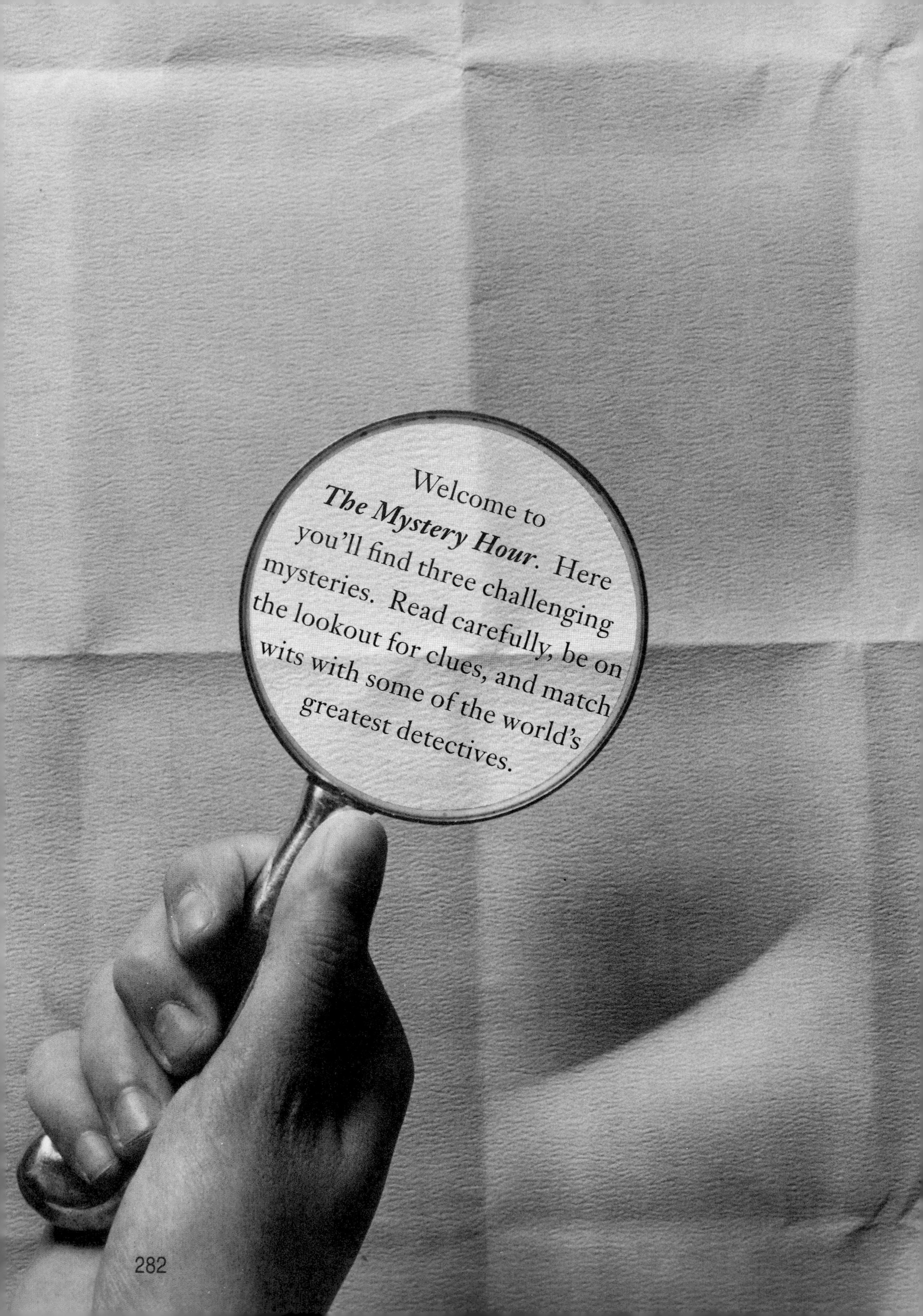
Welcome to
The Mystery Hour. Here
you'll find three challenging
mysteries. Read carefully, be on
the lookout for clues, and match
wits with some of the world's
greatest detectives.

Contents

The Tarantula Legion in Mystery in the Park

by Pedro Bayona
translated from Spanish
illustrated by Carlos Castellanos

1. The Man with the Envelope

One evening Green Bear and Andrés were sitting under a tree in a park in Guadalajara reading a letter that their friend Marifreckles had written from Merida, where she had gone on vacation. Green Bear was a leader of the Tarantula Legion; he was given that name because he was a stocky boy who always dressed in green, including his tennis shoes and socks. Even his bed, his school bag, and his books were that color.

Marifreckles was called this because she was freckled and her name was María. With Green Bear, she had solved many mysteries. The two of them had a diary filled with their adventures.

Andrés, who was looking around, interrupted Green Bear's reading.

"There's a suspicious type," he said.

"Where?" asked Green Bear, looking around at the people wandering through the park.

Andrés pointed at a man in checked pants who was heading for a nearby fountain and glancing all around.

The boys pretended to read but in fact followed the subject's movements closely as he stopped next to the fountain. After looking around nervously to see if he was being watched, he reached into a crack in the fountain and pulled out a white, letter-sized envelope, and then moved away quickly.

"He's getting away!" exclaimed Andrés as the man lost himself in the crowd.

But Green Bear, who was an expert at finding people in crowds, soon located the suspect.

Can you find him too?

2. A Message in Code

"He's behind the man with the balloons," said Green Bear, speeding up his pace. "I saw the envelope and his pants."

The suspect moved across the park and crossed the street. He stopped in a small store, asked for a soda, and opened the envelope. He took out a small piece of paper and read it carefully for several minutes.

"Good heavens!" Andrés exclaimed. "It looks like that guy doesn't know how to read, he's taking so long. . . ."

"Now he's leaving."

The man crumpled the paper and threw it into the street.

"Someone should tell him where to put his trash," said Andrés angrily.

The boys waited until the man disappeared and then went to pick up the paper. When they unfolded it, they read the following message:

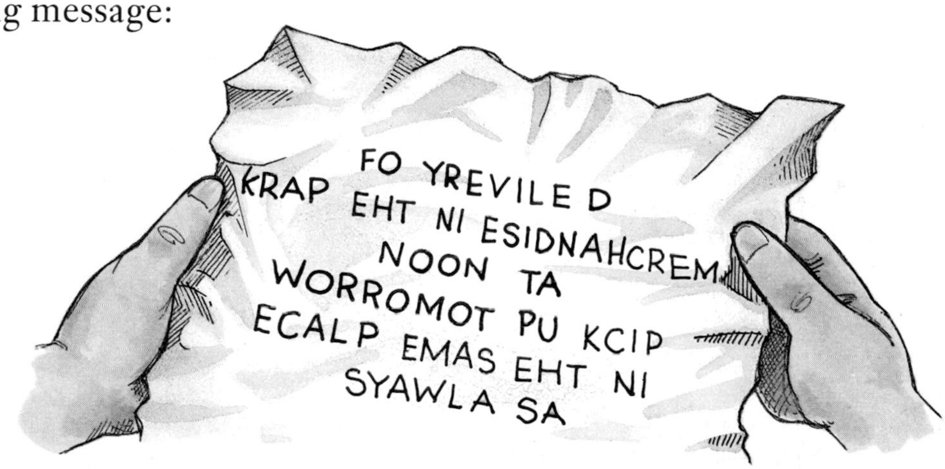

"No wonder he couldn't read it faster — it's in code!" exclaimed Andrés.

The boys went back to their park bench. After examining the message a long while, Green Bear announced, "I know what this says! Tomorrow we'll have a job to do."

Have you figured out the message yet?

3. Stakeout at Noon

Green Bear explained to Andrés that the order of the letters was reversed, so that the message had to be read from right to left. He read:

DELIVERY OF
MERCHANDISE IN THE PARK
AT NOON
PICK UP TOMORROW
IN THE SAME PLACE
AS ALWAYS

"Will it be in this park?" asked Andrés.

"Definitely," answered Green Bear as he got up. "Let's go tell the others. Tomorrow will be an interesting day."

The next day Green Bear and Andrés were beneath their usual tree. The heat was intense and people were sweating under the noonday sun. Since all they had to do was wait and watch the crowd as it moved through the park, Green Bear began to recite a tongue twister, his favorite pastime.

"The volcano of Parangaricutirimicuaro wants to disparangaricutirimicuarate, which disparagari . . . ," he was saying when suddenly he stopped and said to Andrés: "There's our man, the one making the delivery."

Andrés looked at all the people but didn't notice anyone who looked suspicious. Green Bear gave him another clue: "Only a suspect would dress that way in this heat."

With that lead, Andrés figured out who Green Bear was referring to.

Have you found the suspect yet?

4. *Disappearance in the Park*

It was obvious that the man with the thick overcoat among the trees to the left was highly suspicious.

Andrés noted that the man in the overcoat was carrying a metal box under his arm and guarding it very carefully. The man stopped next to a thick stand of trees and looked around nervously.

At that moment Isabel 21 arrived jumping rope. Her greeting distracted Green Bear and his friend. Isabel 21 was so named because she had been born on the 21st and her street address number was 21. As if that weren't enough, she was also the 21st student on the class roll. Furthermore (of course) she had 21 dolls. She was one of the most daring legionnaires.

"What are you looking at?" she asked.

"Shhhh!" said Green Bear as he crouched behind a bush.

They quickly brought Isabel 21 up-to-date, but when they peered over the top of the bush again the man had disappeared.

The three children carefully surrounded the stand of trees, and then Green Bear saw the suspect come out.

"Hmmm," murmured Andrés. "Now I know why he went in there."

"Me too," said Green Bear.

Why did the man go into the trees?

5. In Search of Puzzling Objects

"He left his overcoat in the trees," said Andrés.

"And the box too," added Green Bear.

"We'll need some help," said Green Bear after a while. "Isabel 21, go get Tai so he can keep a lookout while we look for the overcoat and box."

Tai was another member of the Tarantula Legion. His parents were Chinese. He arrived, accompanied by his white mouse, Chop Suey, who always traveled in one of his pockets or on his shoulder. Chop Suey was very smart and quickly learned all the tricks Tai taught him, which he then used to help his master in his detective work.

"If someone comes, play your harmonica," Green Bear told Tai.

Tai took out his little red harmonica and remarked, "As they say: 'One eye on the cat and the other on the hook.'"

The three legionnaires entered the trees, and after looking awhile Andrés found the box. Isabel 21 found the overcoat.

Where were the box and overcoat?

6. The Secret Combination

The box was found under a pile of rocks, and the overcoat had been rolled up and put on a tree limb, hidden in the foliage.

"I'd like to know what's in the box," said Andrés as he pulled it from under the rocks.

The box was metal and didn't weigh much. It looked like one of the old trunks Andrés had seen at his grandfather's house. Metal bands protected the edges and were adorned with gold rivets in the shape of flowers. The box had a round lock plate and a big padlock.

"It's a combination lock," noted Green Bear, pointing to three small disks with numbers.

Isabel 21 tried some combinations. First she tried 5 and 6. Then 8, 4, 2 and 1, 2, 3, but the lock didn't open.

"I don't think we'll be able to open it," she sighed.

But Andrés thought otherwise. He put the box on the rocks and looked at it carefully. Meanwhile, Isabel 21 wanted to get the overcoat down from the tree, but Green Bear wouldn't let her.

"If someone comes we won't have time to put it back up," he explained. "They would realize we're watching them and . . ."

"I've got it!" Andrés shouted.

The others ran over and Andrés told them: "Look at the front of the box. There's the combination!"

Can you discover the combination?

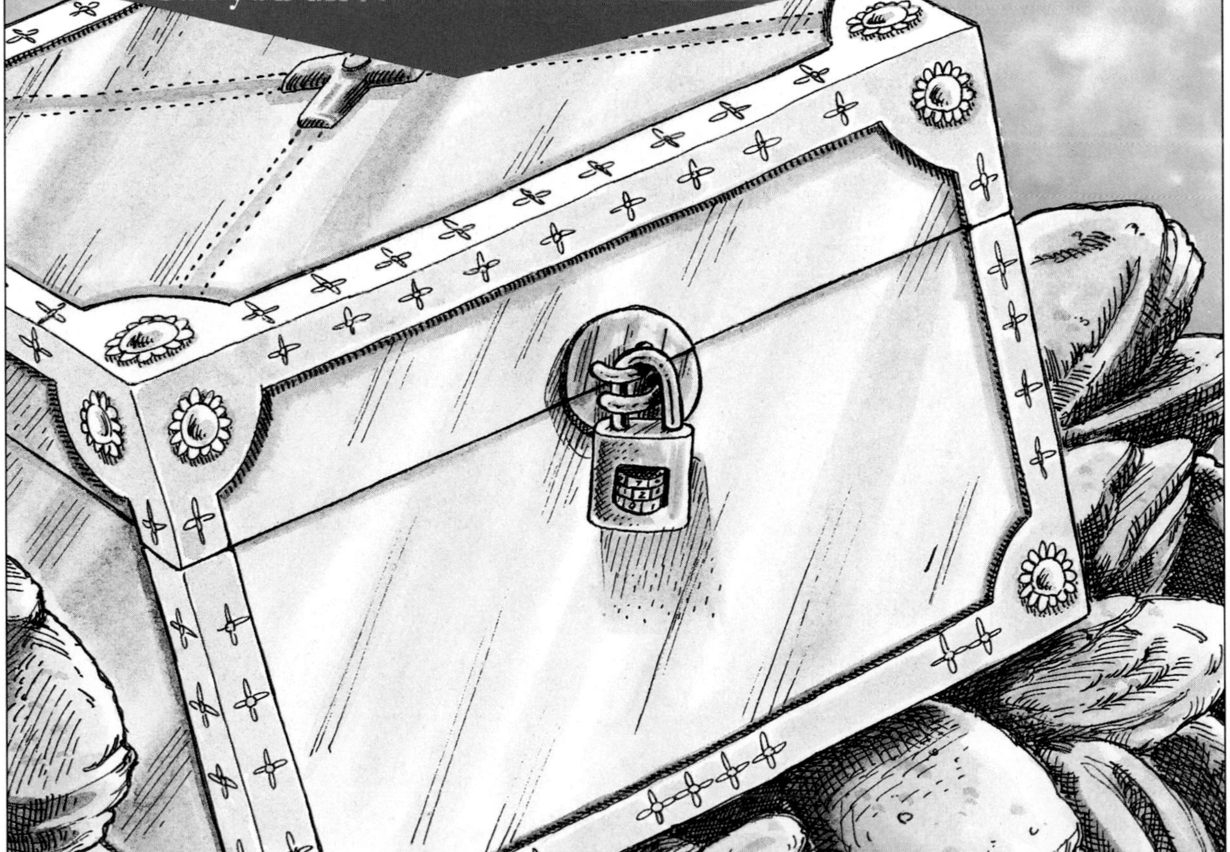

7. *A Woman in a Flowered Dress*

Andrés had figured out that the rivets were placed in a regular pattern everywhere except on the bottom edge of the box. There they found three rivets together, then a space, then four together, followed by another space and two more rivets. So the combination was revealed by the placement of the rivets: 3, 4, and 2.

They were about to open the box when they heard Tai playing the song *Cielito Lindo* loudly on his harmonica. Someone was coming!

They left the box where it was and scampered to the other side of the grove of trees. Tai, who had hidden himself behind a tree, saw that a woman in a flowered dress had stopped and was looking around to make sure no one was watching her. Then she entered the trees and moments later came out wearing the overcoat and carrying the box under her arm.

The legionnaires followed her to a nearby building, which she entered.

"This building has only one apartment per floor," noted Isabel 21. "I know because a friend of mine lives here. . . . How can we figure out which floor the woman lives on?"

"Well, as they say," Tai remarked, "if your eyes can't see great distances, use a magnifying lens." With that, he took out his binoculars and began to examine the windows of the building until he located the woman.

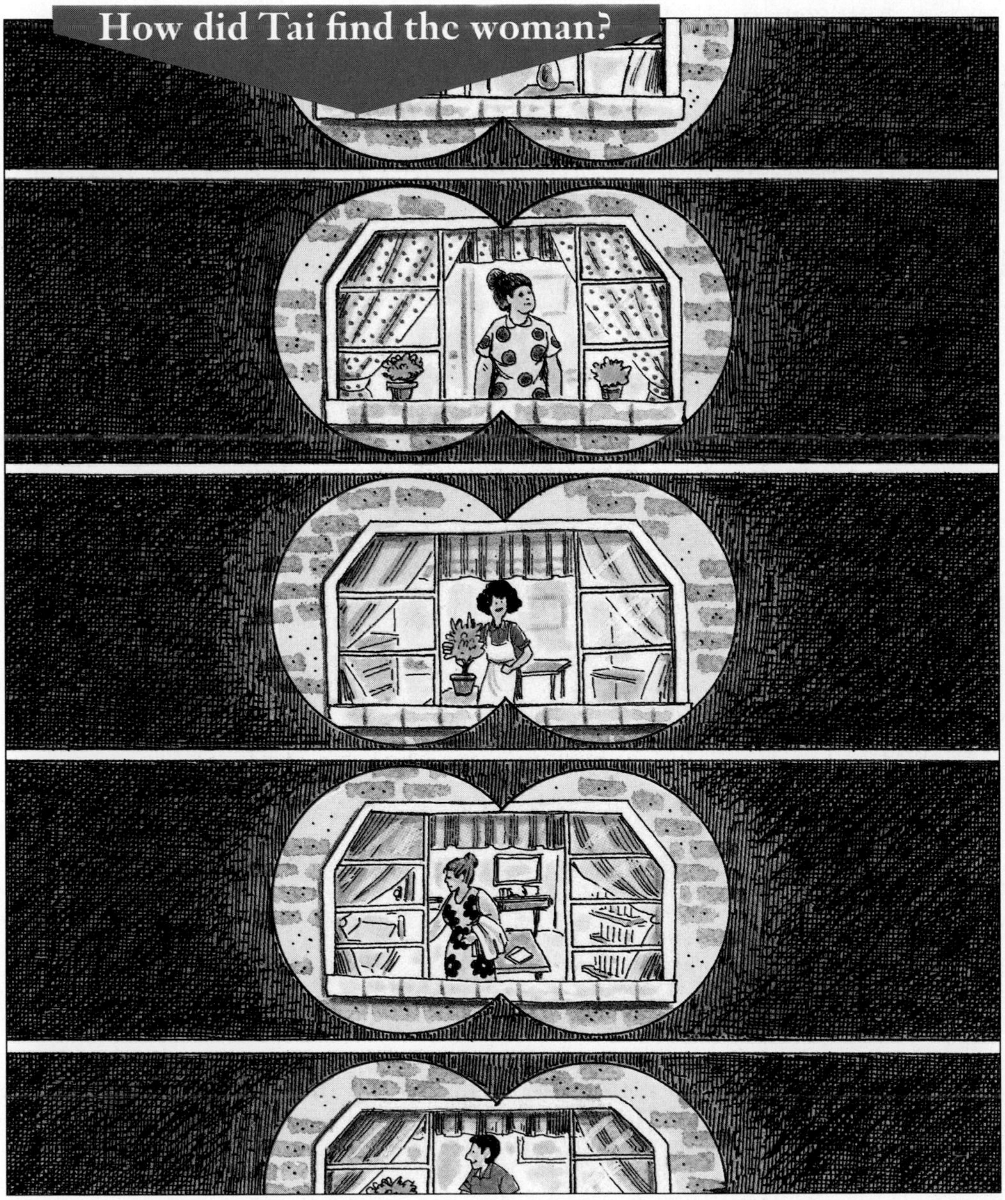

8. Maid Service

Tai figured out that the woman lived on the second floor since her flowered dress was easy to spot with the binoculars.

The legionnaires sat down to think about what to do next. They had to find out what was in the box and what was the significance of the overcoat. But getting inside the woman's apartment without being seen seemed almost impossible.

"We could go in after she leaves," Tai suggested.

"No! It isn't right to enter a house that way," said Green Bear. "They could say we broke in to rob the place."

The legionnaires tried to come up with a plan. Finally Isabel smiled and said, "I know how. Tai, you stay here and keep a look-out. The rest of you come with me, and I'll explain on the way."

Isabel 21 knocked on the door of apartment number 2. The woman in the flowered dress opened the door a crack to see who was there.

"Good morning," said Isabel 21 in her sweetest voice. "We're working to buy a bicycle and will clean your house for whatever pay you think is right. Since there are three of us, we'll finish in no time. . . . Can you help us?"

The woman let them in and gave them brooms and feather dusters. The apartment was full of electronic goods and toy animals. Andrés found the overcoat in a flash, but the box was more difficult.

Have you found the overcoat and box yet?

9. The Puzzling Wardrobe

Isabel 21's plan was to distract the woman in the flowered dress so that Andrés and Green Bear could check out the overcoat, which was on the sofa, and the metal box half-hidden under some books on the TV table.

Isabel 21 took the woman into a bedroom with the pretext of asking her how she wanted it cleaned. Andrés quickly opened the box and saw that it contained a valuable diamond necklace. Meanwhile, Green Bear examined the overcoat. What a surprise! Inside the coat was a complicated system of wires, miniature electronic devices, plugs, and tiny electrical connections. That was why they had had to wear the coat; it was too heavy to carry under their arms. In one pocket Green Bear found a candy wrapper and a piece of paper, which he kept as clues.

Andrés called the woman over so that Isabel 21 could investigate on her own. Ever since she had entered the bedroom, a wardrobe had attracted her attention. Once she was alone, she tried to open it but couldn't. As she swept the room she looked for the key to the wardrobe; she looked through boxes and under the bed, but the key was nowhere to be seen. Only after a long time did she discover it in the most unlikely place.

10. A Valuable Discovery

Isabel 21 took the key from the open book on the table and opened the wardrobe. It was full of metal boxes! Since they didn't have locks, she opened some of them: they all contained valuable jewels.

Just as Isabel 21 was closing the wardrobe, the telephone rang and the woman ran to answer it.

"Yes. . . . Yes, it's me, Emma. . . . Ah, Mr. J.K., how nice! Yes, tomorrow at 11:00 A.M. you can come and pick up your merchandise. . . . Yes, sir. . . . It just arrived this morning. Of course, yes, good-by."

The children swept and dusted until Andrés said he had a stomachache and felt terrible. Green Bear told the woman that they would come back the next day to finish up and that she shouldn't pay them until they had left the apartment spotless. The woman agreed, but before letting them go she made them empty out their pockets to prove that they weren't taking anything that didn't belong to them.

They went back to the park, still angry at being thought of as thieves. Then they told Tai what had happened.

"The lion believes that everyone else is just like him," pronounced Tai.

"Why would she want so many toy animals?" wondered Isabel 21. "Of all of them, the one I liked most was the rhinoceros."

"The rhinoceros?" asked Green Bear and Andrés, who hadn't seen it.

Did you see the rhinoceros in the living room?

11. Identity Revealed

That afternoon Tai came running to the Legion's clubhouse. Isabel 21 had just finished telling Green Bear and Andrés that the rhinoceros was under the piece of furniture next to the window.

"I know who our suspects are," said Tai, holding out a newspaper. He began to read: "Last night a valuable diamond necklace was stolen from the Jewelers' Museum in this city. The police can't explain the robbery since the necklace was kept in an unbreakable crystal box, which could only be opened by means of a complicated electronic combination. Furthermore, there are alarms, also electronic, that ring if the box is even touched. The police are convinced that the box could only be opened with the help of an electronics laboratory."

"Good heavens!" exclaimed Andrés. "The overcoat was used to open the box and deactivate the alarms."

"And tomorrow they're going to hand over the necklace to their accomplices!" said Isabel 21. "We have to get it back first."

"In such cases," noted Tai, "the wise man first plans, then acts."

In less than a half hour, the Tarantula Legion had come up with a plan.

"We need to know where the man in the overcoat is," said Andrés.

Green Bear got out the piece of paper and the candy wrapper. The paper, which he had found in the coat, was from a hotel, but the name wasn't complete. They took out a phone book and looked through the yellow pages until Green Bear found the name of the hotel.

Which hotel was it?
HOTEL
RENA
MEXICALI86
86-775
HOTELES...
CORONA
MEXICO 1114
COMERCIAL
86-1115
MEXICAN
86-7756
CAMARENA
AV. MEXICO 3
TEL. 71-0108
141 ROOMS
HOTEL CABRERA
AV. MEXICAN 186 Tel. 86-7115
HOTEL CREMONA
AV. F. GARRIDO 1001
TEL. 86-2222
HOTEL
MORENA
IN FOUR AREAS
OF THE CITY.
HOTEL
VERBEN
IN THE BES
AREA
AV. PERITENCIA 13
Tel. 24-1118
HOTEL
ARENAL
ROOMS WITH TURKISH
BATH
86-7071
HOTEL
SERENATA
AV: MEXICALI 86
TEL: 86-775

12. In Search of the Man in the Overcoat

The Tarantula Legion had only two clues to help them find the thief: the candy wrapper from a Two Parrots candy bar, and the Hotel Serenata, which Green Bear discovered in the phone book.

The Two Parrots candy was foreign and Andrés's father had told him that it was rarely seen in Guadalajara.

When they got to the hotel, Green Bear said, "We need to find out which room the man is in."

"But we don't even know his name," commented Isabel 21.

"We could knock at every room," Andrés suggested. "The hotel has four floors, so we could each take one."

"And if they don't open?" asked Isabel 21.

"We note the room number in our notebooks and come back later," replied Andrés.

"Some rooms could be unoccupied," Green Bear observed. "Besides, we don't know for sure if the man is even staying here. . . . Your plan is complicated and might not work."

Feeling discouraged, the legionnaires sat down in the hotel lobby to figure out what to do next. Suddenly Andrés jumped up and shouted, "Our man is in the hotel!"

How could Andrés know that the man was in the hotel?

13. The Eccentric Uncle

Andrés had seen a Two Parrots candy wrapper on the table in front of them. That's how they knew the man was there; all they had to do was find out his room number.

"I know!" said Isabel 21, and she headed over to the hotel reception desk.

"Sir . . . sir . . . , I've come to see my uncle," said Isabel 21.

"And who is your uncle?" asked the hotel employee, looking at her curiously.

"Don't tell me you haven't seen him!" exclaimed Isabel 21. "He's the most handsome uncle in the world, with his big, big overcoat. . . ."

"Ah, Mr. Laurel," interrupted the manager. "Imagine dressing like that in this heat. . . . My dear, you have a very eccentric uncle."

"I know," said Isabel 21, without knowing what "eccentric" meant.

The manager asked his assistant: "Is Mr. Laurel in?"

The assistant replied: "No, sir . . . he's the only guest who's out at the moment."

Isabel 21 thanked the manager and asked him not to say anything to her uncle since she wanted to surprise him, and she was a bit eccentric herself.

"Why didn't you ask which room he was in?" Andrés asked when she had rejoined her friends.

"Because I figured it out," she replied with a smile.

How did Isabel 21 know which room the suspect was in?
9
201

14. Chop Suey Gets Involved

At 10:30 the next morning, the Tarantula Legion arrived at the building where the woman in the flowered dress lived.

"Did you inform the police?" Isabel 21 asked Green Bear.

"Of course! I left a message with all the facts and the time of the appointment. It's great that you noticed that the key to room number 201 was the only one in its box."

The children hurried up to the second floor and knocked. The woman opened the door and said, "Hurry up, I'm going to have a visitor in a half hour!"

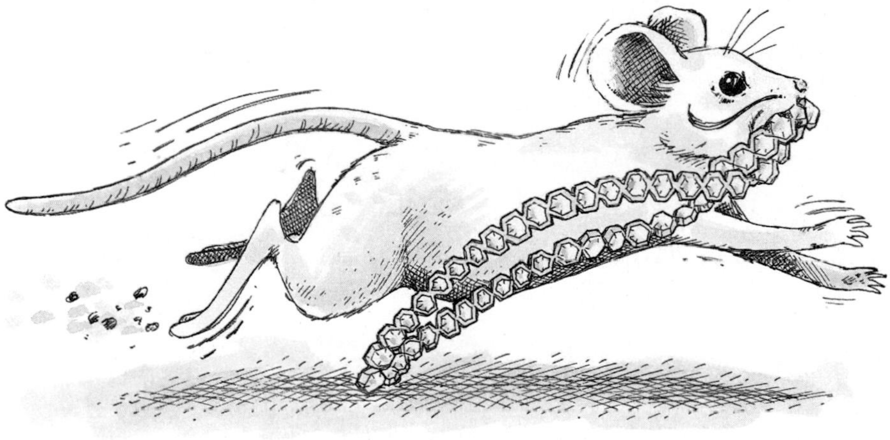

After fifteen minutes of sweeping and dusting, Isabel 21 slipped into the kitchen and dropped a plate. When the woman went to scold her, Andrés opened the box and took out the necklace. At that moment, Tai's pet mouse, Chop Suey, appeared. Andrés gave him the necklace, and the mouse disappeared down a vine outside the window and onto the sidewalk where Tai was waiting. Andrés signaled to Green Bear, who was watching the kitchen where the woman was still scolding Isabel 21.

Green Bear noisily dropped a crystal ashtray, and the woman became furious. After first checking their pockets again, she ran the children out of the apartment without giving them a cent.

"And don't even think about coming back!" she yelled as she slammed the door.

The legionnaires raced down the stairs and saw Tai running toward a nearby alley. When they caught up with him, he told them what had happened.

"After Chop Suey came down, a cat began to chase him. They ran in here. . . . I hope we can find him."

The alley was full of cans, boxes, and all kinds of old junk. Nevertheless, Tai had no problem finding Chop Suey.

Where was Chop Suey?

15. The Necklace Is Lost

Green Bear began to climb a wall overlooking a vacant lot. He called to Chop Suey, who was perched on a light pole. Tai pulled out his slingshot and shot at the cat to scare it off.

Meeeooowww! shrieked the cat as it fled into the boxes and cans, completely forgetting its mouse hunt.

Meanwhile, Chop Suey scurried down the wires to the vacant lot. They found him chewing on some grass, but the necklace was gone.

"We'll have to figure out where Chop Suey dropped the necklace," said Green Bear.

"But that's impossible," said Andrés. "We have no clues."

"Yes, but remember how Marifreckles investigates such cases," answered Green Bear. "She would reconstruct the scene . . . so we should think about the route Chop Suey would have taken."

The legionnaires carefully examined the site, trying to imagine how the mouse would have arrived there. After a while Isabel 21 said, "I think I have it." She took a few steps and then pointed to the necklace.

Where did Isabel 21 find the necklace?

16. Final Discovery

The next day the Tarantula Legion met at their clubhouse to read the newspaper. It described how the police, thanks to a detailed message, had captured the man in the overcoat in his hotel room and the woman in the flowered dress, along with a buyer of stolen jewels.

The newspaper commented: "It appears that the woman and the buyer had a terrible fight. . . ."

"I can believe it!" said Tai. "Opening the box and finding a rubber tarantula rather than a necklace must have infuriated him."

They all burst out laughing.

The newspaper account continued: "The valuable necklace was found, carefully wrapped, in the mailbox at the Jewelers' Museum. . . ."

"What with all the effort that it took me to find the necklace dangling from a wire and concealed inside a tin can, I think we did quite enough," said Isabel 21.

"Let me finish reading," commanded Green Bear, and he continued: "'. . . The police discovered a wardrobe filled with stolen jewels from many countries, which confirmed that they had caught a dangerous band of jewel thieves sought around the world. In the box where the stolen necklace had been kept for several days, a note was found that read: *We regret to inform you, dear thieves, that we have returned the necklace to its owner.* The note was signed *The Tarantula Legion.*'"

"Hooray!" shouted the legionnaires all together. "Now we have a lot to tell Marifreckles when we see her next week."

"Look!" said Andrés, examining the newspaper photo with his magnifying glass. "I just figured out why they wanted all those toy animals."

The toy animals had been used for hiding jewels, as you can see from the striped cat in the right side of the picture. And now let's see:

Were you able to solve this mystery? Are you a good enough detective to join the Tarantula Legion?

A Trail of Clues

A metal box, a scrap of paper, a candy wrapper, and a striped cat were all clues that the Tarantula Legion used to solve the mystery in the park.

With a small group, use the clues below to make up a mystery. Add details to take your mystery from one clue to the next. Someone in your group should write the mystery down.

a comic book

a ticket stub from a movie

a rusty old key

a baseball cap with the letter *Z* on it

a talking parakeet named Petey

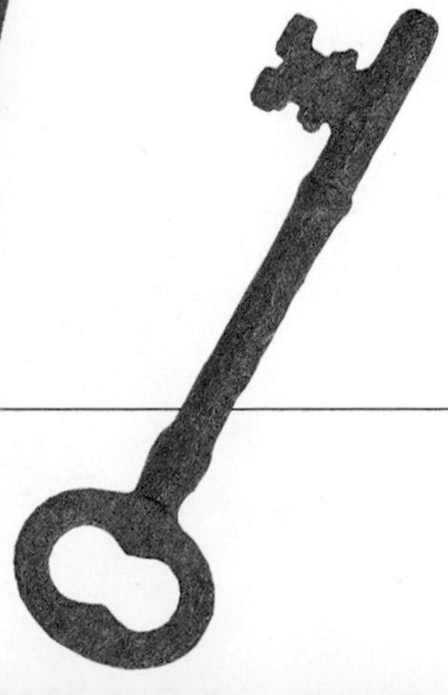

ENCYCLOPEDIA BROWN: BOY DETECTIVE

THE CASE OF THE MISSING ROLLER SKATES

from
Encyclopedia Brown: Boy Detective

by Donald J. Sobol
illustrated by Paul Van Munching

Between nine and nine-thirty on Tuesday morning Sally Kimball's roller skates disappeared from the waiting room in Dr. Vivian Wilson's office.

And where was Encyclopedia Brown, boy detective? He was not ten feet away from the scene of the crime. He was sitting in a chair, with his eyes shut and his mouth wide open!

In a way, he had an excuse.

Dr. Wilson was pulling one of Encyclopedia's teeth.

"There!" said Dr. Wilson. He said it cheerfully, as if he were handing Encyclopedia an ice cream cone instead of a tooth.

"Ugh!" said Encyclopedia.

Dr. Wilson said, "All right. Hop down from the chair."

Encyclopedia hopped down and put the tooth in his pocket. He was going to give it to Charlie Stewart, who collected teeth and kept them in a flowered cookie jar.

Encyclopedia went into the waiting room. The chair on which he had left Sally's roller skates was empty!

He looked behind the chair. He dropped to his knees and looked under the chair.

"The skates — they're gone!" he exclaimed.

"Are you sure you brought them with you?" asked Dr. Wilson.

"I'm sure," answered Encyclopedia. "They were broken. I fixed them last night for my partner, Sally Kimball. I was going to take them over to her house on my way home from your office."

Dr. Wilson shook his head sadly. "I'm afraid you will never get them back."

But Dr. Wilson knew nothing about detective work. Encyclopedia liked the dentist, though he felt that Vivian was a better first name for a woman than a man.

"I'll find the skates," said the boy detective. He spoke with certainty. But he felt no such thing. What he felt was the blow to his pride; it hurt worse than his jaw.

Imagine a detective being robbed!

In the corridor outside Dr. Wilson's office, Encyclopedia leaned against the wall. He closed his eyes and did some deep thinking.

Dr. Wilson's office was on the ground floor of the new Medical Building. The building had three floors

and fifteen offices. All the offices were used by doctors or dentists.

What if the thief had followed him into the building in order to steal the skates? Then the case was closed. "I could spend the rest of my life looking through closets, school lockers, and garages all over Idaville," Encyclopedia thought.

But suppose the thief had simply come into the building to see a doctor. Suppose, on his way in, he had noticed a boy carrying a pair of roller skates. Well, that was something else!

Encyclopedia reasoned further. "The thief could be a grown-up, a boy, or a girl."

He ruled out a grown-up. First, because it was unlikely that a grown-up would steal an old pair of small skates. Second, because a grown-up would be too hard to catch. Too many men and women went in and out of the Medical Building every hour.

"I'll have to act on the idea that the thief is a boy or girl," he decided. "It's a long chance, but the only one I have."

He opened his eyes. The case called for plain, old-fashioned police leg work!

Encyclopedia began on the ground floor. He asked the same question in every office: "Were any boys or girls here to see the doctor this morning?"

The answer was the same in every office: "No."

Things looked hopeless. But on the top floor he finally got a lead. The nurse in room 301 told him a boy named Billy Haggerty had been there this morning to have a sprained wrist treated.

Encyclopedia asked in the last two offices, just to be sure. Neither doctor had treated children that morning.

Billy Haggerty became suspect number one!

Encyclopedia got Billy Haggerty's address from the nurse in room 301. He hurried back to Dr. Wilson's office to use the telephone. He called Sally. He told her to meet him in front of the Haggertys' house in half an hour.

"We may have some rough going ahead of us," he warned.

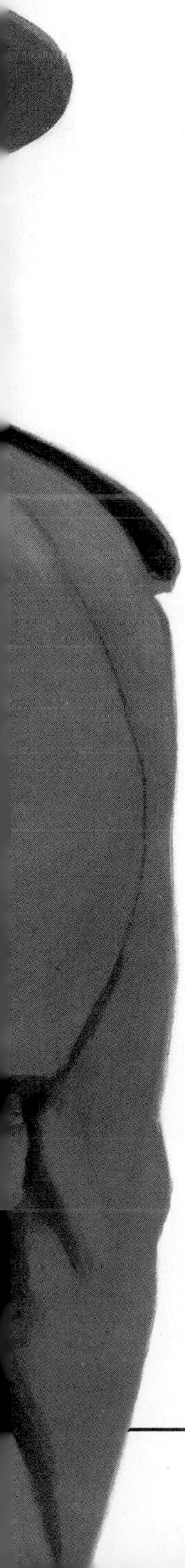

But Billy Haggerty turned out to be only an inch taller than Encyclopedia, and shorter than Sally.

Billy drew himself up to his full height at Encyclopedia's first question:

"Were you in Dr. Vivian Wilson's office this morning?"

"Naw," snapped Billy. "I don't know any Dr. Wilson."

"You didn't ask anyone about Dr. Wilson?" put in Sally.

"I never heard of him before you spoke his name," said Billy.

"Then you went straight to your own doctor on the third floor?" said Encyclopedia.

"Yeah. Dr. Stanton in room 301. What's it to you?"

"Dr. Wilson's office is down the hall from both the stairs and the elevator," said Encyclopedia thoughtfully. "You wouldn't pass his office going up or coming down."

"I don't know where his office is, and I don't care," said Billy. "It's none of your business where I was."

"We just want to be sure you weren't in Dr. Vivian Wilson's office this morning. That's all," said Sally.

"Well, I wasn't. I had a sprained wrist, not a toothache. So why should I go near his office?" demanded Billy. "I don't like snoopers. What are you after?"

"A pair of roller skates," said Encyclopedia. "Do you mind returning them? You've given yourself away."

WHAT GAVE BILLY AWAY?

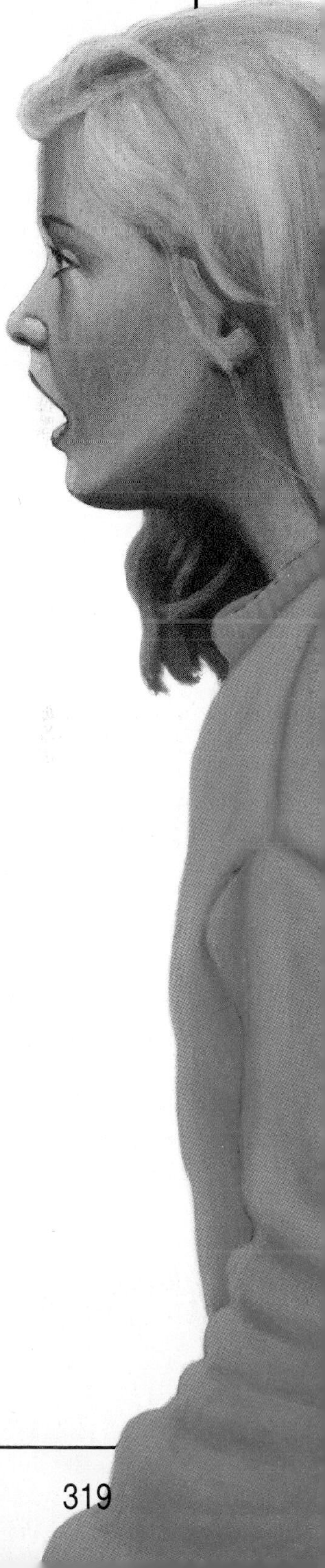

Solution to *The Case of the Missing Roller Skates*

Billy Haggerty said that he had never heard of Dr. Vivian Wilson and that he didn't know where his office was. But he knew too much about him.

He knew that Dr. Vivian Wilson was (1) a man, not a woman, and (2) a dentist, not a doctor.

When he was tripped by his fibs, Billy returned the roller skates to Sally.

CASE CLOSED

After Encyclopedia Brown solves a case, he might fill out a case report. Make up a case report like the sample on this page. Then fill it out for *The Case of the Missing Roller Skates.*

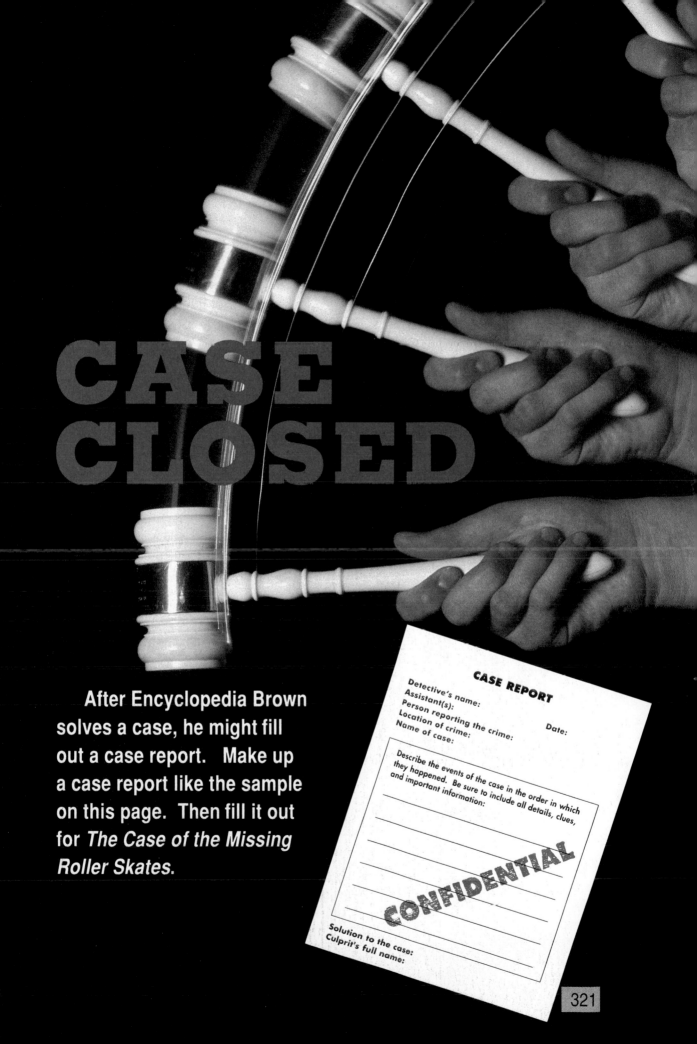

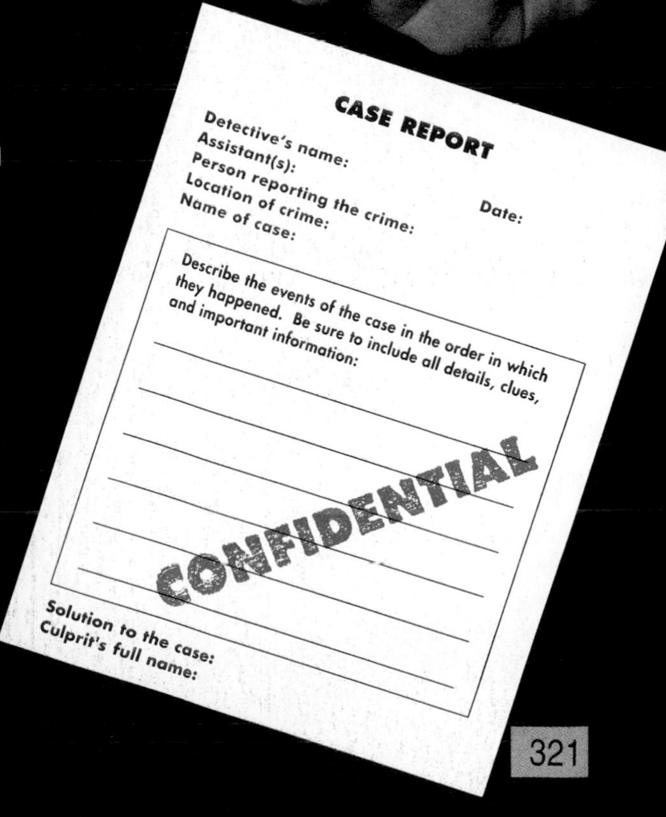

CASE REPORT

Detective's name:
Assistant(s):
Person reporting the crime: Date:
Location of crime:
Name of case:

Describe the events of the case in the order in which they happened. Be sure to include all details, clues, and important information:

CONFIDENTIAL

Solution to the case:
Culprit's full name:

Meg Mackintosh and The Case of the Missing Babe Ruth Baseball

A Solve-It-Yourself Mystery

Written and illustrated by
Lucinda Landon

"Hmm, I do detect a bit of family resemblance," said Meg Mackintosh, as she examined Gramps's old family photo album.

"You've got some funny-looking relatives," remarked Liddy. "And look at these pictures of you and Peter!"

Meg turned another page. "Gramps, who's this?"

"That's me," explained Gramps, "and that's my cousin Alice. She was always bossing me around. She used to drive me crazy, teasing me about my little dog and calling me 'Georgie Porgie.' I called her 'Tattletale Al' because she was always getting me in trouble.

"I'll never forget the day that photo was taken. We went on a picnic," Gramps reminisced. "That was the day she lost my prize possession."

"What was it?" Meg asked.

"My baseball, signed by the Babe himself."

"A baby signed your baseball?"

"Of course not. Babe Ruth, the greatest baseball player ever. He autographed the ball and gave it to my father and my father gave it to me. I took it to that picnic and Alice lost it. I never saw it again."

Meg examined the photo. Alice *did* look like a troublemaker. Then Meg spied something else.

The corner of a piece of paper was sticking out from behind the old photograph. Meg pulled it out and carefully unfolded it.

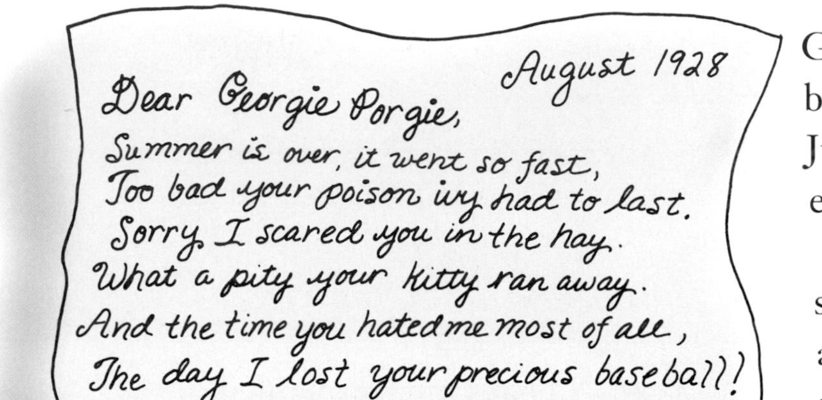

August 1928

Dear Georgie Porgie,
Summer is over, it went so fast,
Too bad your poison ivy had to last.
Sorry I scared you in the hay.
What a pity your kitty ran away.
And the time you hated me most of all,
The day I lost your precious baseball!
Well here's a mystery, here's a clue,
Maybe I can make it up to you.
The answer could be with you right now,
But you wouldn't know it anyhow.

Your Cousin
Alice

Clue one
Not a father
Not a gander
Take a look
In her book

"Hear that, Gramps? Maybe your baseball's not lost. Just follow the clue!" exclaimed Meg.

"I doubt it's that simple, Meg-O. Just another of her pranks. I saw that note years ago, but I couldn't make head nor tail of it," Gramps sighed.

"It's probably too old to make sense now," added Liddy.

"But it might really mean something. I've got to investigate," insisted Meg.

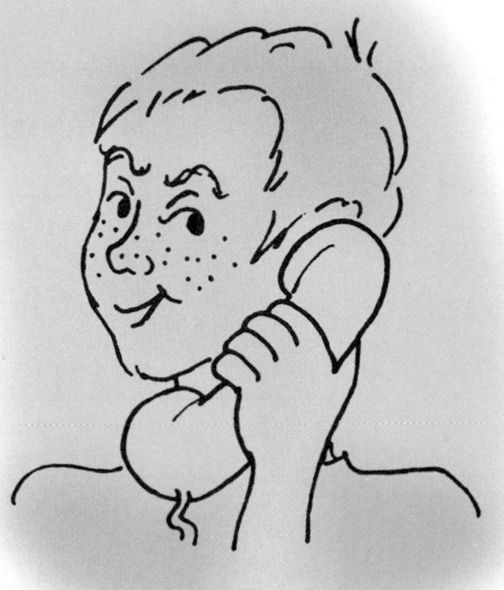

Just then the phone rang.

"Hey, Nut-Meg, Peter here. Remind Gramps that I'll be there in the morning."

"Take your time. I've found a mystery. Something to do with a Babe Ruth baseball," Meg teased.

"A Babe Ruth baseball? That's worth a fortune! Don't touch anything until I get there!" shouted Peter.

"Tough luck, Sherlock, I can solve this one myself. Bye."

Upstairs in Gramps's boyhood room, where Meg always stayed, she took out her notebook and pencil.

"Finally. The chance I've been waiting for!" Meg told Liddy. "Peter won't let me join his Detective Club until I have 'proof' that I can solve a mystery."

"Well, you'd better do it before he gets here tomorrow," warned Liddy. "He'll never give you a chance."

Meg knew Liddy was right. She sat down at the desk and started a list.

"Take a look in her book." Meg looked at the clue again. "Alice's diary? A nature book about birds?" She gazed up at the shelf of Gramps's old books.

"The Old Woman and the Little Red Hen," Liddy suggested as she squinted at the dusty titles. "Doesn't that fit?"

"I don't think so," said Meg, still jotting in her notebook. Suddenly she reached for a book. "I think I've got it!"

Which book did Meg reach for?

"Not a father, that's mother. Not a gander, that's goose. The Mother Goose book!" Meg explained.

She carefully opened it.

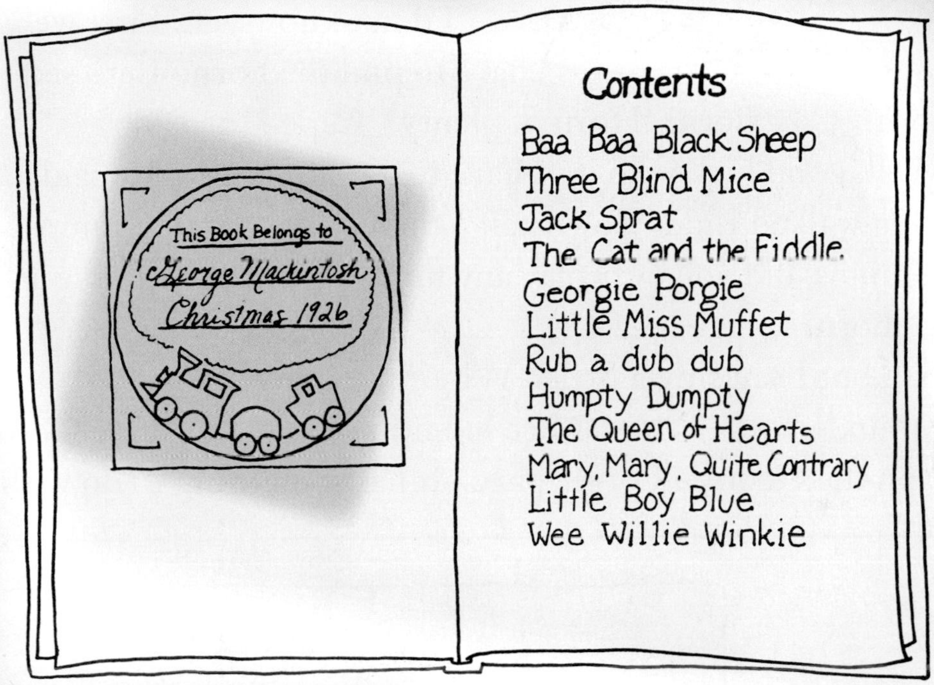

"This is definitely Gramps's old book. We must be on the right track," Meg said. After a moment she added, "I think I know where to look."

Which rhyme did Meg turn to?

"Georgie Porgie, pudding and pie . . ." said Meg.

"Kissed the girls and made them cry . . ." added Liddy as she twirled a pencil in her hair. "So?"

"Georgie Porgie. That's what Alice called Gramps," Meg reminded her. Sure enough there was a small note tucked tightly between the pages. Another clue!

Clue two
Little boy blue
with the cows
in the corn
Whatever you do
Don't blow this ?

"Little boy blue, come blow your horn," Meg recited.

"But what does a horn have to do with a baseball?" wondered Liddy.

"I don't know yet. First we have to find the horn. Let's see. Foghorn? Cow horn? Horn of plenty? Cape Horn?"

"Well, good luck with it. I have to get home," Liddy said.

Meg walked Liddy downstairs, then went to find Gramps.

"Gramps, did you ever play any musical instrument, like a French horn?"

"No, but I can sing a little. Why?" Gramps replied.

"I found another clue. Alice hid it in your old Mother Goose book, on the Georgie Porgie page. It has something to do with a horn."

Family Album

"That's easy." Gramps grinned as he pointed to the bookshelf. Meg followed his finger to the old bugle there. She took it down to inspect it. She removed the mouthpiece, shook it, and peered inside with her flashlight. But no clue.

Gramps got up from the couch. "Well, my dear detective, it's time to turn in. I wouldn't get my hopes up over these clues. Old Alice, she was a sly one."

"Maybe this isn't going to be as easy as I thought," Meg whispered to Skip as they went upstairs to bed.

Meg checked her detective kit. Everything was in order — a magnifying glass, a pair of tweezers to pick up small clues, flashlight and extra batteries, tape measure, scissors, envelopes, and, of course, her detective notebook and pencils.

"I have to be sure to write everything down," she said to Skip as she got under the covers. "The tiniest fact can solve the biggest mystery. Track, write, decode, deduce . . . then I'll have

plenty of proof to show Peter and his Detective Club." After a while she slid her notebook under her pillow and dozed off to sleep.

"Yikes," shrieked Meg. "Stop! Please stop that awful noise!"

Gramps put the bugle down. "If you think that's bad, Meg-O, you should have heard your father play it. I got this bugle for him when he went to Scout Camp. He was a pitiful horn player. Ah well, rise and shine for breakfast."

When Meg got downstairs, Gramps was making pancakes. "All this talk about Alice reminds me of when we were kids. Once she challenged me to a pancake-eating contest. I ate sixteen, while she watched with a miserable grin on her face. When it was her turn, she ate three and forfeited the contest. She had decided from the start to let me win. All I won was a stomachache!" Gramps laughed. "Alice was always getting the best of me."

But Meg was only half listening. She was still puzzled over something Gramps had said earlier. Something had to be wrong with the horn clue.

What was it?

"Wait a minute!" Meg shouted. "Gramps, if you got this bugle for Dad when he was a kid, it *couldn't* be the right horn. It wasn't even *around* when Alice drummed up this whole mystery."

"Guess that's so," Gramps admitted sheepishly.

Meg looked at the clue again. "Whatever you do, don't blow this horn." Remembering another kind of horn, she raced into the living room.

"You wouldn't want to blow this horn, eh, Skip," Meg said as she took the old powder horn off the hook. She pulled off the cap. There was no powder inside, but there was something else. Meg took her tweezers out of her detective kit and slowly pulled out a small, tightly rolled piece of paper.

ucle reeth
tillet ob epep
stol reh ?

"I guess I'm not surprised that nobody has looked in there lately," said Gramps. "Maybe you really are onto something, Meg-O. What does it say?"

"I don't know. Does it mean anything to you, Gramps?"

"Never cared much for word puzzles myself," confessed Gramps, "but if you find one of those jigsaw puzzles with the pictures, I'll be glad to help you."

Meg shook her head and sighed. Peter would be arriving soon. She had to solve this mystery fast. Just then the back door slammed and Meg jumped.

"Whew, it's only you," Meg said with a sigh as Liddy came into the room.

"Only me? Only me might help you solve this," Liddy replied as she read the clue. "It looks like a secret-alphabet code. You know, when each letter stands for a different letter in the alphabet."

"Or maybe the letters in each word are just scrambled around," said Meg. She took out her notebook and began trying different combinations.

Before long the door slammed again. Peter was peering over their shoulders.

"Here's a clue for you, Nut-Meg, *drop it*!" Peter said. "I can have this solved in no time!"

"I found it, I followed it, and I'll finish it," protested Meg, covering her notes. But not quickly enough.

"What's this? A word puzzle? I could put it on my computer and have it decoded in a flash," Peter persisted. "What's it got to do with a Babe Ruth baseball, anyway?"

Meg snatched the clue back. "Don't bother. I've already figured it out with my own brainpower!"

And she had. Have you?

"Well, what does it say?" asked Liddy, as Peter stomped out of the room. "I counted seven *E*'s, but what does that mean?"

"Nothing. It's not an alphabet code. It *is* a scrambled-letter code. The letters in each word are just mixed around."

"It says: 'Clue three little bo peep lost her' — her sheep, of course," said Meg.

"Why didn't I see that?" said Liddy, shutting the dictionary.

"Is it something to do with sheep's wool, or an old spinning wheel?" wondered Meg.

"Or a sheepskin?" suggested Liddy.

Meg and Liddy looked high and low. Meanwhile, Peter was eagerly searching the old photo albums, jotting down notes. He was more nerve-racking than Alice and her crazy clues, thought Meg.

It wasn't until later in the afternoon, when Liddy had gone home, that Meg realized what the answer to the sheep clue was.

Do you know where Bo Peep's lost sheep can be found?

"Right in front of me all along," Meg sighed. She carefully unhooked the old painting. On the back, tucked tightly between the canvas and the frame, was another small note. But it had crumbled over time.

Meg wrote down what she could decipher.

"Aha! Another scrambled code," said Peter, and Meg jumped. She hadn't heard him come up behind her. "Wait until the guys see that baseball!"

"Stay out of this! You don't even know what it's all about," Meg answered. "Anyway, it's Gramps's baseball."

"I think I've got it unjumbled . . . B-U-D-D-H-A!" Peter raced to the statue in the living room.

But Meg knew he was wasting his time. Taking her notes with her, she slipped off to find the answer to the clue.

What did the clue mean and where did Meg look?

Peter was way off. It wasn't a scrambled-letter code at all. It was a line from another Mother Goose rhyme. Alice must have meant *tub*.

Meg was scouring the bathroom for clues when Gramps leaned in the door. "Sorry to disappoint you, Meg-O, but you won't find much here. You see, it's like the horn. This bathroom isn't as old as those clues."

"A new bathroom? Then where's the old one?" asked Meg.

"Well, we put a bathroom *in* the house, but we didn't take one *out*, so to speak. Back when I was a youngster, we just had an outhouse. We took baths in an old tub in the kitchen," Gramps said.

"This can't be a dead end," sighed Meg. "There's got to be a solution, after I've gotten this far."

"Alice was cunning," Gramps said.

Meg had to agree.

Later that night, Peter knocked on Meg's door. "Are you still sleeping with Gramps's old stuffed animals? A little babyish, don't you think? I gave up that pathetic old dog years ago."

"What do you really want, Peter?" Meg said suspiciously.

"Hey, Meggy, let's put our heads together on this mystery. I could help you out. For instance, the old outhouse, where Gramps keeps his gardening stuff now. I bet that has something to do with it. Well, see ya in the morning, Nut-Meg."

"I'd already thought of that," Meg said to herself, "but I'd better not wait until tomorrow to check it out. Peter might get there first." When she thought that Gramps and Peter were safely asleep, she pulled her raincoat and boots over her pajamas and tiptoed outside. The air was cool and the ground still damp from rain. Meg flicked on her flashlight and headed for the rickety old toolshed.

The flimsy door swung open. Meg spied a pile of tools and flowerpots and an old rain barrel. Was it an old washtub? It must be — there was a note wedged between the wooden slats! She pulled it out and opened it up.

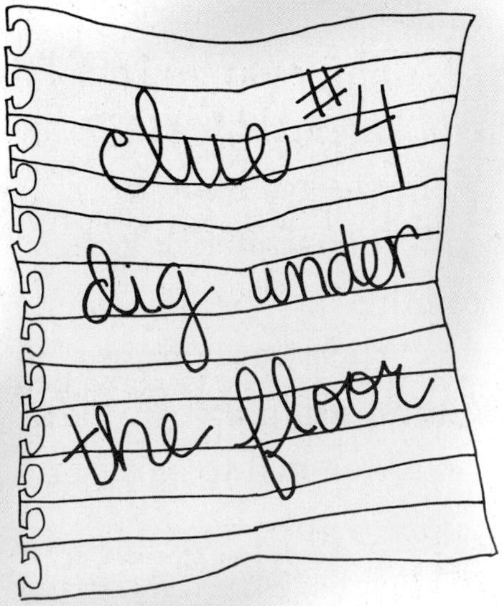
clue #4
dig under
the floor

But instead of reaching for the shovel, Meg sat back on her heels and thought. There was something funny about this clue.

How did Meg know?
Hint: There are five telltale signs.
Can you spot them all?

1. It was on lined paper. All the other clues were on unlined.
2. It was ripped out of a spiral notebook. None of the others were.
3. The handwriting slanted to the left. Alice's slanted to the right.
4. It said "Clue #4" — but Meg had already found the fourth clue.
5. It had nothing to do with Mother Goose rhymes.

Clearly, this was a fake clue. Someone was trying to throw her off the track. Meg was sure she knew who . . . and after looking around the toolshed again, she knew where.

Someone had been here recently. There were fresh, muddy footprints and the dust marks showed that the cabinet had been emptied. Ten to one, Peter was inside.

Meg picked up the shovel and scraped it around on the floor, pretending to dig. After a moment, she came up with the perfect plan to turn the tables on Peter.

"Yikes!" she said loudly. "Spiders — a whole nest of them! Come on, Skip, let's split!" She slammed the toolshed door behind her, then tiptoed around the side and peered through the window. In a flash, Peter tumbled out of the cabinet and bolted back to the house.

Meg held her breath to keep from laughing. "I'm not scared of spiders," she said to herself, "but you-know-who is . . . Mr. Big-shot Detective! It serves him right for leaving that careless clue."

But, as she headed back to bed, she had to admit she was still no further along in solving the mystery. And time was running out. Mom and Dad would be picking them up the next day at noon.

In the morning, Gramps asked Meg to get some kindling for the wood cookstove. He kept it in a funny-shaped old metal bin. The old bathtub!

Meg searched the old tub for a clue, but there was no note, not a scrap of paper.

"Rats! How else could Alice have left a clue?" wondered Meg as she stirred figure eights in her oatmeal. Gramps always gave her huge spoons. This one had a fancy big *M* engraved on it.

As Meg stared at the spoon, she suddenly had an idea of how a message could have been left.

Just as she suspected, there was something scratched on the bottom of the tub:

"Another clue!" Meg exclaimed. This one looked too authentic to be one of Peter's tricks.

"Gramps, did you have any dogs when you were little?" Meg asked.

"Oh, yes," he replied, "probably a dozen or so. Let's see, there was Nippy and Nicky and Lucky and Flippy and twice as many cats. Gosh, we had a lot of pets — ducks, pigs, ponies, even a parrot."

Then the phone rang. It was Liddy.

"What's happening with the mystery?" she asked.

"Can't talk now," Meg whispered as she noticed Peter at the top of the stairs.

"Is that Lydia-the-Encyclopedia on the phone? Tell her I've got this case just about wrapped up," Peter said as he came down the stairs and glanced over Meg's shoulder. "So what's this latest clue?"

"It has something to do with Little Miss Muffet," Meg teased, "and the spider that sat down beside her, you know, scaring Miss Muffet away!"

"What are you talking about?" said Liddy. "Whatever you do, don't let him get it."

"Don't worry, he's bluffing." Meg hung up. She hoped she was right and that this wasn't all a wild-goose chase. She had some deducing of her own to do — fast. Her only hope was to go back to the beginning.

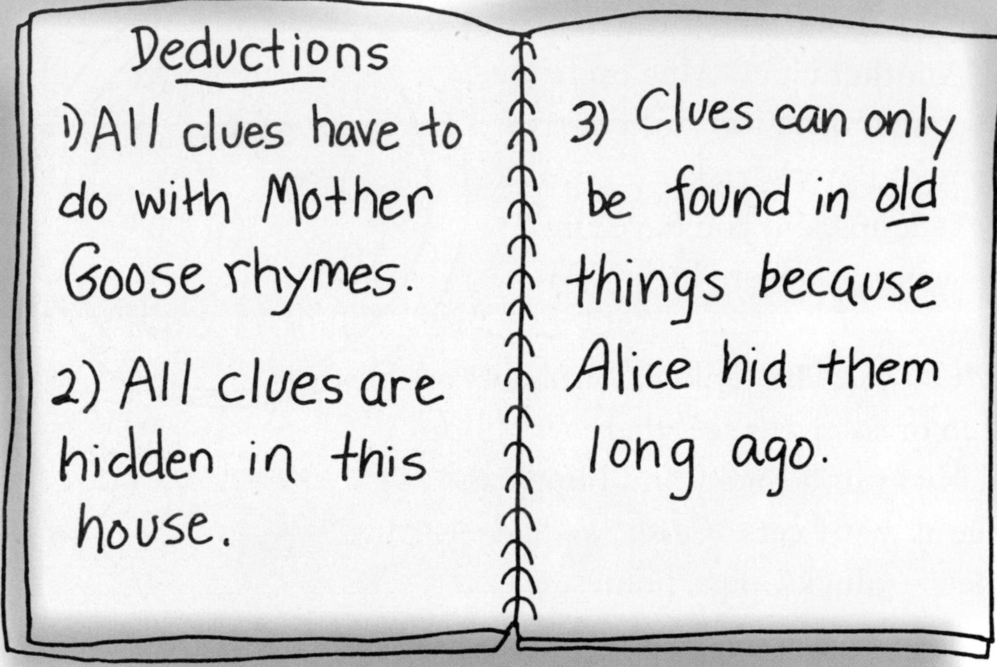

Deductions
1) All clues have to do with Mother Goose rhymes.
2) All clues are hidden in this house.
3) Clues can only be found in old things because Alice hid them long ago.

Meg studied the old clues, then looked at the new one. "'The little dog laughed.' If I'm right, it's part of a Mother Goose rhyme, too. And I think I know which one."

Which nursery rhyme was it?

Meg found the rhyme in Gramps's Mother Goose book.

"This could lead anywhere! Cat, fiddle, cow, moon, dish, or spoon?" Meg tried not to panic. She took out the old photo of Gramps and Alice that had started her on this investigation and reread Alice's letter and clues.

Peter had been upstairs and down, rummaging through all sorts of old stuff. Was he really onto something and she the one off the track?

Meg was determined to solve the mystery. And as she stared at the photo and clue, it all fell into place.

What was the answer?

Meg ran to her bedroom. Safely tucked under the covers was the old stuffed animal that had once belonged to Gramps. The old toy dog. It was the same one that was in the photograph, the one Peter had teased Meg about.

"The little dog laughed," Meg said to herself. "Of course! 'The answer could be with you right now, but you wouldn't know it anyhow' . . . just as Alice said in the letter."

Meg looked at the old toy intently. He was musty and worn. His body was very hard, stuffed with straw.

On his back was a loose thread. It was a different color, as if someone had tried to mend a seam but hadn't done a very good job.

Meg carefully pulled the thread. Sure enough, deep inside the old straw was something you'd never expect to find in an old doggie doll.

The baseball. Just as she had hoped! There was one final note with it, but Meg decided to let Gramps read it.

"What's this?" He woke with a start. "I must be dreaming. My baseball? It couldn't be!"

"It is," said Meg.

"It's what?" Peter burst in.

"It's my Babe Ruth baseball, long lost, and now Meg has found it," Gramps said with a big grin.

"That's right," said Meg. "Alice hid the ball in your old toy dog. With all that hard stuffing, no one ever noticed. She left the Mother Goose clues to help you track it down."

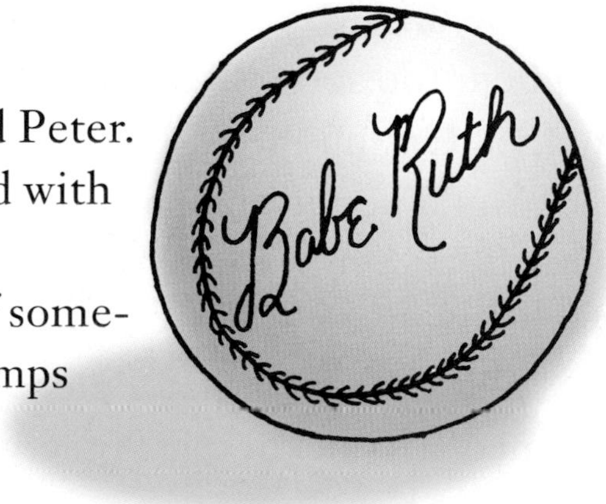

"Amazing," said Gramps.

"Amazing all right," grumbled Peter. "She just got lucky fooling around with those old baby toys."

"Sometimes he reminds me of some-one, but I don't know who." Gramps winked at Meg.

"Maybe this will help you remember. It's a note from you-know-who," Meg said, winking back.

August 1928

Dear Georgie Porgie Pudding and Pie,
This time I really made you cry.
Your baseball was never lost it's true,
But I didn't know how to give it back to you.
I thought a mystery would be fun,
With some little clues—
To keep you on the run!

Your cousin
Alice

P.S. I hope it doesn't take you too long to find it.

"Not *too* long," said Gramps. "Only over fifty years! Wait until I call her and tell her the game is up! And Peter, you be sure to tell everybody back at the Detective Club how Meg-O the supersleuth cracked the case."

Peter groaned. "Oh, all right." Then he even smiled a little.

They heard Mom and Dad's car pull into the driveway. "And solved not a moment too soon," Meg said as she hugged Gramps good-bye.

"You'd better take this along for 'proof,'" Gramps replied, tossing her the baseball.

"Did you catch that, Peter?" Meg laughed. "Wait till the Detective Club sees this!"

FOLLOW THOSE CLUES

Hide an object somewhere in your classroom. Then write a list of clues that tell your classmates how to find it. Remember that each clue should lead to the next one until the hidden object is found.

Lucinda Landon

Lucinda Landon loves mysteries as much as her heroine Meg Mackintosh does. Her eighteenth-century home has a hidden trap door leading to the basement and a secret hiding place behind the chimney.

When Landon was in art school, she would stay up all night just to finish reading a good mystery. Now she writes good mysteries, such as *Meg Mackintosh and The Mystery at Camp Creepy.*

Donald J. Sobol

Is Encyclopedia Brown a real boy? Readers of the more than twenty *Encyclopedia Brown* books constantly ask this question. Author Donald Sobol always answers no. "He is, perhaps, the boy I wanted to be — doing the things I wanted to read about but could not find in any book when I was ten," Sobol says.

The popular author says he writes "to entertain, from the first paragraph to the last."

Other entertaining books by Sobol are *Encyclopedia Brown and the Case of the Disgusting Sneakers* and *Encyclopedia Brown and the Case of the Mysterious Handprints.*

Pedro Bayona

Pedro Bayona says that the idea for *The Tarantula Legion in Mystery in the Park* came to him when he was a Boy Scout living in Guadalajara, Mexico. He and his friends would test their clue-finding skills by playing mystery games and watching Sherlock Holmes movies.

Pedro Bayona is surprised by how popular his mystery stories have been. He even receives letters from adults who want to join the Tarantula Legion. Bayona says that he loves writing mysteries for children. So far he has written three of them, all with the Tarantula Legion, and he plans to write many more.

UNCOVER A MYSTERY

WHO STOLE *THE WIZARD OF OZ*? *by Avi*
A rare copy of *The Wizard of Oz* is missing from the Checkertown Library. Becky is accused of being the thief. Will she and her brother be able to solve this book case?

MYSTERY OF THE PLUMED SERPENT *by Barbara Brenner*
Nothing interesting ever happens in Elena and Michael Garcia's neighborhood. But the twins soon find themselves in the middle of a crime that was committed thousands of miles away.

THE CASE OF THE FUNNY MONEY MAN *by William Alexander*
There's something phony going on next door, and the Clues Kids are determined to find out what their new neighbors are up to.

CAM JANSEN AND THE MYSTERY OF FLIGHT 54 *by David A. Adler*
Cam Jansen must rely on her photographic memory to unravel the mystery of a missing French girl.

SUSANNAH AND THE BLUE HOUSE MYSTERY *by Patricia Elmore*
What secret does the mysterious old Blue House hold? Susannah and her partner hcpe it will lead them to a long-lost treasure.

THE YOUNG DETECTIVE'S HANDBOOK *by William Vivian Butler*
This book contains tips for breaking secret codes, taking fingerprints, making disguises, and much more.

BIOGRAPHY

THEME 6

The Dreamers

Walt Disney, Marian Anderson, Roberto Clemente.
Three extraordinary people. Three dreamers.
Three people who made their dreams come true.

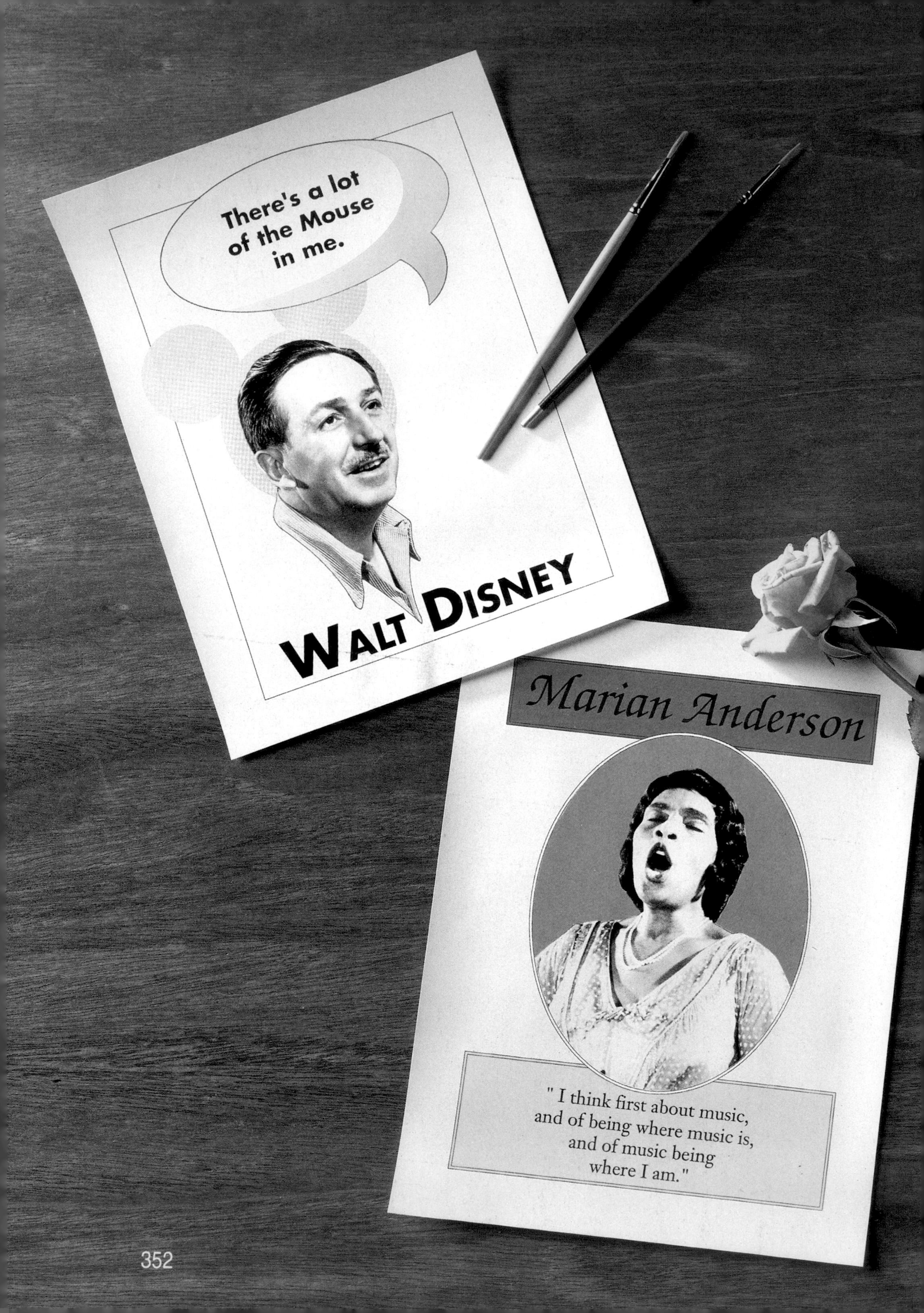
There's a lot of the Mouse in me.
WALT DISNEY
Marian Anderson
"I think first about music, and of being where music is, and of music being where I am."

Contents

ROBERTO CLEMENTE
PIRAT
"I want to be remembered as a ballplayer who gave all he had to give."

Walt Disney

Master of Make-Believe

from the book by Elizabeth Rider Montgomery

Walt Disney was born in 1901. His family lived on a farm for a few years and later moved to Kansas City, Missouri, where his father bought a paper route. Life was hard for young Walt. He had to get up every morning at 3:30 to deliver papers, often in deep snow. But on Saturdays, after delivering papers, Walt took art lessons.

The Disneys eventually moved to Chicago, where Mr. Disney invested in a jelly factory. Walt worked at the factory, but also found time to study cartooning by mail.

By the age of eighteen, Walt had decided to become an artist. He packed his bags, gave his savings to his mother for safekeeping, and headed back to Kansas City to try to get a job at the Kansas City Star.

In Business for Himself

Walt did not get a job on the art staff of the *Star* when he arrived in Kansas City in the fall of 1919. But he did find work with the Gray Advertising Company, making sketches for their catalog.

When advertising slowed down, Walt was laid off. He turned to the post office for work. From 7:30 A.M. to mid-afternoon he delivered mail. He spent the rest of each day looking for another art job. In the evenings he made up drawing samples.

Just before Christmas Ub Iwerks, a fellow artist at Gray Advertising, came to see Walt. Ub had also been laid off.

After a brief conversation Walt said, "Why don't we go into business together, Ub?"

"Doing what?" asked Ub.

"We could do artwork for any business firm that doesn't have an art staff," Walt replied. "We'd make ads and letterheads — things like that."

Ub nodded thoughtfully. "You're good at cartooning, and I'm pretty good at lettering and airbrush painting. We'd make a real team."

Walt took some of Iwerks' samples and his own and showed them to businessmen who might need artwork. He got several orders. A newspaper publisher agreed to give them desk space in return for free artwork.

Walt wrote to his mother, asking her to send the $500 she was keeping for him. She answered promptly, but she sent no money.

"What do you want it for, Walter?" she asked.

Her letter made Walt angry. He was eighteen now — grown up — and the money belonged to him. Why should his parents treat him as if he were a child?

"I'm going into business," he wrote back. "I need my money for supplies. After all, I earned it. Why shouldn't I decide what to do with it?"

His mother sent only half of his money. It was soon spent on desks, drawing boards, an airbrush, and a tank of air.

The partnership got off to a good start. In its first month of operation it took in $135, and more orders were coming in.

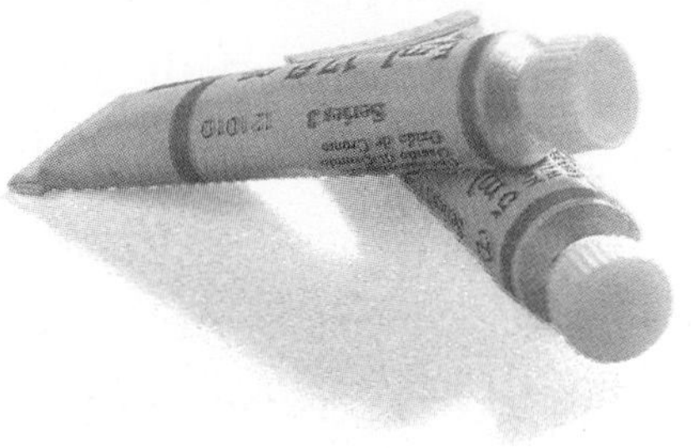

Early in February 1920, Walt saw an ad in the *Star* for a cartoonist at Kansas City Film Ad

Company. He called on the firm, hoping to get an order, but they wanted a full-time artist.

"Our company makes one-minute, animated cartoon ads for local theaters," Walt was told. "The job pays $160 a month — full-time work."

Walt wanted the job, but if he took it he would have no time for Iwerks-Disney orders. He went back to the office to talk to Ub.

"It's too good an opportunity to pass up," Iwerks said. "That's more than the two of us together made last month."

The partners decided to separate. Walt would take the position at Kansas City Film Ad, and Ub would take over Iwerks-Disney work.

Two months later Ub telephoned Walt. "Can you get me a job there with you?"

"What about Iwerks-Disney?" Walt asked.

"I'm going broke," Iwerks confessed. "I'm no salesman like you." So Walt got Ub a job at Kansas City Film Ad.

Walt liked his job as a cartoon animator. The art of animation, or making a cartoon seem to move, was very new and very crude. Walt used little figures cut out of paper, with arms and legs fastened so they could be moved. A cutout was photographed in one position with a motion picture camera. Then the arms and legs were moved a trifle and another picture was taken. Again the figure was changed slightly and another picture taken, and so on. When

the series of photographs was projected on a screen, the cartoon figure seemed to move.

In his spare time Walt tried to find better ways of making cartoons. He read all the books he could find on the subject in the public library. His boss lent him an old box movie camera, and night after night Walt worked with it in a neighbor's empty garage. He tried photographing a series of drawings instead of paper cutouts. It took much longer, but the animated figures were more lifelike.

Soon Walt made a sample reel of cartoon jokes, using drawings in place of cutouts, and sold it to the Newman Theater as a Laugh-O-Gram. The film was so popular that he was asked to make others. Walt decided to leave Kansas City Film Ad and go into business for himself again.

Grudgingly his mother sent him the rest of his money. But it was not enough. He needed thousands of dollars, not hundreds, to start his new business. So Walt visited all the people he had met in Kansas City and tried to get them to invest in his company.

Walt was a good salesman. He soon raised the $15,000 he needed. At not quite 21, Walt Disney became president of Laugh-O-Gram Films. Ub Iwerks was his chief assistant.

Failure

In spite of a promising start, the Laugh-O-Gram corporation had trouble making a profit. In less than a year it went out of business. Walt was left with nothing but his movie camera and a print of his latest movie, *Alice's Wonderland.* This film was a new idea of Walt's, which combined animated cartoon figures with pictures of a live girl.

Walt gave up his apartment and lived in the Laugh-O-Gram office, sleeping in an armchair. Often he had nightmares about delivering newspapers for his father.

He ate one meal a day, in a little Greek restaurant downstairs. Since there was no bathroom in the office, he walked downtown once a week to the Union Station and paid a dime for a tub bath in a public bathroom. He traded artwork for haircuts.

One day Walt got a letter from his brother Roy, now recovering from tuberculosis in a veterans' hospital in Los Angeles.

"I have a hunch, kid," Roy wrote, "that you could use a little dough. I'm enclosing a blank check. Fill it out for any amount up to $30."

Walt used most of the money to pay part of his bill at the Greek restaurant.

Walt tried everything he could think of to make money. He took photographs of news events. He made short movies of babies for parents to show in their living rooms. For the organist of the Isis Theater he made a cartoon that encouraged audiences to join in group singing.

Then a dentist asked Walt to make an animated cartoon that would teach children to care for their teeth. It was to be called *Tommy Tucker's Tooth*.

One evening the dentist telephoned and said, "Your money is ready, the $500 we agreed on. Come on over and get it."

"I can't," Walt replied. "My shoes are at the shoemaker's, and I can't get them until I pay him $1.50."

"Stay right there," the dentist said. "I'll bring the money to you." And he did.

For months Walt kept up this hand-to-mouth life. Once he lived for two days on beans and bread a neighbor gave him. Walt fed the crumbs to the mice that gathered in his wastebasket at night. He had become very fond of these little creatures and built cages for them. They kept him from getting lonely.

One mouse in particular seemed extra bright and curious. Walt named him Mortimer. From time to time Walt set Mortimer free on the drawing board and taught him tricks. Walt drew a big circle on a sheet of drawing paper. He taught Mortimer to stay inside that circle, tapping him gently on the nose each time the mouse tried to scamper across the line.

In the summer of 1923 Walt decided to go to California and join Roy, who would soon be getting out of the hospital. He sold his camera to raise the train fare. He packed his few belongings in a cheap suitcase — one shirt, two suits of underwear, some socks, a few drawing materials, and his film of *Alice's Wonderland.* Then he took the cages with his mice and rode to the end of the streetcar line. In an open field he let the mice go.

Walt turned to leave. After a few steps he looked back. Mortimer sat where Walt had left him. The mouse's eyes seemed very reproachful.

Two Partnerships

In July 1923, at the age of 21, Walt Disney arrived in Los Angeles in a badly worn jacket and mismatched pants. He had only $40 in his pocket. His prospects did not look bright. Walt boarded with one of his father's brothers, Robert Disney, paying him five dollars a week. Day after day he walked the streets looking for work. He also wrote to New York movie distributors, trying to interest them in *Alice's Wonderland.*

One day Walt got a letter that sent him hurrying to the veterans' hospital to see Roy.

"A New York movie distributor, Margaret Winkler, wants a series of *Alice* films!" he crowed, sitting on the edge of Roy's bed. "She'll pay $1,500 each! Think of that!"

"How many does she want?" Roy asked.

"Twelve. We'll do it, won't we, Roy? We'll go into business together. With $500 we could make a start, I'm sure of it!"

Roy shook his head. He was due to be discharged from the hospital in a few days, but he had no money except his $85-a-month pension from the government. "Who would lend us $500?"

However, Roy could not long resist Walt's enthusiasm. He soon found himself saying, "Okay, kid. Let's go!"

Roy persuaded Uncle Robert to lend them $500. Walt went to a neighborhood real estate dealer and asked to rent space for a studio.

"How much can you pay?" the realtor asked.

"About five dollars a month," Walt replied. The man laughed. "We don't need much space," Walt assured him hurriedly. "Just about room enough to swing a cat."

Still laughing, the man agreed to rent the Disneys a cubbyhole in the back of his office for five dollars a month.

Production costs ran higher than Walt had figured. He hired a girl from Kansas City to play "Alice." He worked night and day drawing cartoon figures, and he also built the scenes for the backgrounds. Soon he realized he must have help with the drawings, and he wrote to Ub Iwerks and offered him a job. Ub accepted.

At first Roy did the movie photography, but he could not master the steady cranking rhythm that the old-fashioned hand camera required. So Walt had to hire a real cameraman.

"We've got to raise more money," Roy said one evening as the partners sat down to their usual meal of beans in their little walk-up apartment. "Where can we get it?" Uncle Robert had announced flatly that he would not lend them money again.

"What about that girl Edna you went with in Kansas City?" Walt suggested.

"You leave Edna out of this," Roy snapped. "I'm not going to borrow money from my girl!"

Walt shrugged. "Maybe the organist of the Isis Theater in Kansas City would lend me a few hundred. He liked the animated song sheets I did for him."

Walt wrote to the organist, and he also wrote secretly to Roy's girl, Edna Francis. Both sent some money.

Although Roy was angry because Walt had gone against his wishes, he soon forgave him.

The Disney brothers made one *Alice* film after another, but there was little profit. Walt was always trying to improve the animation and photography, and improvements cost money. He also kept adding to his staff. He took on more artists and began to

train them in animation. Then he decided to hire a girl to do stenographic work and also ink the outlines of the pencil drawings and fill them in to make them ready for photographing.

One day while Walt was working, a pretty young woman appeared in the tiny Disney office and applied for a job.

"I'm Lillian Bounds, from Lewiston, Idaho," she told Walt. "I'm staying with my sister, just a few blocks from here."

"Good," Walt said, looking down at her approvingly. "You won't have to pay carfare."

Lillian took the job without bothering to ask what it paid. By the time she learned that her wages were only fifteen dollars a week, she had become so interested in her dynamic, hardworking boss that she stayed on.

Walt and Roy continued to live as cheaply as possible. They paid themselves salaries of $35 a week and put the rest of their income back into the business.

Walt admired Lillian Bounds, but he had no money or time for dates. Instead he would drive her home after they had worked late. When they reached her sister's house, they would sit in the car and talk.

"Come in and meet my sister," Lillian often urged, but Walt always refused. He was ashamed of his clothes — an old sweater and worn-out pants.

One day he asked Roy, the company's business manager, if he could draw enough money from their account to buy a suit.

Roy grinned. "We'll both buy suits, kid," he replied. "Edna is coming out from Kansas City, and we're getting married."

"That's swell, Roy," Walt exclaimed. "But I guess it means I've got to get a new cook!"

Roy and Edna were married in the spring of 1925. A few nights later Walt was dictating to Lillian in the office. Suddenly he paused. He leaned over and kissed her.

"Which do you think we should pay for first, Lilly, a new car or a ring?" he asked.

"A ring," Lilly replied promptly.

The wedding took place in July 1925, in Lillian's brother's home in Lewiston. Now Walt Disney had a marriage partner as well as a business partner.

The Lesson Oswald Taught

Lillian quickly learned that life with Walt Disney would never be dull, but it could be uncertain and upsetting. One day she worked for hours cooking dinner in their apartment kitchen. When dinner time arrived, Walt had not come home. Hour after hour Lillian waited, getting angrier and angrier.

Long after midnight the door opened softly and Walt tiptoed in. Before Lillian could say a word he said, "I'm sorry, Lilly. I forgot about dinner. I was drawing an awfully funny animation scene, and I didn't realize what time it was."

Lillian laughed helplessly. She just couldn't stay mad at Walt!

The following afternoon Walt came home early. He handed his wife a hatbox tied with a big red ribbon. "Here's a peace offering, Lilly," he said, smiling shyly.

Inside the box was a chow puppy, with another red ribbon around its neck!

Walt loved the puppy as much as Lilly did. He spoiled it with extra food, but he trained it with unlimited patience. Lilly was impressed with Walt's love of animals and his kindness to them.

The first two years of Walt's marriage saw many changes. The business outgrew the real estate office, so Walt leased a store building on Hyperion Avenue and converted it into a studio. He also bought a home near the studio.

After three years the *Alice Comedies* began to lose their popularity.

"I've got to think of a new series idea," Walt told Lilly. He began to spend every spare minute sketching different animals. Finally he drew a long-eared rabbit. His entire staff liked it.

"The rabbit can get into all kinds of scrapes," Walt said, "all of them very funny. It should be a good series."

"What will you name him?" Lilly asked. But Walt had not yet decided.

"Write names for the rabbit on slips of paper," Walt directed his staff. "We'll put them in a hat and draw one." "Oswald" was the name that was drawn.

Charles Mintz, Margaret Winkler's distribution partner, was delighted with Oswald Rabbit. He sent Walt a contract to sign, which named a price of $2,250 for each Oswald picture.

One day in 1927 Walt said to Lilly, "The Oswald contract will end soon. We'll go to New York, and I will bargain for a new contract personally. I'm going to ask for a raise in fees."

Instead of agreeing to a raise, Mintz told Walt bluntly, "I'll give you $1,800 a reel on a new contract."

Walt protested. "I'm not going to take a cut when Oswald is so popular!"

Mintz smiled unpleasantly. "Oh, yes, you are. If you don't, you lose Oswald entirely, and you also lose your best artists." He explained that he had copyrighted Oswald Rabbit in his own name

UNIVERSAL
presents
OSWALD
THE
LUCKY RABBIT
IN
"THE OL' SWIMMIN' HOLE"
A Winkler Production
by WALT DISNEY
HUGH
+MAX

instead of Disney's, so he owned all legal rights. He told Walt that four Disney artists had signed contracts, agreeing to leave Disney and work for him.

It hurt Walt deeply that employees whom he had trained would desert him.

"If those men desert me now," Walt said, "they'll leave you in the lurch some day, too."

Mintz only smiled, sure that Walt Disney had no choice but to meet his terms.

However, Walt did not give in. "I can replace those artists easily," he boasted.

Walt wasn't as confident as he sounded. He and Lilly were sad as they packed for their trip home.

"I'll never work for anybody else again," Walt vowed. "Never!"

Before boarding the train, he sent a telegram to his brother: "Everything O.K. Coming home."

"How can you say that?" Lilly protested. "You know it isn't true!"

"I'll make it come true," Walt said.

The Birth of Mickey Mouse

On the long train trip across the continent, Walt Disney stared unseeingly out of the coach window. Day after day he tried to think of an animal character around which to build a new cartoon series. His mind went back to his childhood on the farm. He drew cows, horses, chickens, pigs, and geese. None of them satisfied him.

As the train reached the Middle West, Walt exclaimed suddenly, "I've got it!" He began to sketch furiously. Soon he thrust a sheet of drawings into Lilly's hands.

"See what you think of these," he said excitedly.

Lilly looked down at the sketches. She saw a cartoon of a mouse — a merry, appealing little creature. In a way the mouse, with his expressive eyes and his pointed face, resembled Walt. The body of the mouse was pear-shaped. He had pipe-stem legs in big shoes. He wore two-button short pants and gloves.

"I'll call him Mortimer Mouse," Walt said.

Lilly objected. "That's a horrible name for a character!"

"What's wrong with Mortimer?" Walt demanded. "I called one of my Kansas City mice Mortimer. He was smart. He learned to stay inside a circle on drawing paper. Mortimer learned . . ."

"I don't care what your Kansas City mouse learned!" Lilly snapped, her nerves on edge from days of worry and inactivity. "You've got to find a better name for that mouse!"

They argued about it while the train crossed wheat fields, deserts, and mountains. Before it reached the Pacific Coast, they had agreed to call the mouse "Mickey."

"Mickey Mouse is going to make a fortune for us," Walt assured his wife. "He's the kind of character who can cook up lots of mischief, like a bad little boy. I'll never run out of story ideas for Mickey."

Walt set to work on a Mickey Mouse film, *Plane Crazy*. He used farm animals as background and as sources of humor. Animators were sent to zoos and farms to draw animals from life.

The whole Disney staff worked night and day. Lilly and Edna, Roy's wife, helped by tracing the animation drawings on celluloid and inking them so they could be photographed. When *Plane Crazy* was finished, a second Mickey Mouse film was started, and then a third. But nobody would buy them! Something had happened that changed the whole movie industry!

In October 1927 a "talking picture," *The Jazz Singer*, had been shown. Before that date, movies had been "silent." That is, the actors moved their lips, but they made no sound in the theater. Movie audiences had to read signs flashed on the screen to find out what characters said. In *The Jazz Singer* audiences really heard for the first time what actors on the screen were saying. The picture was a sensation! After it appeared, owners of movie theaters no longer wanted to show "silent" films.

Walt Disney had spent a great deal of money on his silent Mickey Mouse pictures. Now they seemed worthless.

"What are we going to do with these films?" Roy asked at last, very discouraged.

"We'll make them over," Walt said. "We'll add sound to the film."

Roy stared at his brother. "That's impossible," he said.

"I'll find a way," Walt insisted. "Sound will make our pictures much better." He began to experiment with sound in the third Mickey Mouse film, which he called *Steamboat Willie.*

Lean months followed. It took time and money to solve the problems of adding sound to a film. And when it was accomplished at last, the brothers ran into more trouble. Distributors wanted to buy the Disney films outright.

Walt refused. "Nobody is ever going to own any of our

pictures again," he said stubbornly, remembering Oswald Rabbit. "We'll rent our films, we won't sell them."

Although the Disney Studio needed money badly, Roy stood by his brother.

Walt drove his staff unmercifully. Every detail of every picture had to be perfect, no matter how many times each drawing had to be done over. He drove himself even harder than he did his staff. Often he worked up to fourteen hours a day.

"I have a little work to finish," he told Lilly one evening after dinner. Lilly went with him to the studio. She stretched out on the sofa and watched her husband working at his drawing board. Soon she drifted off to sleep. The next thing she knew Walt was bending over her, shaking her gently.

"What time is it?" Lilly asked sleepily.

"Ten-thirty," Walt replied, glad that she didn't have a watch. He drove her home and somehow managed to keep her from seeing a clock before she went to bed. It was 2:30 in the morning!

The first Mickey Mouse film opened in New York in November 1928. Mickey Mouse, using Walt Disney's voice, quickly became a star. Audiences laughed at Mickey and loved him.

Fame

Walt could not enjoy his success. He had worked too hard too long. He became cross and irritable. He shouted at his staff, at Roy and Edna, and even at Lilly, whom he adored. Finally he went to a doctor.

"You need a long rest," the doctor told Walt. "Drop everything and get away from the studio. Take a trip, and when you come back stop working such long hours. Find yourself some hobbies. Otherwise your health will fail again."

Walt followed the doctor's orders. During several months of leisurely travel he regained his health, his cheerful disposition, and his zest for living.

Soon after he returned from his vacation, Walt learned about a process for color photography.

"That's what I've been waiting for," he exclaimed. "We'll scrap *Flowers and Trees* and reshoot the whole thing in color."

"We've already finished half of that picture in black and white!" Roy protested.

"*Flowers and Trees* is a natural for color photography," Walt insisted.

"But think how much more color photography will cost!" Roy exclaimed.

"Oh, you'll find some way to raise the money," Walt replied cheerfully.

They quarreled about it, but Walt would not give in. Roy finally raised the necessary money, and Walt rushed into color production of *Flowers and Trees*. However, he took time out to buy a peace pipe and place it on his brother's desk. Roy hung the pipe on the wall of his office.

When *Flowers and Trees* was finished, Roy admitted that Walt had been right to gamble on color. The picture won a Motion Picture Academy Award as the best cartoon of 1931–1932, and again the Disney Studio led all of its competitors.

Walt continued to search for perfection. He constantly looked for ways to improve animated cartoons. One day he stopped in to see Webb Smith in the Disney story department. Webb's office wall was covered with a series of sketches that told the story of the picture then in progress.

"I just had these offices redecorated, Webb," Walt complained. "You're ruining the wall with those thumbtacks."

"Sorry, Walt," Webb replied. "I didn't think of that."

Walt stopped frowning at the offending thumbtacks and studied Webb's sketches.

"Um," he murmured thoughtfully. "You can follow the story from these sketches better than from a written outline."

The next day a truckload of corkboard was delivered to the Disney Studio, and a permanent storyboard was installed in each office of the story department.

In the early 1930s the Great Depression swept over the nation. More than 18 million people were out of work. Disney Studio, however, continued to prosper. In five years Walt's staff increased from 150 employees to more than 750. The studio on Hyperion Avenue was enlarged, and Walt started a training class for cartoon artists.

During these years Walt Disney made many cartoon shorts. He made Donald Duck pictures and Silly Symphonies like *The Tortoise and the Hare* and *Three Little Pigs.* These were all very popular.

***Three Little Pigs* (1933)**

Still Mickey Mouse was Walt's best-known character. He had become more than a movie star. He was seen everywhere — on school tablets, watches, toys, and children's clothes. There was also a Mickey Mouse comic strip, printed in 1,000 newspapers, and there were hundreds of Mickey Mouse Clubs in 38 different countries. In 1935 the League of Nations presented a medal to Walt Disney, calling Mickey Mouse "a symbol of international good will." Walt and his cartoon characters had become world famous.

If you want to discover more about the man who created a mouse named Mickey, read the rest of *Walt Disney: Master of Make-Believe.*

CREATE A CARTOON

Walt Disney based the character of Mickey Mouse on his pet mouse. Create your own cartoon character based on a pet or even a person in your life. Draw a picture of your character and give it a name. Then, if you wish, create a four-panel comic strip featuring your new character.

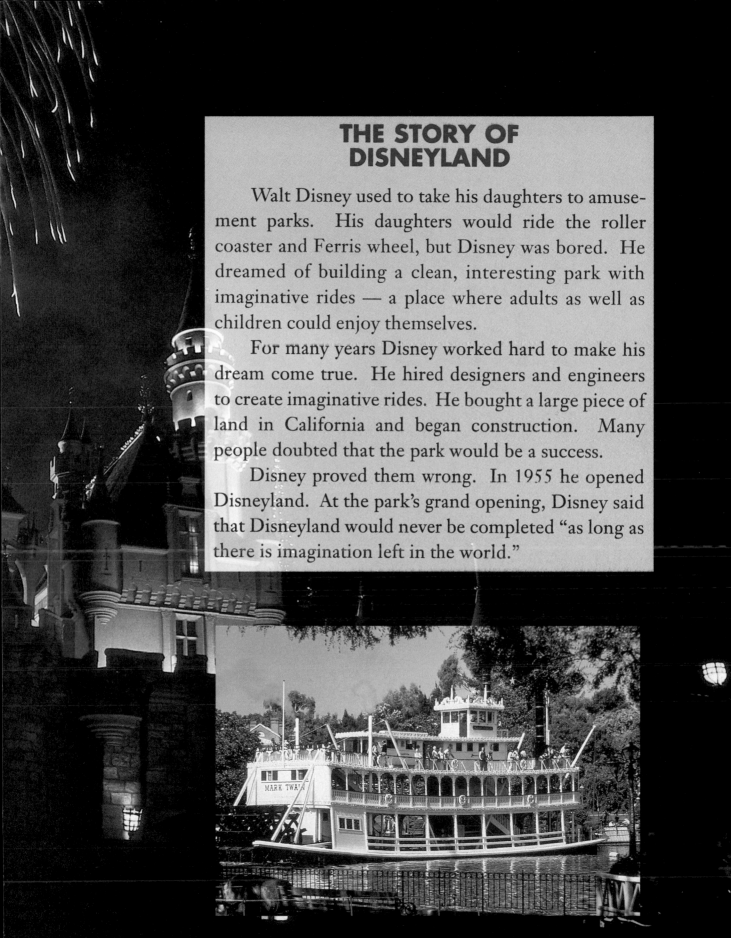

THE STORY OF DISNEYLAND

Walt Disney used to take his daughters to amusement parks. His daughters would ride the roller coaster and Ferris wheel, but Disney was bored. He dreamed of building a clean, interesting park with imaginative rides — a place where adults as well as children could enjoy themselves.

For many years Disney worked hard to make his dream come true. He hired designers and engineers to create imaginative rides. He bought a large piece of land in California and began construction. Many people doubted that the park would be a success.

Disney proved them wrong. In 1955 he opened Disneyland. At the park's grand opening, Disney said that Disneyland would never be completed "as long as there is imagination left in the world."

Marian Anderson

by Tobi Tobias

In a small house in Philadelphia a three-year-old girl was singing. She sat at a little table that she liked to make believe was her piano. The walls of the room were covered with flowered paper. The child thought she saw friendly faces in the flowers, looking down at her as she played and sang. The child's name was Marian Anderson. When she grew up, she became one of the world's best-loved singers.

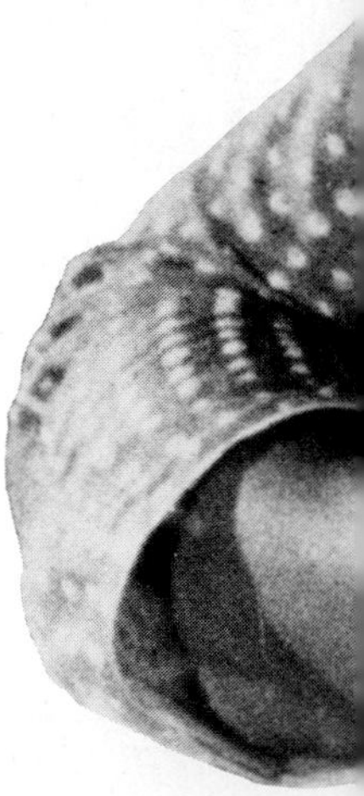

Marian was born on February 17, 1902. Her father, John Anderson, worked long hours delivering coal and ice. Her mother, Anna Anderson, had been a schoolteacher once. Now she was busy keeping the house comfortable for her husband and their three daughters: Marian, Alyce, and Ethel. The Anderson family did not have much money, but they cared about each other and had many happy times together.

As Marian grew older, her father took her to church with him every Sunday. The Union Baptist Church was important to the people in Marian's neighborhood. Often their lives were unhappy. Many of them were poor. Some of them had trouble getting jobs. In church they heard words and music that said to them: "Yes, you have troubles. We know that life can be hard. We must hope for good things to come."

Marian joined the children's choir of the church. As she sang with this group, the choirmaster noticed her beautiful voice. He asked her to practice a duet with her best friend, Viola Johnson. The next Sunday the two girls stood up to sing for the whole congregation. It was Marian's first public performance. She was six years old.

Marian was finding out about music in other ways, too. When she was eight, her father bought an old piano. But there was no money for music lessons. After weeks of trying, Marian taught herself to play simple tunes. She wished she could learn more.

Then one day she saw a used violin in a store window. She went in and asked the man how much it cost. "Three dollars and ninety-five cents," he said. "Is it a good violin?" Marian asked. She knew how hard it would be for her to get that much money. “Oh, it’s a very fine instrument,” the storekeeper said.

Marian went to work after school. She scrubbed steps for her neighbors and ran their errands. If someone gave her a few cents for candy, she put the money carefully away. At last she earned and saved enough nickels and pennies. Proudly she went back to the store and bought the violin. A friend of the family taught her to tune it and to play a few notes. But before long the strings snapped and the wood of the violin cracked. It was no good at all. Marian was sad and disappointed. She wanted so much to make music well.

Still she was never downhearted for long. She loved singing in the choir. Her full, rich voice poured through the church. The sound she made was so loud the choirmaster sometimes laughed and said, “Hold back a little there, Marian. We want to hear the other singers, too.” Friends and neighbors in the congregation, though, had nothing but praise for Marian.

Her voice was deep and velvety, the kind musicians call contralto. But she could reach up to the high soprano notes, too, and even down to the low music of the baritone. When the choir prepared a new song, Marian learned all the different parts, high and low, not just her own. Then, if a singer could not come to church on Sunday, she helped out by singing in his place. It made her happy to know the choir needed her, and she learned a lot about music this way. Secretly she dreamed of being a singer when she grew up.

At home, life was good. The Andersons were a warm, close family. Even though Marian’s father worked hard and came home tired, he was always ready to laugh and joke with his daughters. Sometimes he surprised them with special treats, like new Easter hats or tickets to the circus. And Mrs. Anderson was there whenever the girls needed her, teaching them and loving them.

But when Marian was ten, her father died. Life changed then. Harder times began. Marian's mother had to go out to work. She got a job cleaning other people's houses and bringing their laundry home to wash and iron. Mrs. Anderson was a frail, gentle woman, but she had great spirit. No matter how difficult her tasks were, she never complained. Somehow she found the extra strength to make a good home for her children.

As the years went by, Marian began to realize how hard her mother worked to provide for her family. "I'm getting old enough now," she thought, "I must do something, too." When she entered high school she tried to study useful subjects, like typing. She knew this would help her get a job as a secretary in an office. But all the time her heart was really set on singing.

If only she could earn enough money at it, she could make singing her life's work. Of course she was not paid for singing in church. Ever since she was eight, though, she had been invited to sing in other churches, too. People all over Philadelphia got to know about her splendid voice. They began asking her to perform at their parties and club meetings. By the time Marian was in high school, she was getting $5.00 every time she sang at one of these gatherings.

This seemed like a lot of money to her. Yet she knew she was still a long way from being a professional singer. She had been born with a fine voice and she sang with deep feeling.

But Marian saw how much she still had to learn. The best way, she decided, would be to have lessons, at a music school.

Early one morning she took the trolley car to a well-known school in uptown Philadelphia. She went into the building and got in line with a group of girls who were waiting to apply. When Marian's turn came, the pretty, blue-eyed woman in charge paid no attention to her. Marian stepped aside. After everyone else had been taken care of, the woman said, "What do *you* want?" in a sharp voice. "I'd like to arrange for lessons, please — " Marian began politely. "We don't take colored," said the woman coldly, and turned away.

Marian felt hurt and confused. She had often heard that white people sometimes behaved in this cruel, thoughtless way toward Negroes. But it had never really happened to her before. In her neighborhood black people and white people lived side by side. Most of the time they were comfortable and friendly with each other. True enough, their skins were different, Marian thought, but not their feelings.

Sadly she went home to tell her mother what happened at the school. "The way that woman spoke," she cried, "it bit into my soul." Her mother listened quietly. Was she wrong to think a Negro girl could become a singer? Marian asked. Maybe her dreams were foolish.

Mrs. Anderson thought for a while. Then, in her calm, sure way, she said, "Of course you can be a singer, Marian. You must have faith. There will be another way for you to learn what you need to know."

And there was another way. The people at the Union Baptist Church believed in Marian's talent. These friends and neighbors planned a concert to help her. Every bit of money they got from the tickets was set aside to pay for private singing lessons for Marian.

Marian performed at the concert herself, but the main star was Roland Hayes. Mr. Hayes was the first Negro singer to become famous in the concert halls of America and Europe. He sang the spirituals Marian and her people knew so well. These were powerful songs of sorrow, of joy, and of hope that the Negroes made up when they were slaves. Mr. Hayes also sang lieder, poems set to music by the great European composers. Marian could not understand the French or German languages they were sung in. Still she was quick to hear the beauty of the music. She longed to learn such songs herself.

Roland Hayes

Then, as she listened to Mr. Hayes's pure tenor voice, she suddenly realized, "His skin is dark, like mine. And he has gone so far. They say he has even sung for kings and queens. If he can, perhaps I can too." Slowly, from this time on, Marian's pride began to grow. It was never an angry pride, but full of faith and hope. Throughout her life, no matter what happened, it kept her strong.

With the money raised at the concert, Marian started taking music lessons. She quickly learned everything her teachers could show her. Then Giuseppi Boghetti agreed to listen to her. He was a well-known voice coach with studios in Philadelphia and New York. At first he spoke to her gruffly. "I am seeing you just as a favor," he said. "I don't want any new students. I have too many already."

Marian sang for him. The deep beauty and feeling in her voice instantly changed Mr. Boghetti's mind. "I will make room for you right away," he declared. "Don't think it will be easy, though. You have a grand voice. But it must be trained, so that it can do whatever you want it to do. For this you need many exercises and much hard practicing. We will work together. After that you will be able to go anywhere and sing for anybody."

That year Marian finished high school. With more free time, she could do more performing. She began to travel farther from home to sing in churches, colleges, and small theaters. Finally she earned enough money to make one of her greatest wishes come true. The day came when she could say to her mother, "I can take care of you now. You don't have to work any more." Afterward Marian always said that was the happiest day of her life.

Marian with her mother, Anna Anderson, after receiving an award

When Mr. Boghetti thought Marian was ready, he let her enter a contest of three hundred young singers. The first prize was a chance to perform with the New York Philharmonic Orchestra. By now Marian's amazing voice was well trained. And, as always, she put her whole spirit into the music. After she sang, the other contestants clapped and cheered. Then the judges announced that she had won.

Marian hoped this prize would prove she was ready to sing in America's best concert halls. The people who wrote about music in the newspapers and magazines were beginning to say fine things about her. But several years passed and still she was not often asked to sing in the really important theaters. Most Americans just did not want to believe that a Negro could be an excellent concert singer. They would not give Marian a chance to show them how good she was.

Marian felt that her career was standing still. "What can I do about this?" she wondered. Finally she decided to go to Europe. There she would study with famous singing masters. Then, if she performed for European audiences, and these people liked her work, perhaps America would welcome her back and realize what she could do.

She studied first in England. Then she went to Germany, to learn the language of her favorite lieder. There she met Kosti Vehanen, a pianist from Finland. "Let me become your accompanist," he offered. Marian agreed. Kosti would play the piano while she sang. Together they set out on a tour of the Scandinavian countries in the north of Europe. Here — in Norway, Sweden, Finland, and Denmark — Marian was immediately accepted as a great singer by everyone who heard her. It did not matter to these people that Marian was black and most of them were white. They loved her voice and they loved her.

Arturo Toscanini

A tour of Europe followed. Once again Marian was a huge success. Arturo Toscanini, the famous orchestra conductor, came to one of her concerts. He was so moved by her singing that he went backstage afterward to speak to her. Marian could hardly believe what he said: "A voice like yours is heard only once in a hundred years."

Ordinary people had the same feeling about her. It was Marian's way to end each of her concerts with a group of Negro spirituals. Often the Europeans could not understand the English words. It made no difference. Marian poured the heart and soul of her people into this music. When the songs she planned to sing were over, the audience would not leave the theater. They called for her again and again. Some of them rushed down the aisles and pounded on the stage, shouting out the names of the spirituals they liked best. " 'Deep River'!" they yelled. " 'Heaven, Heaven'!"

Never in America had she had a welcome like this. And yet Marian thought it was time to go back to her own country. Her stay in Europe helped her find her place as a singer. But America was her home. Her family was there. All the people who first believed in her and helped her were there, waiting. She knew she must return to them.

Marian sailed back to the United States on a large ocean liner. Every day she and Kosti practiced together for the important homecoming concert in New York. One morning, as Marian was going down the staircase to the rehearsal room, the rough sea made the ship lurch. Marian lost her balance and fell. She was in great pain. The doctor told her she had a broken bone in her foot. He put her leg in a bulky plaster cast.

But Marian did not disappoint the people who came to her concert. On December 30, 1935, she sang at Town Hall. Her cast was hidden by a long evening dress. And this time her American audience let themselves understand what a wonderful singer this black woman was. Marian sang about the beautiful things in the world, and the ugly things. She sang about happy times and sad ones. She sang about the deepest thoughts and feelings that all people share. When she finished there was a long silence. Then the audience rose to its feet and burst into wild applause.

Marian Anderson performing in Bombay, India

In the next thirty years Marian sang all over the world. She traveled across the United States again and again. She went back to Europe many times. She gave concerts in Russia, Israel, and Japan. She was almost always accepted as she deserved. Sometimes, though, there were difficulties because she was black. But when others were mean-spirited, Marian knew how to be generous and understanding. Once, when she faced this kind of trouble, the whole world was watching.

In the spring of 1939 she planned to give a concert in Washington, D.C., the nation's capital. She hoped to appear in Constitution Hall. It was owned by the Daughters of the American Revolution, a group of women whose families had, long ago, fought for freedom in the United States. But the D.A.R. refused to let Marian Anderson sing on their stage. Why? There could be only one answer. She was a Negro.

Fair-minded people all over America said this was wrong. Throughout the world men and women waited to see what would happen. Marian was not a fighter. But through her music she would do whatever she could to gain freedom and justice for her people. Leaders of the United States government invited her to give her concert outdoors for everyone who wanted to come.

On Easter Sunday Marian came to the Lincoln Memorial. She stood before the statue of Abraham Lincoln, the president who freed the Negro slaves. There she sang for 75,000 people. Black and white together, they joined her in the opening song — "America."

Marian Anderson singing at the Lincoln Memorial in 1939

Four years later Marian married Orpheus Fisher. They had known each other for a long time. Together they chose some beautiful land in the Connecticut farm country. On it they built the simple, comfortable house Marian had always dreamed of. Close by, near a running brook, was a separate studio for Marian to work in. Mr. Fisher, who was an architect, designed everything himself.

Marian with her husband, Orpheus Fisher, at Marianna Farm

Now, although Marian might be on tour most of the year, she always came home to Marianna Farm for the summer. There, with her new accompanist, Franz Rupp, she prepared her concerts for the next season. First Marian and Franz carefully picked out the songs they wanted to do. Then they studied them and practiced them over and over again. They tried to make their performance of each song as close to perfect as they could.

Marianna Farm was also a place of rest. Here Marian could relax with her husband. She enjoyed sewing things for her home and caring for the pet animals they kept. Here, too, her mother and sisters often visited with her.

After twenty years as a successful concert singer, Marian was given a chance to try another kind of music. In 1955 she was asked to appear with the world-famous Metropolitan Opera Company in New York. She took the part of Ulrica, the gypsy fortune-teller, in Verdi's opera *The Masked Ball.* It was the first time a Negro had sung an important role at the Metropolitan as a regular company member.

Marian's part was not easy. She had to reach very high and very low notes, and join in difficult group singing. And as she sang, she had to make the audience believe she was truly a gypsy sorceress. The whole company worked with her. Marian said it was like being part of a big family. Together they gave a wonderful performance of the opera.

That night, as the gold curtain came down at the Met, people called excitedly, "Anderson, Anderson!" Some of them even cried, thinking of all Marian had done to reach this great moment. That night a new audience discovered her glorious voice. More important, Marian opened a door for her own people. From that time on, Negro singers were welcome on the great opera stage.

Marian's talent and her simple, beautiful spirit brought her many honors. Like Roland

Hayes, she sang for kings and queens, and for three presidents of the United States. Two of her best rewards, though, were jobs she was invited to do.

In 1957 the American government asked her to tour the countries of Asia. She sang to the people and then spoke with them. These men and women found it easy to talk to her, to tell her the thoughts deep inside them, to explain what their countries needed and what they hoped for. Marian understood people from different places so well that she was then sent to the United Nations. There she joined the leaders of many countries in trying to bring peace to the world.

Now Marian was growing older. Her singing voice was not as rich and full as it used to be. Of course she would always sing at home, for her family and friends. But it was best to end the days of performing.

In 1965 she made a farewell tour of Europe and America. As she took her last bows from the stage, she thought, "My work is not over. There is still much I can do. I want to help people of different groups come to understand each other. I can make the way easier for young singers. I want to do something for children all over the world — with my hands, and my heart, and my soul. In a way, my work is just beginning."

A Someday Dream

As a young girl, Marian Anderson
secretly dreamed of being a singer when she grew up.
What do you dream of being someday?
Write a paragraph or a poem telling about your dream.

Poetry

GERTRUDE

When I hear Marian Anderson sing,
I am a STUFFless kind of thing.

Heart is like the flying air.
I cannot find it anywhere.

Fingers tingle. I am cold
And warm and young and very old.

But, most, I am a STUFFless thing
When I hear Marian Anderson sing.

Gwendolyn Brooks

DREAMS

Hold fast to dreams
For if dreams die
Life is a broken-winged bird
That cannot fly.

Hold fast to dreams
For when dreams go
Life is a barren field
Frozen with snow.

Langston Hughes

HOLD FAST YOUR DREAMS

Hold fast your dreams!
Within your heart
Keep one still, secret spot
Where dreams may go,
And sheltered so,
May thrive and grow —
Where doubt and fear are not.
Oh, keep a place apart
Within your heart,
For little dreams to go.

Louise Driscoll

Award Winner

Roberto Clemente

by Kenneth Rudeen

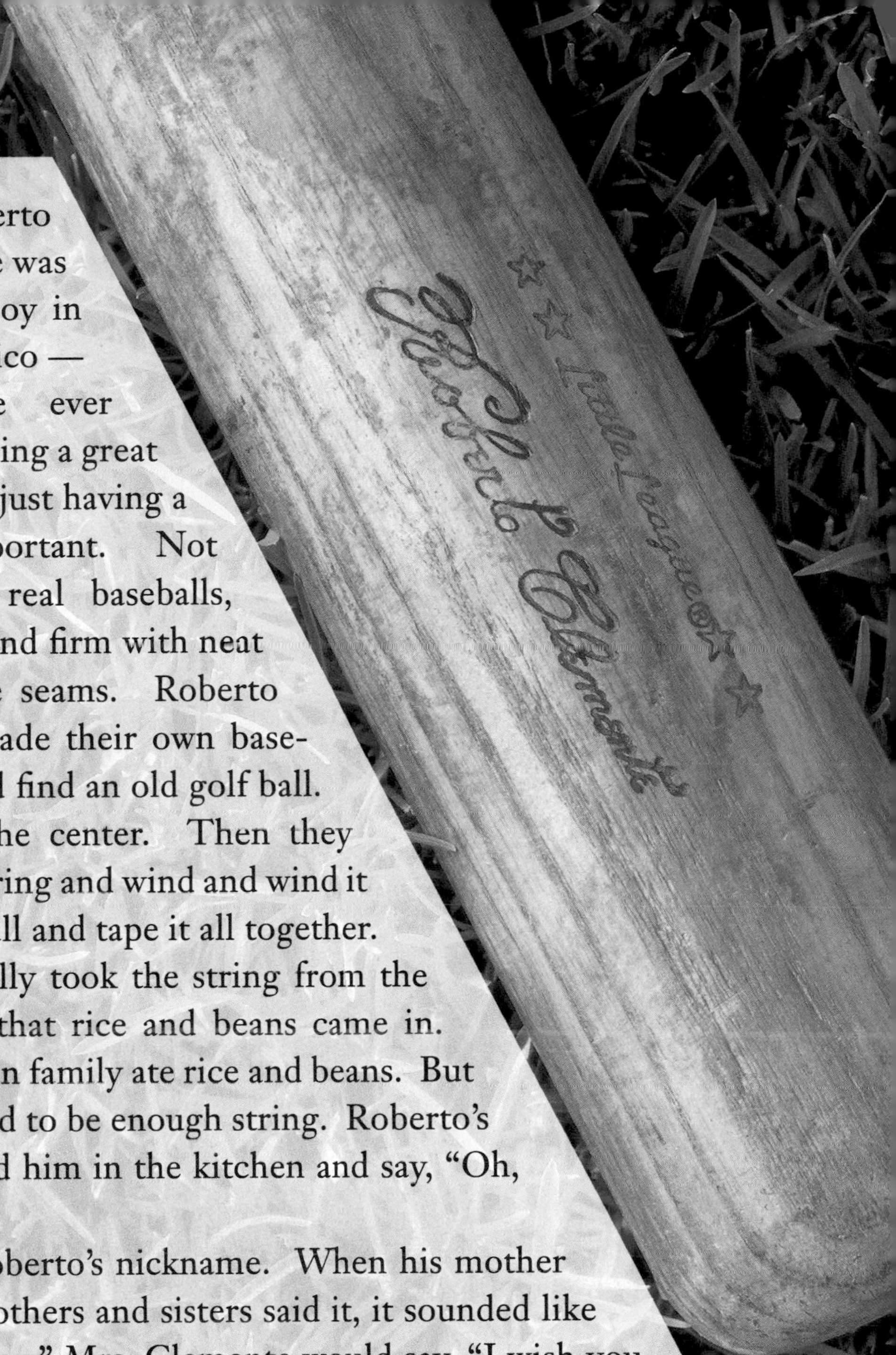

When Roberto Clemente was a small boy in Puerto Rico — long before he ever dreamed of becoming a great baseball player — just having a baseball was important. Not many boys had real baseballs, white and round and firm with neat stitches along the seams. Roberto and his friends made their own baseballs. They would find an old golf ball. That would be the center. Then they would get some string and wind and wind it around the golf ball and tape it all together.

Roberto usually took the string from the tops of the bags that rice and beans came in. Every Puerto Rican family ate rice and beans. But there never seemed to be enough string. Roberto's mother would find him in the kitchen and say, "Oh, *Mome*, not again."

Mome was Roberto's nickname. When his mother and father and brothers and sisters said it, it sounded like Mo-may. "Mo-may," Mrs. Clemente would say, "I wish you would not take the string out of the bags."

And Roberto would say, "But I have to have a baseball, Mama."

In Puerto Rico baseball was the favorite sport. Baseball players were heroes to Roberto.

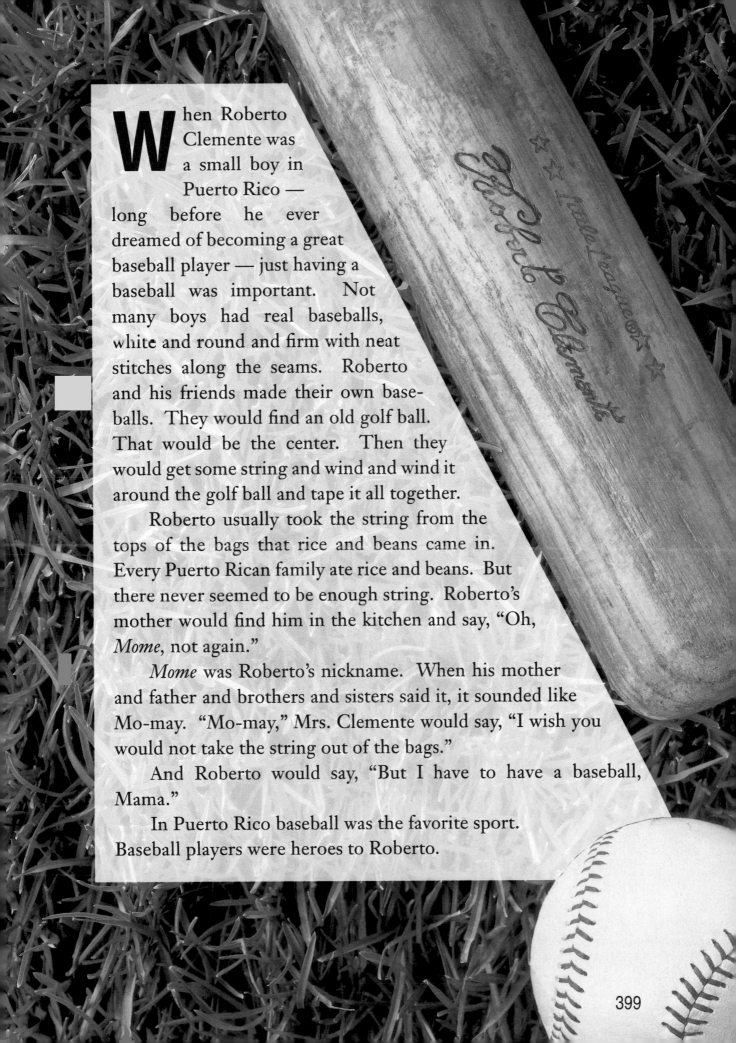

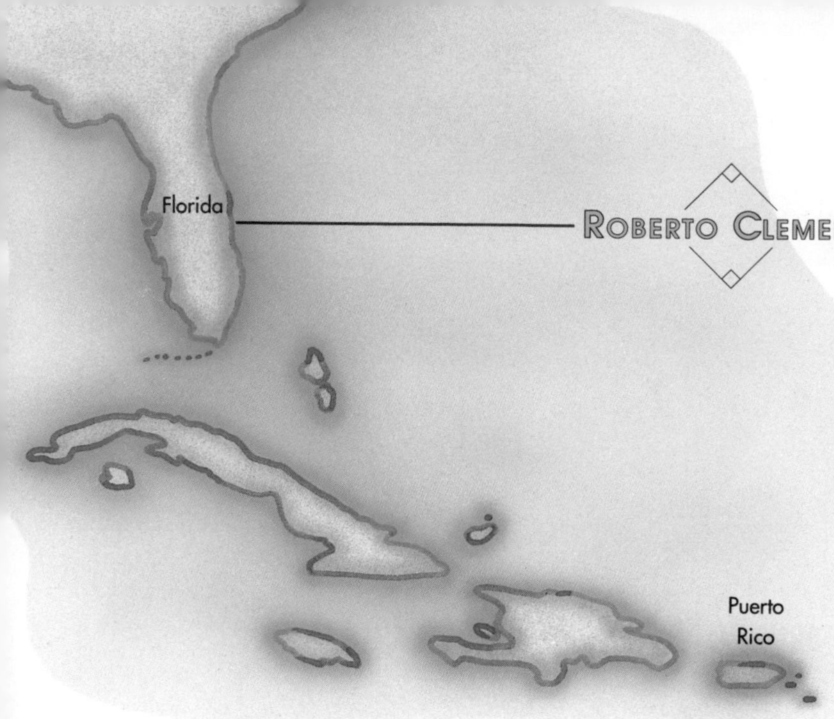

Puerto Rico is one of the islands that stretch out like steppingstones from the southern tip of Florida into the warm, blue sea. The island is beautiful, but for most of the people life is hard. In the sky the sun shines brightly. Foamy waves splash against the shore. Green mountains rise up from the sea. Birds with gaily colored feathers sing in the trees.

But men are not free to fly like birds. They must work long hours in the cities or in the fields. To be a baseball player is to be like a bird. That is a way to fly up from the hard life.

Roberto Clemente was born in the town of Carolina on August 18, 1934. The town is nestled in a valley not far from the big city of San Juan. When Roberto was growing up, there were large fields of sugar cane all around Carolina. They looked a little like the cornfields of the United States. The canes were slender and tall, growing to a height well above a man's head. They had sharp, narrow leaves that cut like a razor if you brushed against one by mistake.

To Roberto and his friends the sugar cane was like candy. They would peel back the bark on a piece of cane and bite and suck on the chewy pulp inside to get its sweet taste.

Roberto knew the fields especially well. His father was a foreman for a big sugar cane company. He saw that other workers in the fields did their jobs properly.

A man did not get rich working in the cane fields. An ordinary worker received only $2 a day. A foreman like Roberto's father received $3 or $4 a day.

In Roberto's family there was no money for luxuries like new baseballs. But there was always enough rice and beans and chicken and pork on the table. Roberto's house, which was made of wood and had a zinc roof, stood near a grove of bamboo trees.

Roberto's father was strict. When he gave his sons jobs to do, they did them. One day he asked Roberto and another son to move a large pile of sand. It was hard work to shovel the heavy sand, and the sun was hot.

"Roberto, I feel sick," his brother said.

Roberto looked at his brother. Sweat stood out on his forehead and his face was pale.

"Go on home," Roberto said. "I will finish the job."

It was easy to say, but when his brother was gone, Roberto had to face the pile of sand all by himself. It looked so high he wanted to give up. But he didn't.

Roberto worked harder than he ever had before. When he was finished at last, he ran for home, because his father had told

sugar cane

him not to be late for dinner. He was tired and he ached, but inside he felt good.

From Monday to Friday, Roberto went to school. Often his thoughts were tugged from his books by the warm sun and gentle breezes outside the classroom window — tugged to the ball park, where someday he hoped to play.

In the meantime he had to be content, after school, with balls made of string and tape and games played in a rough clearing that was not even level.

There were other boys much better at baseball than Roberto. People did not say, "Roberto is going to be a great ballplayer." He was small and thin. He could not hit the ball as hard or throw it as far as the bigger boys of his age.

Roberto and his friends played a game that was more like softball than baseball. They did not have the gloves or catching masks and pads to handle the hard, stinging baseball that the big-leaguers use.

But they saw the real game played in the park in Carolina — and they longed to play there, too, someday.

While he loved baseball and played as much as he could on the field the boys used, after school Roberto always ran first to the sugar cane fields. There he met his father and rode home with him on his horse. Papa Clemente climbed into the saddle and Roberto scrambled up behind him. Then off they rode to the house with the bamboo trees.

One day, when Roberto was nine years old, he was late. Papa Clemente rode off without him. A car came along and crashed into the horse. Papa Clemente was thrown. He was badly hurt and had to spend two months in a hospital.

"It is a miracle Roberto was spared," his father said. "If he had been riding with me as usual, I am afraid he would have been killed."

When time came for Roberto to go to high school, he was happy. The high school had a real baseball field. It had real baseballs, gloves, and masks.

Roberto played in the outfield. He had to run fast to get to balls that were hit in his direction and throw hard to keep the hitter from running to extra bases.

Roberto had always been a fast runner. Now he worked hard to become a good thrower and a good hitter. Roberto's high school had a track team. Besides running on the team, Roberto also threw the javelin, which is like a spear. When you throw it, the javelin sails through the air and then comes down and sticks in the ground.

Roberto threw the javelin to make his arm strong for baseball. In time he became one of the best throwers on his baseball team.

In high school Roberto was a quiet and serious boy. "He did not want to be just an ordinary person, he wanted to be the best," one of his friends says.

Just before Roberto was graduated from high school he was chosen to play for the team in Santurce. Santurce is a town near

Roberto (kneeling, second from left) with the Santurce team

Carolina. Roberto was paid to play baseball for this town. He did not make a great deal of money, but it was more than anyone in the sugar fields could make.

Even better, now Roberto was *somebody*. People turned their heads to look at him when he walked in the plaza. To his old friends he was still *Mome*, but to everyone else he was the new young ballplayer, Roberto Clemente.

It was a name soon to be heard in the United States, where the best players in baseball perform in two major leagues. They are called the National League and the American League.

Roberto wanted to be the best. He wanted to play in the major leagues. Men who look for new players for the major leagues came to see him in Puerto Rico. They saw him hit the ball hard. They saw him catch it in the outfield with sure hands. They saw him throw the ball fast and true. They saw him run swiftly.

In 1954, when Roberto was nineteen years old, he was chosen by one of the most famous teams in the National League, the Brooklyn Dodgers.

He was happy to have this chance. The Dodgers was the team of Jackie Robinson. Jackie was the first black man to play in the major leagues. He was a wonderful player, but he had many problems with white people who did not accept black men as equals.

Like Robinson, Roberto Clemente was black. But while growing up in Puerto Rico, he did not think about the color of a person's skin. Black men and men with light skin had always played baseball together in Puerto Rico.

So while Roberto was happy, he was also scared. He was going far from home for the first time in his life, and to places where black men still were not always treated fairly.

First Roberto was sent to Montreal in Canada to play for a farm team of the Dodgers. A farm team helps prepare young players for the major leagues.

Roberto probably was good enough to be on the Dodgers. But this was still a time when there were not very many black men in the major leagues. Some people said that the major leagues did not want to have more than four black players on any one team.

The Brooklyn Dodgers already had four black players. That was one of the reasons, people said, why Roberto was sent to the Montreal farm team.

But now the Dodgers had a problem. They wanted to keep Roberto for the future, but by sending him to a farm team just then they ran the risk of losing him. Scouts for other teams might discover him. One of these teams might take him.

The Dodgers did not want that to happen. They wanted to hide Roberto from these scouts. But how were they to do it? The Dodgers could not put him in a cave, or a closet. They had to try to hide him right out in the open as he played baseball for Montreal. They tried to do this by making it look as if Roberto were not as good a player as he really was.

It was not easy to hide Roberto. The manager of the Montreal team did his best. When Roberto was doing fine in a game, the manager would take him out. When Roberto was having just an ordinary day, the manager would leave him in.

Roberto did not know why he was being treated this way. He became confused and angry. He was lonely, anyway, living among strangers so far from home. He had grown up speaking Spanish. The people on his team spoke English, and the people in Montreal mostly spoke French.

There were trips to other cities to play other farm teams, so there were new sights for Roberto to see and new people to meet. He had money to spend. He had a good-looking uniform, and he had time to practice batting and throwing and running.

Roberto might have enjoyed all these things, but life seemed upside-down. The better he played, the quicker he was taken from a game. The worse he played, the longer he stayed in. At times he thought about quitting baseball and going home to Puerto Rico.

But his desire to play, and to be the best, was stronger than his loneliness and his anger. He kept on playing.

The Dodgers just could not make him look bad enough. Other teams could see that he was a fine player. Scouts for the Pittsburgh Pirates, another team in the National League, watched Roberto closely. They decided to take him and have him play for them.

Pittsburgh is not a place of tall sugar cane fields and gaily colored birds. It is a big, smoky city. But its people do have one thing in common with the people of Carolina, Puerto Rico. They love their baseball team.

Right from the start they loved Roberto. He was tremendous as a fielder. He had a trick of catching a ball way up in the air, with both of his feet off the ground, and then whirling to throw the ball back to the infield before his feet came down to earth. He thought nothing of crashing into walls and fences if he had to do that to catch a ball.

He became an excellent hitter. In baseball a really good hitter is one who gets three hits in every ten chances at bat. If he does that, he is said to be batting three hundred. In his second year with Pittsburgh, Roberto was batting better than three hundred.

More and more black men, more and more Spanish-speaking players like Roberto were coming into major league baseball. Soon there was no more talk of keeping the number of black players on a team down to four.

But still there were times when Roberto felt that he and other Spanish-speaking players were treated unfairly. He believed that they were not given as much praise and publicity as the others, even when they were just as good. Roberto was the kind of man who could make people listen to him. He asked for equal treatment for Spanish-speaking players. Whenever he could help one of them, he did.

Once the regular Pittsburgh shortstop could not play. A Spanish-speaking player was put in his place. This player was new to the team and nervous. He made some mistakes. Other players on the team were angry with him.

Roberto found him later, crying in the dressing room. "You are coming to dinner with me tonight," Roberto said. At dinner Roberto cheered him up. Then he asked the other Pirates to be more patient with the shortstop. They were, and he played well in some very important games.

By 1960 Roberto's Pirates were strong enough to win the championship of the National League. They played the American

P
P
P
PIRATES
PIRATES

League champions, the New York Yankees, in the World Series. There were seven games in that World Series. Roberto made a hit in every game and the Pirates won.

Roberto was getting better and better as a player, but he was not always happy. Often he was sick or injured. Playing as hard as he did, he would tear muscles. Once he had malaria, an illness of chills and fevers.

Even so, Roberto went on to win four batting championships in the National League. Nearly every year he was a member of the All-Star team — the best players from all the teams in the National League.

Every winter, after the major league baseball season ended in the United States, Roberto went home to Puerto Rico. Once when he was in Carolina he met one of his old high school teachers in a drugstore. As he was talking to her, a lovely girl walked past.

"Do you know her?" Roberto asked his friend, the teacher.

"Yes, I do," the teacher said. "That is Vera Zabala."

"Will you introduce me?" Roberto asked.

That is how Roberto met the woman he married. They built a beautiful house in the town of Rio Piedras, which is near Carolina, and in time they had three little boys.

Roberto with his sons
Enrique, Luis, and Roberto, Jr.

The basement of the house in Rio Piedras was Roberto's workshop. As a child he had liked to make things of clay. He had shaped small figures of people and animals and let them bake in the Carolina sun until they were hard. Now in Rio Piedras he took clay and made it into baseball gloves and bats.

When Roberto talked to young Puerto Ricans, he remembered the rough playing field of his boyhood and he began to dream of a sports city for the island. There young people would be able to play baseball, basketball, tennis, and soccer with the best equipment.

Each spring he returned to the United States to play for the Pirates. But not until 1971 did he and the Pirates win another National League championship and go into another World Series.

Now the Pirates faced the Baltimore Orioles. Nearly everybody thought Baltimore was a better team than Pittsburgh, and the Orioles won the first game easily. The next day they won again. Those games were played in Baltimore on the Orioles' home field. It is often easier to win at home than on the opponent's field.

There were to be three games in Pittsburgh. To the great joy of that city, the Pirates won all three games. To win a World Series one team must win four games. So now the Pirates needed just one more victory. But the next game would be played in Baltimore.

Baltimore won that game by the close score of 3 to 2. The winners of the next game would be the world champions. And again the game would be played in Baltimore.

The stadium in Baltimore was packed with cheering fans. Millions of people were watching the game on television.

The score was zero to zero when Roberto stepped up to bat in the fourth inning. He made a twisting motion with his head to relieve the pain he had been feeling all week in his neck. He looked out at the Baltimore pitcher, Mike Cuellar.

Cuellar was a man who threw slow, tricky pitches that were difficult to hit. He threw. The ball floated in toward Roberto. Crack! went the bat. The ball flew over the outfield and into the seats beyond. It was a home run. Pittsburgh was ahead in the game, 1 to 0.

Roberto connects for a home run in the 1971 World Series.

In the eighth inning the Pirates scored another run. Baltimore scored a run in the eighth inning, too, but the Orioles could do nothing after that to draw even. The game ended. The Pirates had won the Series in the last possible game by the score of 2 to 1. Without Roberto's home run, who knows what might have happened?

Just as he had in 1960, Roberto made a hit in every game of the World Series. He was voted the most valuable player of the Series by the reporters who wrote about it. Of all the players on both teams, Roberto Clemente was the very best.

Roberto rounds the bases after homering in the Series.

He went home to a hero's welcome in Puerto Rico. A huge crowd was at the airport in San Juan to meet his plane. The governor of the island presented him with a gold medal.

There was just one more thing left in baseball for Roberto to do. That was to make 3,000 hits. He would soon be thirty-eight years old — very old for a ballplayer. Only ten men in the entire history of baseball had ever played long enough or well enough to make 3,000 hits. These were special heroes.

At the very end of the 1972 season, on September 30 in Pittsburgh, Roberto hit Number 3,000.

Roberto went home to his family in Rio Piedras. He wanted to rest and also to plan for the sports city for the boys and girls of Puerto Rico.

Roberto hits Number 3,000.

In December he heard terrible news. In the city of Managua in the Central American country of Nicaragua there had been an earthquake. The ground trembled and shook beneath the city. Buildings cracked and fell. Fires broke out. More than 10,000 people were killed. More than 200,000 people lost their homes.

Around the world people began sending money and food and medicine and clothing to help the earthquake victims. Roberto asked the many Puerto Ricans he knew to help out as much as they could. He did more.

On December 31 he climbed aboard a plane loaded with supplies to take them to the people of Managua. The plane, heavily laden, rose slowly from the San Juan airport and headed out to sea. Then, when it was just a mile away, it plunged into the ocean.

That night was New Year's Eve, usually a time of gaiety and celebration, but there was no gaiety in Puerto Rico. Thousands of people went to the beach to look for the wreckage of the plane. When it became clear that Roberto had drowned, Puerto Ricans and many people in the United States felt sad. A great player — and man — was gone.

In the United States Roberto was elected to baseball's Hall of Fame. This is the greatest honor a baseball player can receive. The Hall of Fame building is in Cooperstown, New York. In it there are pictures of the best players, and things like their bats and caps.

A sign was placed on the door of the room Roberto had lived in during spring training with the Pirates in Florida. It read, "I want to be remembered as a ballplayer who gave all he had to give."

It was signed,

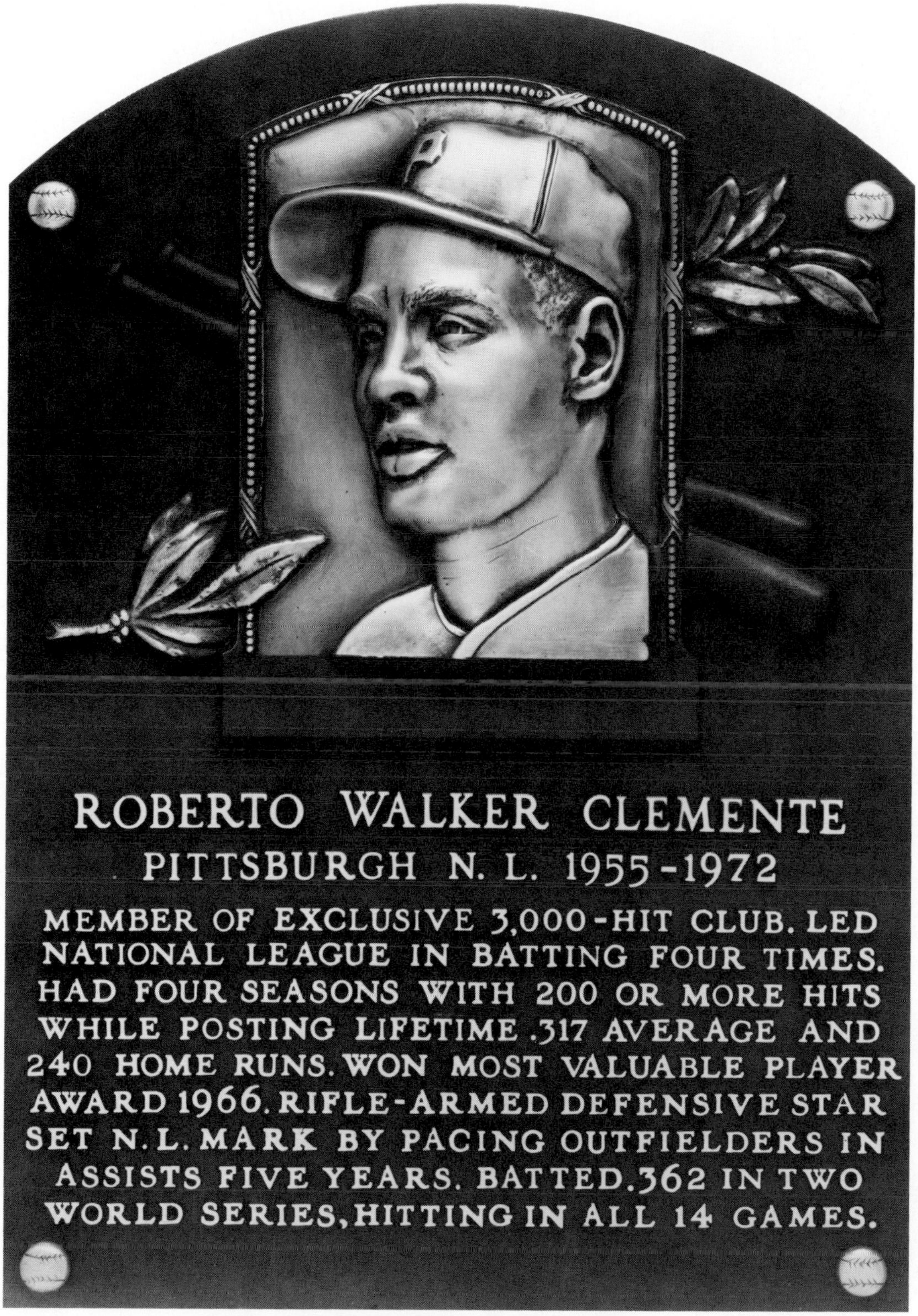
ROBERTO WALKER CLEMENTE
PITTSBURGH N. L. 1955-1972
MEMBER OF EXCLUSIVE 3,000-HIT CLUB. LED NATIONAL LEAGUE IN BATTING FOUR TIMES. HAD FOUR SEASONS WITH 200 OR MORE HITS WHILE POSTING LIFETIME .317 AVERAGE AND 240 HOME RUNS. WON MOST VALUABLE PLAYER AWARD 1966. RIFLE-ARMED DEFENSIVE STAR SET N.L. MARK BY PACING OUTFIELDERS IN ASSISTS FIVE YEARS. BATTED .362 IN TWO WORLD SERIES, HITTING IN ALL 14 GAMES.

plaque from the Hall of Fame

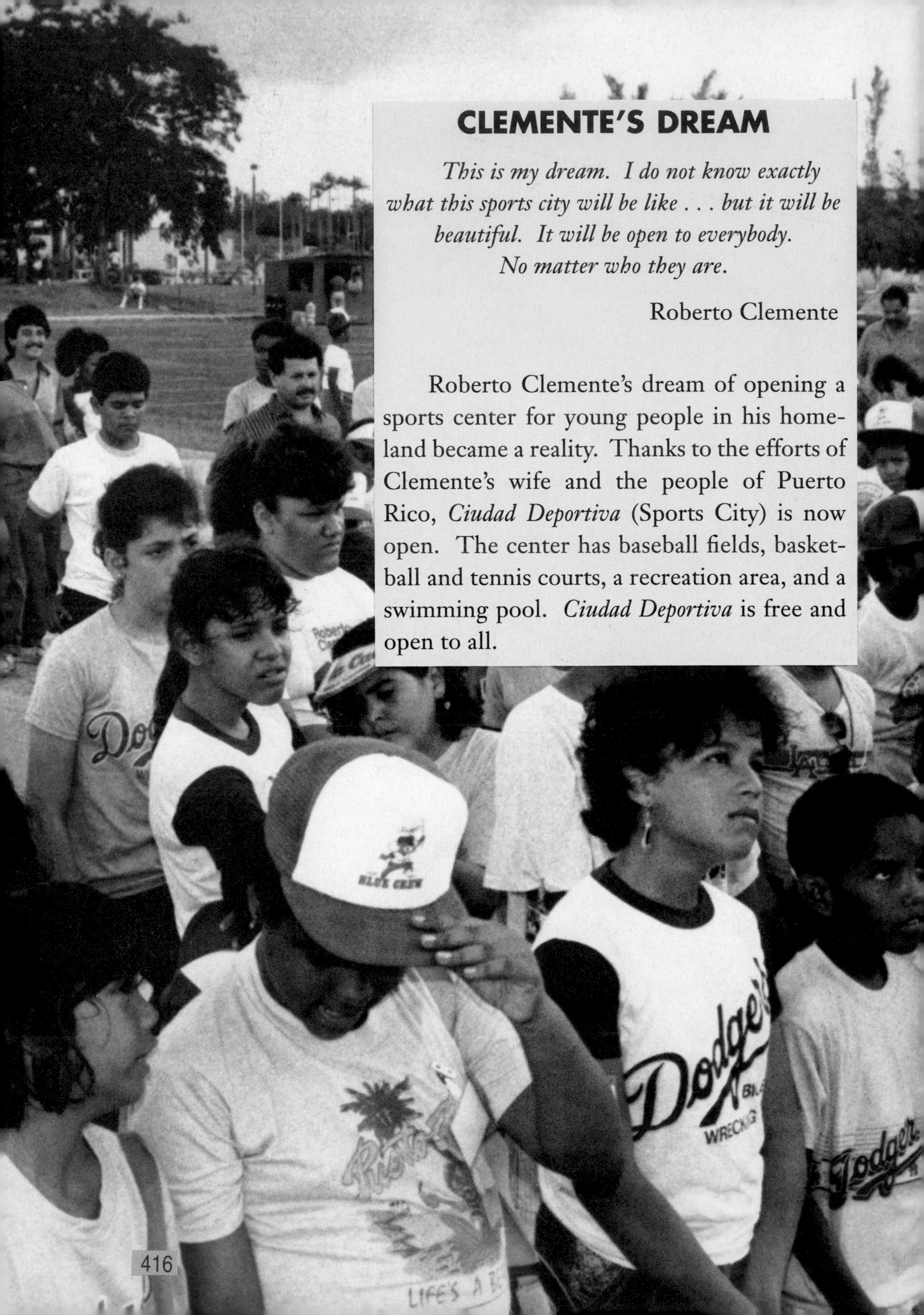

CLEMENTE'S DREAM

This is my dream. I do not know exactly what this sports city will be like . . . but it will be beautiful. It will be open to everybody. No matter who they are.

Roberto Clemente

Roberto Clemente's dream of opening a sports center for young people in his homeland became a reality. Thanks to the efforts of Clemente's wife and the people of Puerto Rico, *Ciudad Deportiva* (Sports City) is now open. The center has baseball fields, basketball and tennis courts, a recreation area, and a swimming pool. *Ciudad Deportiva* is free and open to all.

MY HERO

As a boy in Puerto Rico, Roberto Clemente admired baseball players. When he grew up and played baseball himself, Clemente became a hero to many people.

Who are your heroes? They might be famous people or they might be people who are close to you. Write a paragraph about one of your heroes and tell why you admire that person.

The Authors

ELIZABETH RIDER MONTGOMERY

Elizabeth Montgomery never intended to be a writer. She wanted to illustrate books, not write them. Winning an essay contest at age six for "The Good and Bad Uses of the Apple" didn't convince her. Winning several other writing contests didn't convince her either. Finally, her parents convinced her that she couldn't make any money as an illustrator. So she gave in and became a writer.

Montgomery wrote many biographies, including these:

- ***Hans Christian Andersen, Immortal Storyteller***
- ***Alexander Graham Bell: Man of Sound***

TOBI TOBIAS

When Tobi Tobias was nine years old, her father predicted that one day she would become a writer. She made his words come true.

Tobias has written many books, including several other biographies. Her love of the performing arts, especially dance, is seen in books such as these:

- ***Maria Tallchief*** — the story of the Osage Indian who became a ballerina.
- ***Arthur Mitchell*** — the biography of the man who became a star with the New York City Ballet.

KENNETH RUDEEN

Kenneth Rudeen, the author of *Roberto Clemente*, had something in common with Walt Disney. While Rudeen was still in high school, he worked as a copy boy for the *Kansas City Star*, the same newspaper that Disney once delivered. By age seventeen, Rudeen had become a reporter for the *Star*. Rudeen has written several biographies of sports heroes. Here are two you might enjoy:

- ***Jackie Robinson*** tells the story of the man who broke the color barrier in major league baseball.
- ***Wilt Chamberlain*** tells how one of the greatest basketball players got his start.

Sitting Bull
by Kathie Billingslea Smith

This is the story of Sitting Bull, or Tatanka Yotanka, who became Chief of the Sioux Nation and fought to preserve a way of life for his people.

Go Free or Die: A Story about Harriet Tubman
by Jeri Ferris

Although she had to walk more than a hundred miles to become free, Harriet Tubman returned to the South to lead other slaves to freedom.

Ann Bancroft: On Top of the World
by Dorothy Wenzel

Having a learning disability didn't stop Ann Bancroft from becoming the first woman to reach the North Pole by dog sled.

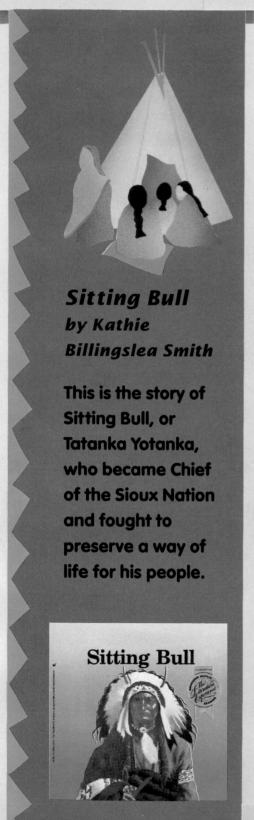

El Chino
written and illustrated by Allen Say

Billy Wong believed his father when he told him, "In America, you can be anything you want to be." Against the odds, Billy became the first Chinese bullfighter.

Cesar Chavez and La Causa
by Naurice Roberts

As a boy, Cesar Chavez worked in the fields of California. Years later, he became the leader of La Causa, a movement to promote better working conditions for farm workers.

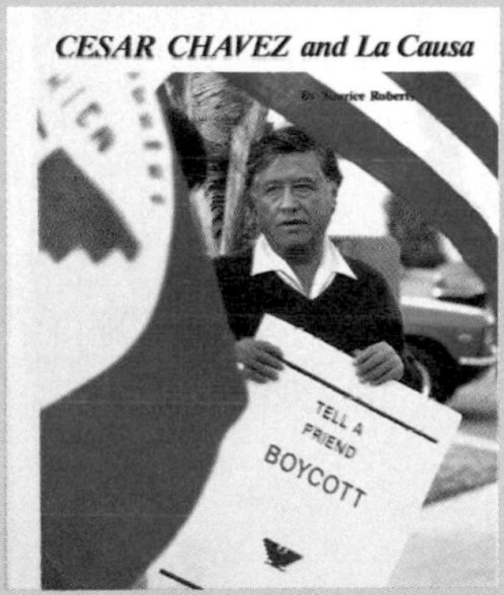

Martin Luther King, Jr.
by Patricia McKissack

"I have a dream that my four little children will one day live in a nation where they will not be judged by the color of their skin but by the content of their character."
Martin Luther King, Jr., lived by these words.

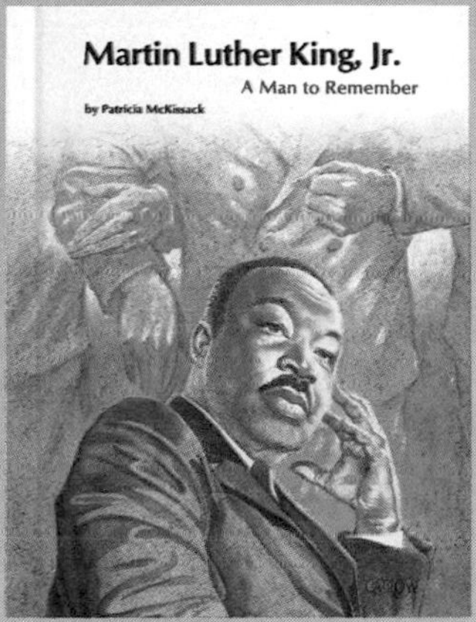

They Lived Their Dreams

Meet

Kazue Mizumura

"For as long as I can remember, I have always liked to draw," says Kazue Mizumura. Her love of art began when she was a child growing up in Kamakura, Japan. Years later, after coming to the United States, she became an author and illustrator of children's books.

Mizumura has combined her love of art with a love of nature in writing and illustrating *Flower Moon Snow*, a book of haiku — a type of traditional Japanese poetry. Mizumura's illustrations are woodcuts printed in another traditional Japanese style — the use of soft colors. Her illustrations and poems show and tell of the simple pleasures of nature. Mizumura says, "The title I have used, *Flower Moon Snow*, is a translation of a Japanese phrase that is used to suggest the beauty of nature."

You will be reading twelve of Kazue Mizumura's haiku. The poems and the pictures are all from *Flower Moon Snow*.

Flower

Tulips open one by one;
Each is bringing you
A cupful of spring.

Why are all of these flowers
In bloom? Don't they know
This house is for sale?

Who tossed those golden coins,
The dandelions glittering
On my lawn?

A flash of lightning sparks,
Forsythia;
Spring opening here today!

MOON

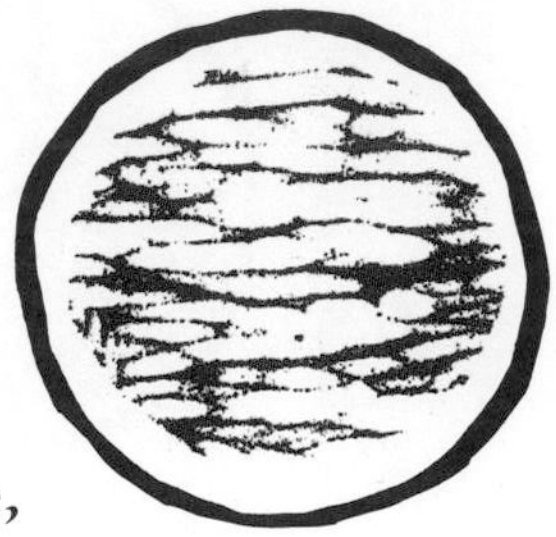

Coming home late,
Only my moonlit shadow
Dances on the street.

The moon is hiding.
And how the jack-o'-lanterns
Grin there in the dark!

The party is over.
The moon in the swimming pool
Is all alone.

Following me all along the road,
The moon came home
With me tonight.

SNOW

Snow makes a new land.
One step, two steps. I explore
The way to my school.

All through the long night,
Snow is falling and falling
Upon the snowman.

A lonely sparrow
Hops upon the snow and prints
Sets of maple leaves.

Squeals of children
Tumble down the snowy hill.
Spring is still far away.

FICTION

THEME 7

Dear Diary

April 14
Dear Diary,
Oh no!
Miss Simmons wants me to sing a solo!
July 16
Dear Diary,
Today I found out that Uncle Joe is coming to live with us.
CHORUS RECITAL TODAY
I ♥ TO SING
I ● CHOIR
May 1
Dear Diary,
Guess what?
Annie Alpert likes me! (I think.)
Sept. 25
Dear Diary,
Don't ask me why, but I signed up for the school talent show today.
La Bamba

Contents

The contents of a diary are PRIVATE. But you'll find out what each of these diary entries means when you read the stories in this theme. So go ahead and take a peek.

Louella's Song

by Eloise Greenfield • illustrated by Gil Ashby

Louella leaned forward in her seat and raised her hand. Of all the things in the world she didn't want to do, the thing she most of all *didn't* want to do was sing by herself, on a stage, in front of a lot of people. Everybody knew the song. She didn't know why Miss Simmons had to go and pick her!

She shook her hand in the air. "Miss Simmons," she said. "Miss Simmons, I can't sing by myself."

Miss Simmons looked up from the paper in her hand. "Yes you can, Louella," she said. "I know you've been trying to hide that sweet little voice, but I hear it every time we sing. All you have to do is sing out and make it a sweet big voice."

"But Miss Simmons . . . ," Louella said.

Miss Simmons looked worried. "I've already planned the whole program," she said. "Please, Louella?"

Louella looked around the room for sympathy, but most of her classmates wouldn't look at her. And those who would were frowning. She had to say yes, but she didn't want to. She nodded her head at Miss Simmons, and everybody smiled.

Miss Simmons smiled too and looked down at her paper. "Let's see, now," she said. "After Louella's solo, we'll close with *Lift Every Voice and Sing*. Now, listen everybody, tomorrow's the last rehearsal and when you get here Friday morning, the bus will be here to take us to the hospital. Be sure to . . ."

Louella stopped listening and looked at her classmates again. They would do anything for Miss Simmons. And so would she. Anything *except* sing by herself, on a stage, in front of a lot of people.

It wasn't that she didn't like to sing. At home, she sang a lot, and she sang loud, sang in her big voice — but only in her room with the door closed and just her mirror for an audience. And maybe Dwayne. And when she'd go downstairs, her mother would say, "Why didn't you bring Diana Ross down for some dinner, too?" Or she'd say, "You mean Aretha's up there, too? It must be getting pretty crowded."

But Louella didn't let anybody hear her sing except her brother. And she was going to keep it that way. Dwayne would help her.

"You could tell Mama you were sick," Dwayne said that night when they were watching television in her room, "and she'd make you stay home."

"Wouldn't nobody believe it," Louella said, "and they'd be all mad and everything. But maybe if I fell down and broke my leg . . ."

"You don't sing with your leg, dummy," Dwayne said. "You sing with your . . ." He stopped talking and stared at her.

"What's the matter?" Louella asked.

"You got to hurt your voice!" Dwayne said.

"Fall down and break my *voice*?" Louella said.

"Naw," Dwayne said, laughing. "But something's got to be wrong with your voice."

"I know!" Louella said. "How does this sound?" She made her voice low and scraped it against her throat. "I have a cold. I can't sing."

"Not too good," Dwayne said. "You have to whisper."

Louella practiced whispering and sniffling and sneezing and coughing until it was time to go to bed, and the next day, she sneezed twice at reading time and Miss Simmons handed her a tissue. All through arithmetic, she sniffled loudly. And when she opened her mouth to rehearse her solo, she had a coughing fit and had to run for a drink of water. Miss Simmons told her to rest her voice.

On Friday, when Louella got to school, Miss Simmons was at the door of the bus, crossing names off a list as the children got on.

"Good morning, Miss Simmons," Louella whispered.

Miss Simmons smiled. "Good morning . . . ***Louella! Oh no!***"

Louella nodded her head and tried to look sad.

When they were all on the bus, Miss Simmons announced that Louella had lost her voice and they would all have to sing her song together. Louella kept looking sad, but inside she was smiling. She had fooled them. She didn't have to sing and nobody was mad at her either.

The children at the hospital were waiting for them when they got there. They were sitting in the small auditorium, some of them in the regular seats, some in wheelchairs and one small boy in a bed.

A girl in a peach-colored dress rolled her wheelchair up to a microphone in front of the stage and welcomed the class to the hospital. Then Miss Simmons hit the first chord on the piano and they were singing.

Louella whisper-sang and felt good. Soon it would be over. All she had to do was remember for the rest of the day that she couldn't talk.

After the fourth song, the girl in the pretty, peach dress took the microphone over to the boy in the bed. She held it to his mouth.

"I made up a thank-you poem," he said, "'cause I was glad you were coming to sing for us and I want to tell you my poem."

As the boy said his poem, Louella's good feeling started to fade away. By the time he had finished, a very bad feeling had taken its place. She felt too bad to even whisper while they were singing the next song. She just moved her mouth.

She looked at the children in the audience and she looked at her classmates. They were friends, they were all friends and she was left out. They were giving each other songs and smiles and clapping, and even a thank-you poem, but she wasn't giving anything. She wanted to be part of the giving.

She heard Miss Simmons start to play the introduction to her song and she wanted to sing it. She was scared, but it was something she could give. She stepped out in front of the class the way they had rehearsed at school.

Louella sang softly at first. Then she forgot to be nervous and pushed her voice out into the audience. She *wanted* to give them her music. She liked them, and they liked her.

And then it was time for *Lift Every Voice*, and all of her old friends and her new friends were singing together. Some were standing up and those who couldn't stand lifted their hands in the air.

Louella looked at Miss Simmons. She was smiling as she played. And Louella smiled, too.

A Gift from the Heart

At first Louella didn't want to sing a solo with her class. But at the hospital she changed her mind because she wanted to be "part of the giving" with the others. Her gift was her song.

Think about a time when you gave someone a gift that wasn't bought at a store, but that came from the heart. Write about that time.

Eloise Greenfield

When Eloise Greenfield was in the fifth grade, her teacher talked her into taking a solo part in the school play, although she didn't want to do it.

During the play, Eloise didn't say her lines loudly enough. No one could hear her. She ruined the play.

"For the rest of the day, I was famous," she remembers. "Children passing by my classroom door, children on the playground at lunch time, kept pointing at me saying, 'That's that girl! That's the one who didn't talk loud enough!'"

Two good things came out of the experience: Her teacher told Eloise that she would never be in another school play. And years later, when Eloise Greenfield became a writer, she had the idea for a story called *Louella's Song*.

Greenfield is the author of many books, including *Talk About a Family*, *Mary McLeod Bethune*, and *Rosa Parks*.

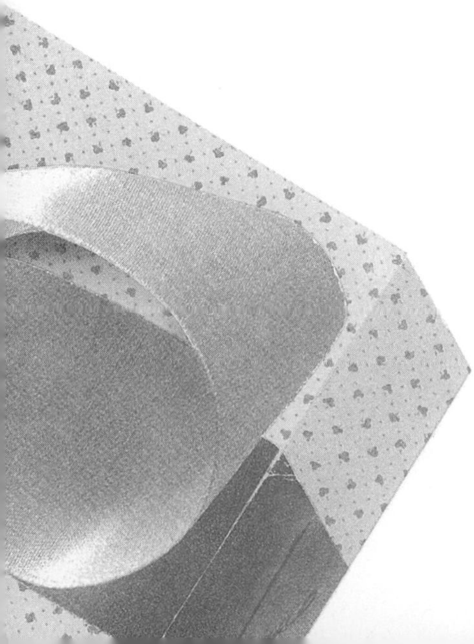

Award Winner

MAKING ROOM FOR UNCLE JOE

by Ada B. Litchfield with illustrations by Gail Owens

Mom looked really serious as she read us the letter from Uncle Joe's social worker.

Uncle Joe is Mom's younger brother. He has Down's syndrome. People with Down's syndrome are mentally retarded and need help taking care of themselves. After Uncle Joe was born his mother died, and no one else in the family could give him the care he needed. That's why he had been in a state hospital school for such a long time.

Uncle Joe had been happy at his school. But now it was closing, the letter said, and the people who lived there had to find other homes. Uncle Joe would have to live with us for a while. We were his only family.

"The social worker says she's looking for an apartment for Uncle Joe, but they are hard to find," Mom explained. "So your dad and I think Joe should stay with us until — "

"He'd better find an apartment fast," my older sister, Beth, shouted. "We can't have a retarded person living here forever!"

"But he won't be here forever, Beth," I said. "It's just until he finds another place."

"You keep out of this, Dan," Beth told me. "It might as well be forever. I won't be able to have any of my friends here. What will they say when they see Uncle Joe creeping around? They'll make fun of him and of me, too."

"Now Beth, stop that," Dad said. "No real friend would ever make fun of you for doing somebody a kindness. Besides, Uncle Joe won't bother you and your friends."

"Good grief," Beth said. "Doesn't anyone see how embarrassing this will be for all of us?" She burst into tears and ran out of the room.

"Let her go," Dad said when Mom tried to call Beth back. "She needs to think things over."

I needed to think things over, too. Suppose Uncle Joe *was* a nuisance? Suppose he hung around me all the time? Suppose he messed with my baseball cards?

"Dan, helping Uncle Joe is something our family has to do together," Dad said, as if he were reading my thoughts. "Your mother and I will appreciate any help you and Beth and Amy can give us."

"I'll help Uncle Joe," Amy said.

Amy is only five and a half. What kind of help could she be?

"I'll help, too," I said, trying to sound cheerful. But to tell the truth, I didn't feel cheerful at all.

I felt worse when I talked to my friend Ben the next day.

"Down's syndrome, eh?" Ben said with a know-it-all look on

his face. "You should be upset. I saw a TV program about people with Down's syndrome. Their eyes slant and their noses look squashed in." He showed me with his fingers what he meant. "Does your uncle look like that?"

"I don't remember," I said. "I only saw him once when I was little. My mom and dad always visited without us kids."

"Doesn't matter," Ben said. "All retarded people are funny looking and most of 'em drool. You'll probably have to wipe his chin all the time."

"A fat lot you know!" I shouted.

I didn't know if what Ben said was true or not, but it made me mad just the same. I didn't think it was a very helpful thing for a friend to say.

When I got home, I found Mom and Dad moving furniture around. They had moved the TV from the family room into the living room and the record player into Beth's room.

"We're making room for Uncle Joe," Mom said when she saw me. "You're just in time to help."

Dad and I brought an extra bed up from the basement into the family room. Uncle Joe would sleep there.

"Whew," said Mom when everything was in place. "The social worker just called to say Uncle Joe will be here tomorrow. I wish we'd known sooner."

Tomorrow!

Beth was sitting on the back porch with her hands over her face. I could tell she'd been crying.

"I had to cancel my slumber party for tomorrow night," she told me between sobs.

"Why?" I asked. "Did Mom make you?"

"No," she said. "But how can I have the girls over with *him* around?"

"I don't know," I said. I understood how Beth felt.

Early the next day, Mom and Dad drove to the state school to bring Uncle Joe home. All morning, Amy and Beth and I waited at the front window, watching for them to return. Finally, about noon, we saw our car turn into the driveway. In a few minutes, Mom and Dad came up the walk. Behind them came a short man carrying a suitcase and a small blue bag.

As soon as Beth saw them, she left the window and went into her bedroom.

Uncle Joe came into the house very slowly. His cap was on crooked. He was wearing a jacket with sleeves too short for his arms. His pants were too long for his legs. I was glad to see he wasn't drooling. But to tell the truth, his eyes did slant a little, and his nose did look a little squashed in.

He looked around at everything in the room and at Amy and me. Then he smiled, showing a gap between his small, even teeth.

"Hi," he said. "My name's Joe. What's . . . uh . . . yours?"

"This is Dan," my father said. "And here's Amy."

Amy made a little bow, and I bobbed my head.

"And, oh, yes," Dad said, "there's one more." He left the room and came back holding Beth by the arm.

"This is Beth," Dad said.

"Hello, Beth," Uncle Joe said. "You're pretty."

"Thank you," said Beth. She looked surprised.

Dad took Uncle Joe's suitcase into the family room. But Uncle Joe wouldn't let him take the blue bag. Instead, he brought it over to me.

"This is my bowling ball," he said, holding the bag up almost in my face. "My friend Ace gave it to me. Can you bowl?"

"I don't know," I said. "I never tried."

"That's okay," he said. "I'll . . . uh . . . show you."

Soon after that we all sat down for lunch. All except Uncle Joe, that is. He sat in a chair by the china cabinet, holding his bowling ball on his lap.

"Come sit here, Joe," Mom said, pointing to the empty chair beside Amy. "Put that bowling ball down somewhere and come eat."

"No," Uncle Joe said, shaking his head. "I don't want to. I can't eat without my friend Ace. I miss Ace. I need a friend with me . . . uh . . . when I eat lunch."

He hung his head and looked sad. Nobody seemed to know what to do, except Amy. She slid out of her chair, went over to Uncle Joe, and put her hand in his.

"I'll be your friend, Uncle Joe," she said. "You can eat with me." And she pulled him to the table.

It was a terrible meal. Amy chatted away, but nobody else seemed to know what to say. Uncle Joe dribbled catsup on the tablecloth and forgot to use his napkin. The mustard from his hot dog got all over his face. Beth watched him in disgust.

Then Amy spilled her milk. "See?" she said cheerfully. "Everyone spills sometimes." I think she was trying to make Uncle Joe feel better.

That was the beginning of Amy's friendship with Uncle Joe. As soon as we finished lunch, she showed him her library book. Every day after that, Uncle Joe and Amy spent a lot of time together with their heads bent over Amy's books. I don't think he always knew if she read the right words or not, but he listened carefully anyway, nodding his head. And showing off for someone made Amy very happy.

Every night Uncle Joe would sit on the stairs with Amy while she told him bedtime stories. He'd laugh and clap his hands and join in when she came to something like the huff and puff part in "The Three Little Pigs." When he said, "Time for bed, Amy," she scooted off without any fuss.

Yes, Amy and Uncle Joe got along fine right away, but for the rest of us, having Uncle Joe around wasn't easy.

He had to be reminded to wear his glasses, comb his hair, take a shower, and things like that. And somebody had to see that he put on matching socks.

When he ate, he always left bits of food all over the table and floor. He did like everything Mom cooked though, and he always said, "Mmmm . . . good!" no matter what we had for dinner. Mom liked that.

Most of the time Uncle Joe was cheerful, but sometimes he sat in his room or on the back porch just staring into space. Then even Amy couldn't cheer him up. He'd just mutter something about being a no-good dumbhead who couldn't take care of himself.

Uncle Joe offered to help around the house, but he often seemed to get directions mixed up. Usually he was more trouble than help.

One day Dad asked him to weed the garden. I was supposed to help, too. By the time I got out to the yard, Uncle Joe had already started — and he had pulled up as many flowers as he had weeds! When I told him what he'd done, he was really upset.

"It's not your fault, Uncle Joe," I said over and over. "Nobody showed you which plants not to pull up."

But Uncle Joe was so mad at himself he disappeared into his room and wouldn't come out.

We didn't know what to do. Finally Mom got the idea that I should take him bowling. I didn't want to go, but before I knew what was happening, Uncle Joe had come out of his room wearing his bowling jacket and carrying his blue bag.

All the way to Bowl-a-rama, I hoped none of my friends would see us. I hadn't seen any of them — even Ben — for a few weeks. I guess I was afraid they would make fun of Uncle Joe. I didn't want them staring and saying things like "How's Danny Dan and the retard man?"

But we didn't see anyone I knew, and as soon as we started bowling I forgot about everything else.

Uncle Joe was a good bowler. Sometimes he got a spare. And sometimes he got a strike.

Me? I was lucky if I knocked down any pins at all.

"It's okay, Danny," Uncle Joe kept saying in his slow way. "I . . . uh . . . know you can do it. You'll get a strike. Just . . . uh . . . keep trying."

And I did. I got a strike. On the very last frame, all the pins went down — whack, whack, whack — just like that!

We both shouted and jumped up and down.

Everyone around us looked. But I didn't care. I didn't even care when I saw Ben and two other guys from my school watching us.

At first, they just stared and nudged each other. I could tell they were looking for something to laugh at.

When they finally came over to us, I introduced them to Uncle Joe.

"I'm glad to meet you . . . Ben . . . and John . . . and Eli," Uncle Joe said. He shook each of their hands and smiled at them. They looked down at the floor and shuffled their feet, but Uncle Joe didn't seem to notice.

"Would you like to bowl with us?" he asked.

They all nodded yes. Ben and Eli had bowled before, but John hadn't. Uncle Joe showed him how to hold the ball and encouraged him the way he had encouraged me.

In no time at all, everybody seemed to forget that Uncle Joe had Down's syndrome. We were all just trying to knock down bowling pins. We were all just having fun.

After that, Ben and my other friends started coming over to the house again. They were always kind to Uncle Joe, and he loved to talk with them.

And after a while, things seemed to go better at home. Mom and Dad took more time showing Uncle Joe how to do simple jobs. Uncle Joe began to be a real help around the house. He could carry in groceries and help put them away. He liked to peel carrots and potatoes for dinner. He helped wash and polish the car. He helped Amy put the new bell on her tricycle, and he helped me paint a display rack for my baseball cards.

And Uncle Joe was good at weeding, once he knew which plants to leave alone. One day I went out with him to be sure he didn't pull out the flowers. But I think my checking up on him hurt his feelings. "You don't have to watch me, Danny," he told me. "This is my job, and I . . . can do it by myself."

I didn't watch anymore, but I stayed outside anyway. I liked being out in the backyard with Uncle Joe. Sometimes after he finished his work we tossed a Frisbee around for a while.

But what about Beth?

For a long time, Beth acted almost as if Uncle Joe didn't exist. He never bothered her, but sometimes he would sit quietly in the living room and listen while she practiced her piano lesson. Once he clapped, but that startled her so much he never did it again.

Then one day, when he thought no one was around, Uncle Joe sat down at the piano and played "Chopsticks."

Everyone in the family came running, and we clapped so loudly for him that he played it again.

"My friend Ace showed me how to do that," Uncle Joe said, grinning.

Beth went over to the piano. "I know how to play another part of that piece," she said. She sat down next to Uncle Joe and taught him how to play "Chopsticks" as a duet.

Later, Beth showed Uncle Joe how to play other tunes. Sometimes he played them over and over so many times we all got tired of listening, but we felt good because Beth was being kind to Uncle Joe. She started inviting her girl friends over again, and one day I heard her tell a friend that she was giving Uncle Joe piano lessons. I think Beth liked being a teacher, and I know Uncle Joe liked being her pupil.

By the time spring came, things had settled down into what Mom called a "comfortable routine."

Then another letter came from Uncle Joe's social worker.

Mom read the letter to us. It said that Uncle Joe would be leaving. Everything had finally been arranged. Uncle Joe would share an apartment with two other men in the city. He would work at a sheltered workshop close to where he lived.

A sheltered workshop is a place where handicapped people are taught to do special jobs. They sort nuts and bolts, put together small motors, package things to send through the mail, or do other simple tasks. The work is easy enough for them, and they are paid for doing it.

At first, Uncle Joe seemed pleased. He had Mom read the letter again and again.

I was sure he felt good about having a place of his own and a job of his own. He wanted to take care of himself.

I was sure my parents felt good about not having to be responsible for Uncle Joe anymore.

We would all be glad to have the family room back again so we could entertain our friends there.

We'd always known that Uncle Joe would be leaving sometime. So why did everyone look so sad that night at dinner?

"I'm going to miss you, Uncle Joe," Amy said. She burst into tears.

"I'll miss you, too," said Uncle Joe. He began to look very unhappy.

"Who will listen to me practice for my recital now?" Beth said. Tears were running down her cheeks, too.

"And who will teach me new songs?" Uncle Joe asked her, looking sadder than I had ever seen him look before.

"Hey, I'm not going to cry about this," I said to myself, taking a drink of water. But there was a lump in my throat, and I choked so badly I had to leave the table.

I knew I was going to miss Uncle Joe something awful.

When I came back, even my father looked as if he'd been crying. He cleared his throat and blew his nose.

"Listen," he said at last, "your mother and I have been talking this over for quite a while. We thought you all might be pretty upset if Joe leaves. We don't see why Uncle Joe has to live somewhere else if he doesn't want to. We are his family. I can drive him to that workshop every day on my way to the office, and he can take the bus back. What do you say, Joe? Would you like to stay with us?"

Uncle Joe looked thoughtful for a long time. He pulled at his hair. Then he started to grin. "I want to stay here. Yes, I do. . . . I can work hard and . . . uh . . . pay for my food. I want to stay here all the time forever with my family."

"Then it's settled," Mom said. "I'll call the social worker right away and tell her we'd all like Uncle Joe to stay with us."

"Yippee!" shouted Amy. She climbed into Uncle Joe's lap and gave him a big hug.

And Uncle Joe? He looked so happy nobody cared that he had forgotten to comb his hair. Or that there was a mess of crumbs around his plate and more on the floor. We all knew that in many ways Uncle Joe is a neat guy.

We were glad he had come to stay with us . . . all the time, forever.

"I used to think . . ."

Before they got to know Uncle Joe, Dan and Beth were uncomfortable with the idea of his staying with them. But after getting to know Uncle Joe, they realized how foolish their worries were.

Write a poem about Uncle Joe as either Dan or Beth might write it. Write four verses, each of which begins

"I used to think ______________________________

But now I ____________________________________"

Ada B. Litchfield

Ada Litchfield was thrilled to receive a letter one day from a teacher whose class had read *Making Room for Uncle Joe*. "Your book has made an impact on our lives," the teacher wrote.

After reading the book, the class had visited a workshop where they met handicapped employees who made coin bags for the U.S. Treasury. The students later invited their new friends to Thanksgiving dinner at their school.

Litchfield says she hopes people will gain "a little better understanding and compassion" if they read books such as *Making Room for Uncle Joe*. Two of Litchfield's other books are *A Cane in Her Hand* and *Words in Our Hands.*

la bamba

by Gary Soto
with illustrations by Melodye Rosales

Manuel was the fourth of seven children and looked like a lot of kids in his neighborhood: black hair, brown face, and skinny legs scuffed from summer play.

But summer was giving way to fall: the trees were turning red, the lawns brown, and the pomegranate trees were heavy with fruit. Manuel walked to school in the frosty morning, kicking leaves and thinking of tomorrow's talent show. He was still amazed that he had volunteered. He was going to pretend to sing Ritchie Valens's "La Bamba" before the entire school.

Why did I raise my hand? he asked himself, but in his heart he knew the answer. He yearned for the limelight. He wanted applause as loud as a thunderstorm, and to hear his friends say, "Man, that was bad!" And he wanted to impress the girls, especially Petra Lopez, the second-prettiest girl in his class. The prettiest was already taken by his friend Ernie. Manuel knew he should be reasonable, since he himself was not great-looking, just average.

Manuel kicked through the fresh-fallen leaves. When he got to school he realized he had forgotten his math workbook. If the teacher found out, he would have to stay after school and miss practice for the talent show. But fortunately for him, they did drills that morning.

During lunch Manuel hung around with Benny, who was also in the talent show. Benny was going to play the trumpet in spite of the fat lip he had gotten playing football.

"How do I look?" Manuel asked. He cleared his throat and started moving his lips in pantomime. No words came out, just a hiss that sounded like a snake. Manuel tried to look emotional, flailing his arms on the high notes and opening his eyes and mouth as wide as he could when he came to *"Para bailar la baaaaammmba."*[1]

After Manuel finished, Benny said it looked all right, but suggested Manuel dance while he sang. Manuel thought for a moment and decided it was a good idea.

"Yeah, just think you're like Michael Jackson or someone like that," Benny suggested. "But don't get carried away."

During rehearsal, Mr. Roybal, nervous about his debut as the school's talent coordinator, muttered under his breath when the lever that controlled the speed on the record player jammed.

"Darn," he growled, trying to force the lever. "What's wrong with you?"

"Is it broken?" Manuel asked, bending over for a closer look. It looked all right to him.

Mr. Roybal assured Manuel that he would have a good record player at the talent show, even if it meant bringing his own stereo from home.

Manuel sat in a folding chair, twirling his record on his thumb. He watched a skit about personal hygiene, a mother-and-daughter violin duo, five first-grade girls jumping rope, a karate kid breaking boards, and a skit about the pilgrims. If the record player hadn't been broken, he would have gone after the karate kid, an easy act to follow, he told himself.

As he twirled his forty-five record, Manuel thought they had a great talent show. The entire school would be amazed. His mother and father would be proud, and his brothers and sisters would be jealous and pout. It would be a night to remember.

Benny walked onto the stage, raised his trumpet to his mouth, and waited for his cue. Mr. Roybal raised his hand like a symphony conductor and let it fall dramatically. Benny inhaled

---

[1]**Para bailar la bamba** (PAH•rah bye•LAR lah BAHM•bah): In order to dance the bamba.

and blew so loud that Manuel dropped his record, which rolled across the cafeteria floor until it hit a wall. Manuel raced after it, picked it up, and wiped it clean.

"Boy, I'm glad it didn't break," he said with a sigh.

That night Manuel had to do the dishes and a lot of homework, so he could only practice in the shower. In bed he prayed that he wouldn't mess up. He prayed that it wouldn't be like when he was a first-grader. For Science Week he had wired together a C battery and a bulb, and told everyone he had discovered how a flashlight worked. He was so pleased with himself that he practiced for hours pressing the wire to the battery, making the bulb wink a dim, orangish light. He showed it to so many kids in his neighborhood that when it was time to show his class how a flashlight worked, the battery was dead. He pressed the wire to the battery, but the bulb didn't respond. He pressed until his thumb hurt and some kids in the back started snickering.

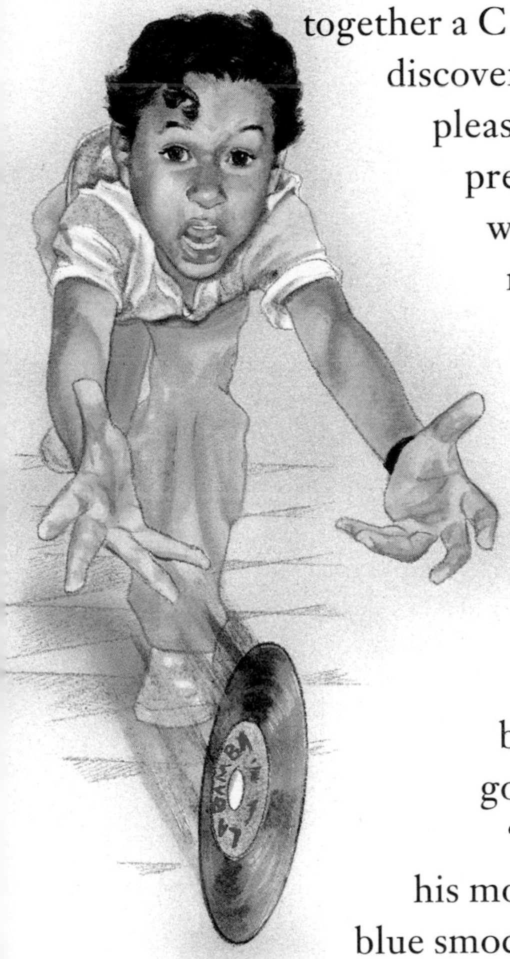

But Manuel fell asleep confident that nothing would go wrong this time.

The next morning his father and mother beamed at him. They were proud that he was going to be in the talent show.

"I wish you would tell us what you're doing," his mother said. His father, a pharmacist who wore a blue smock with his name on a plastic rectangle, looked up from the newspaper and sided with his wife. "Yes, what are you doing in the talent show?"

"You'll see," Manuel said with his mouth full of cereal.

The day whizzed by, and so did his afternoon chores and dinner. Suddenly he was dressed in his best clothes and standing next to Benny backstage, listening to the commotion as the cafeteria filled with school kids and parents. The lights dimmed, and Mr. Roybal, sweaty in a tight suit and a necktie with a large knot, wet his lips and parted the stage curtains.

"Good evening, everyone," the kids behind the curtain heard him say. "Good evening to you," some of the smart-alecky kids said back to him.

"Tonight we bring you the best John Burroughs Elementary has to offer, and I'm sure that you'll be both pleased and amazed that our little school houses so much talent. And now, without further ado, let's get on with the show." He turned and, with a swish of his hand, commanded, "Part the curtain." The curtains parted in jerks. A girl dressed as a toothbrush and a boy dressed as a dirty gray tooth walked onto the stage and sang:

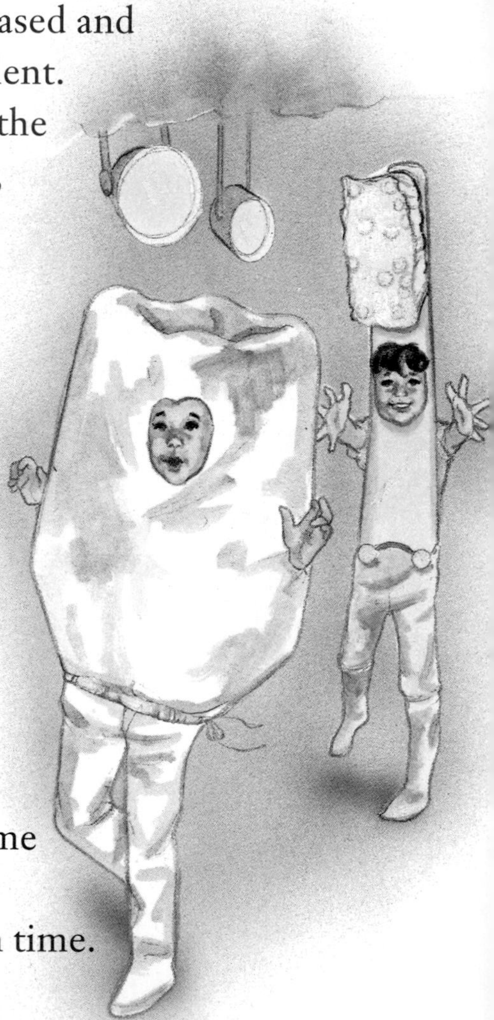

Brush, brush, brush
Floss, floss, floss
Gargle the germs away — hey! hey! hey!

After they finished singing, they turned to Mr. Roybal, who dropped his hand. The toothbrush dashed around the stage after the dirty tooth, which was laughing and having a great time until it slipped and nearly rolled off the stage.

Mr. Roybal jumped out and caught it just in time. "Are you OK?"

The dirty tooth answered, "Ask my dentist," which drew laughter and applause from the audience.

The violin duo played next, and except for one time when the girl got lost, they sounded fine. People applauded, and some even stood up. Then the first-grade girls maneuvered onto the stage while jumping rope. They were all smiles and bouncing ponytails as a hundred cameras flashed at once. Mothers "awhed" and fathers sat up proudly.

The karate kid was next. He did a few kicks, yells, and chops, and finally, when his father held up a board, punched it in two. The audience clapped and looked at each other, wide-eyed with respect. The boy bowed to the audience, and father and son ran off the stage.

Manuel remained behind the stage shivering with fear. He mouthed the words to "La Bamba" and swayed from left to right. Why did he raise his hand and volunteer? Why couldn't he have just sat there like the rest of the kids and not said anything? While the karate kid was on stage, Mr. Roybal, more sweaty than before, took Manuel's forty-five record and placed it on a new record player.

"You ready?" Mr. Roybal asked.

"Yeah . . ."

Mr. Roybal walked back on stage and announced that Manuel Gomez, a fifth-grader in Mrs. Knight's class, was going to pantomime Ritchie Valens's classic hit "La Bamba."

The cafeteria roared with applause. Manuel was nervous but loved the noisy crowd. He pictured his mother and father applauding loudly and his brothers and sisters also clapping, though not as energetically.

Manuel walked on stage and the song started immediately. Glassy-eyed from the shock of being in front of so many people, Manuel moved his lips and swayed in a made-up dance step. He couldn't see his parents, but he could see his brother Mario, who was a year younger, thumb-wrestling with a friend. Mario was wearing Manuel's favorite shirt; he would deal with Mario later. He saw some other kids get up and head for the drinking fountain, and a baby sitting in the middle of an aisle sucking her thumb and watching him intently.

What am I doing here? thought Manuel. This is no fun at all. Everyone was just sitting there. Some people were moving to the beat, but most were just watching him, like they would a monkey at the zoo.

But when Manuel did a fancy dance step, there was a burst of applause and some girls screamed. Manuel tried another dance step. He heard more applause and screams and started getting into the groove as he shivered and snaked like Michael Jackson around the stage. But the record got stuck, and he had to sing

Para bailar la bamba
Para bailar la bamba
Para bailar la bamba
Para bailar la bamba

again and again.

Manuel couldn't believe his bad luck. The audience began to laugh and stand up in their chairs. Manuel remembered how the forty-five record had dropped from his hand and rolled across the cafeteria floor. It probably got scratched, he thought, and now it was stuck, and he was stuck dancing and moving his lips to the same words over and over. He had never been so embarrassed. He would have to ask his parents to move the family out of town.

After Mr. Roybal ripped the needle across the record, Manuel slowed his dance steps to a halt. He didn't know what to do except bow to the audience, which applauded wildly, and scoot off the stage, on the verge of tears. This was worse than the homemade flashlight. At least no one laughed then, they just snickered.

Manuel stood alone, trying hard to hold back the tears as Benny, center stage, played his trumpet. Manuel was jealous because he sounded great, then mad as he recalled that it was

Benny's loud trumpet playing that made the forty-five record fly out of his hands. But when the entire cast lined up for a curtain call, Manuel received a burst of applause that was so loud it shook the walls of the cafeteria. Later, as he mingled with the kids and parents, everyone patted him on the shoulder and told him, "Way to go. You were really funny."

Funny? Manuel thought. Did he do something funny?

Funny. Crazy. Hilarious. These were the words people said to him. He was confused, but beyond caring. All he knew was that people were paying attention to him, and his brothers and sisters looked at him with a mixture of jealousy and awe. He was going to pull Mario aside and punch him in the arm for wearing his shirt, but he cooled it. He was enjoying the limelight. A teacher brought him cookies and punch, and the popular kids who had never before given him the time of day now clustered around him. Ricardo, the editor of the school bulletin, asked him how he made the needle stick.

"It just happened," Manuel said, crunching on a star-shaped cookie.

At home that night his father, eager to undo the buttons on his shirt and ease into his recliner, asked Manuel the same thing, how he managed to make the song stick on the words "*Para bailar la bamba.*"

Manuel thought quickly and reached for scientific jargon he had read in magazines. "Easy, Dad. I used laser tracking with high optics and low functional decibels per channel." His proud but confused father told him to be quiet and go to bed.

"Ah, *que niños tan truchas,*"[2] he said as he walked to the kitchen for a glass of milk. "I don't know how you kids nowadays get so smart."

Manuel, feeling happy, went to his bedroom, undressed, and slipped into his pajamas. He looked in the mirror and began to pantomime "La Bamba," but stopped because he was tired of the song. He crawled into bed. The sheets were as cold as the moon that stood over the peach tree in their backyard.

He was relieved that the day was over. Next year, when they asked for volunteers for the talent show, he wouldn't raise his hand. Probably.

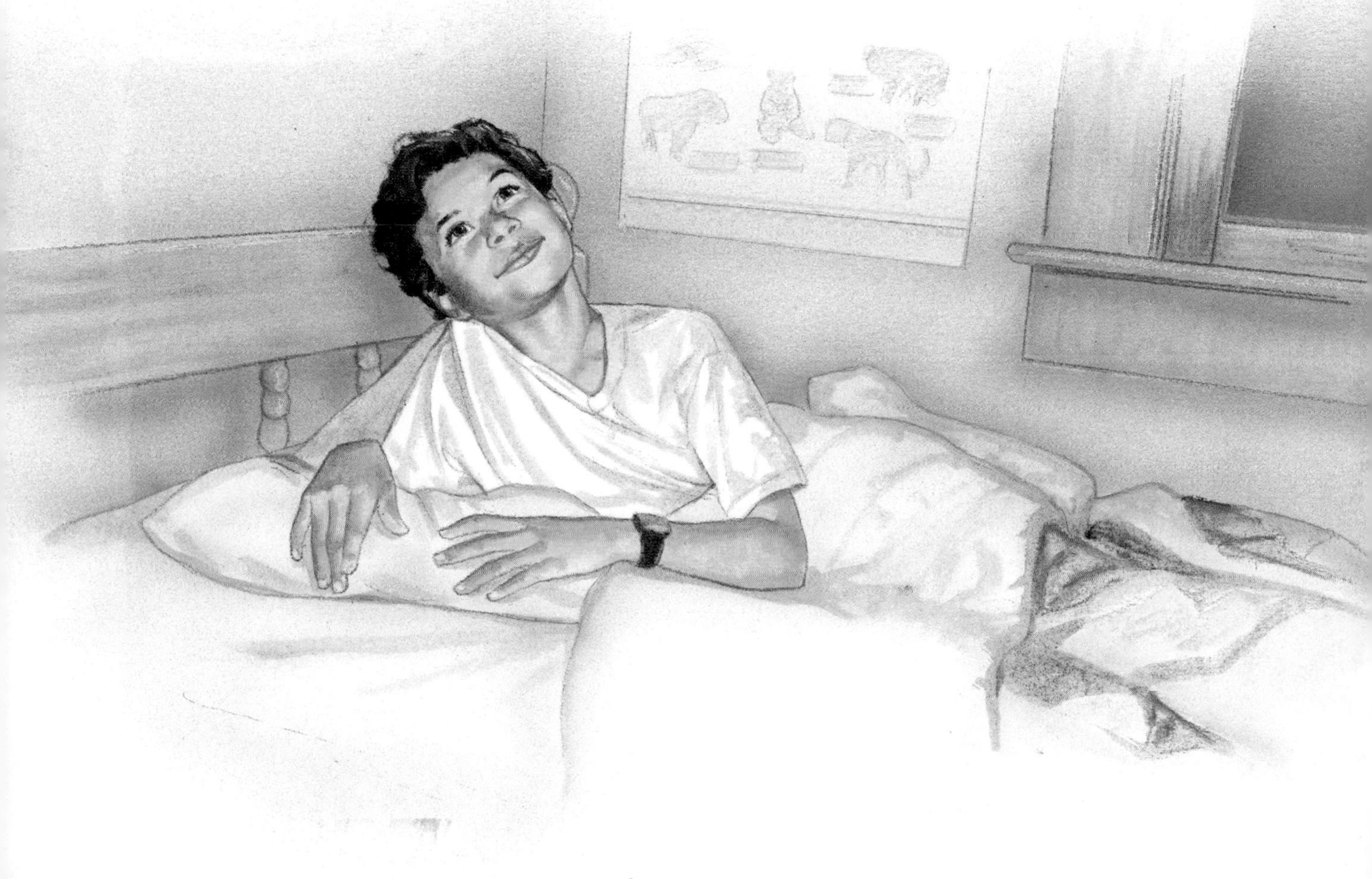

[2]**que niños tan truchas** (KAY NEE•nyose TAHN TRUE•chahs): An expression meaning "These kids are so clever!"

The Show Must Go On...

When the record got stuck on *"Para bailar la bamba,"* Manuel was very embarrassed — but he went on with the show. He kept singing the same words over and over until Mr. Roybal finally took the record off.

With a group, think of ways to deal with other sticky school situations such as those below. Then act out your solutions.

- You're playing the lead role in the school play and you forget your lines.

- You're asked to feed the class's pet hamster and when you open the cage, the hamster runs down the hall.

- You're in the lunch line and you spill a tray of food on the principal.

Please...
HELP KEEP
THIS LUNCHROOM
CLEAN

and On...

Gary Soto

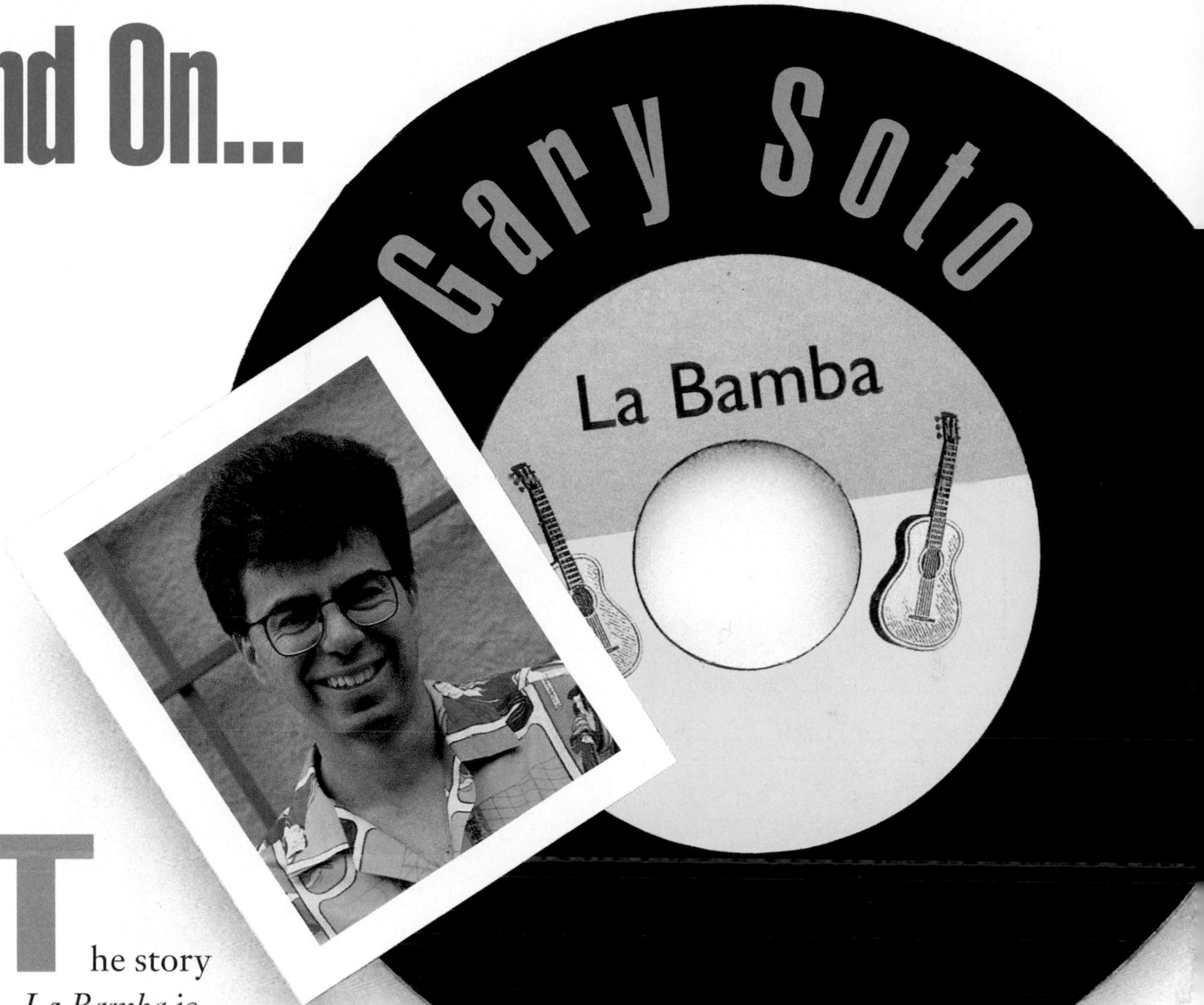

The story *La Bamba* is based on something that Gary Soto remembers from his days as a student at Jefferson Elementary School in Fresno, California. One year, the school held a talent show, and a classmate of Gary's decided to pantomime to the song "Sugar Shack." On stage, in the middle of the song, his friend forgot the words.

Growing up in California, Gary Soto played a lot of baseball, soccer, and four-square. "I was a playground kid," he says.

Today he is a writer and a college professor. *La Bamba* is from a book by Soto called *Baseball in April and Other Stories.*

CHASING AFTER ANNIE

by Marjorie Weinman Sharmat

with illustrations by Marc Simont

May 3 **Richie**

Dear Journal,
I think Annie Alpert likes me. She probably thinks I'm the greatest! Because of my muscles, my A's, and my famous fish scrapbook. Annie likes everything about me including a few things she doesn't even know about yet.

May 3 Annie

Dear Diary,
I can't stand Richie Carr. I totally dislike him. More than bugs, more than itches, more than liver. Bugs don't brag, itches don't brag, liver doesn't brag. But Richie Carr brags all the time.

May 4 **Richie**

Dear Journal,
The way I can tell Annie likes me is because she pretends so hard that she doesn't.

Today I saw her walking to school. So I chased after her, kind of slowly of course. Then I yelled, "Annie!"

She dropped a book. How about that? I ran to pick it up. "Hey, Annie," I said. "Let me do that."

"I can pick up my own book," she said.

"There's a special way to pick it up," I said. "Bend your knees and keep your back straight. I know these things. I'm an athlete."

"That's not all you are," Annie said.

DID YOU HEAR THAT, JOURNAL? Annie must have been checking up on me. She must have found out I can play chess, spell *microgroove* without checking the dictionary, as well as high dive.

Annie Alpert likes me so much she can't stand it!

May 4 **Annie**

Dear Diary,

Well, I almost told Richie Carr off today. He made me drop a book and then he bragged when he tried to pick it up. How can anyone brag about picking up a book? Richie Carr can.

On my way home from school I told Frances what happened. "Isn't Richie Carr the worst braggart in the world?" I said.

"I think Richie Carr likes you," she said.

"Hmmpph!" I said.

Then when I got home, Mom told me that Fritz was lost. The back gate was open and he ran out after another dog and didn't come back.

I wish Richie Carr would get lost.

Come home, Fritz.

May 5 **Richie**

Dear Journal,

Annie is down today. I mean *down*. She didn't even do her Annie Walk, where she hops every few steps or twirls in circles and laughs. I saw her in school, and she looked like somebody sad and droopy. Her dog ran away and Annie likes that dog almost as much as she likes me. That's a whole lot, Journal.

So I'm going to look for Annie's dog. Who else can Annie count on? And I'll *find* him. Because when Richie Carr does something, he does it right.

May 5 **Annie**

Dear Diary,
Maybe I'll never see Fritz again. Maybe some people took him into their house and they're moving to California and so Fritz is, too. If Fritz comes home, I'll never make him take a bath again.

May 6 **Richie**

Dear Journal,
Tired! That's me. I've been looking and looking for Annie's dog. I mean I looked an hour and a half today for that creature. I, Richie Carr, have been to alleys, parks, stores, dumps, delicatessens, parking lots, and garbage cans.

Still, Annie said *thanks* to me today. What happened was that I saw Annie in an alley. I said, "I'm looking for Fritz, too." And that's when Annie said, "Thanks!"

May 6 **Annie**

Dear Diary,
Mom and Dad put an ad in the newspaper about Fritz being lost. But I'm saving up my allowance so I can go to California and look for Fritz. Every day I think of something else I loved about him. Today it's his tail. I don't know why Richie Carr is looking for Fritz. How could someone like *him* be a dog person?

May 7 **Richie**

Dear Journal,
I've increased my dog hunt. Three hours! I added meat markets to my looking places, and also under the benches of the school cafeteria. I even drew a picture of Fritz, because I draw very well. I put it up at school under LOST.

May 7 **Annie**

Dear Diary,

It's been 3 days now, and I'm still looking for Fritz. Richie Carr is, too. He's strange, Richie is. I was at the supermarket asking if anyone had seen a black-and-white dog with a long tail and a sad face and there was Richie. "A very sad face," Richie said.

Oh, and Richie draws pretty good.

May 8 **Richie**

Dear Journal,

No. 1: A sore knee.

No. 2: A hole in my sneakers.

No. 3: Sweat. Sweat. Sweat.

These are the things I've gotten so far looking for Fritz. The sneakers were guaranteed to last through 75 baseball games. I wish I had worn them out that way.

P.S. I think Fritz got married or something.

May 8 **Annie**

Dear Diary,

Richie has been walking a little funny. Should I tell him to look in his socks for a pebble?

May 9 **Richie**

Dear Journal,

You won't believe what happened today.

Zitts came over in the morning and said, "Guess what I'm getting today."

I answered, "A skyscraper."

And Zitts said, "Wrong. A dog."

Then Zitts asked me to go to the animal shelter with him and his dad to help pick out a dog. Well, I've had enough of looking for a dog this week. So I almost said no. ALMOST. What if *Fritz* was at the dog shelter! I went with Zitts and his father. I've never seen so many dogs at one time in my life! I've never heard so many yelps and barks and dog sounds. And I've never felt so sorry for so many dogs. All behind bars and wanting to get out.

"You can have any one you want, Zitts," his dad said. "Except for the big monsters."

Zitts kept looking at one dog, then another, then another. At last he said, "*That* one!"

That one was brown and white with a bushy tail. I didn't know what kind of dog it was. Zitts's dad went to get someone in charge.

Suddenly I saw something that made me stop. Stop like a red light, Journal.

Right there at that animal shelter I found Fritz!!!!

Black except where he was white, sad face, long tail.

I ran after one of the people in charge. Then I pointed to Fritz. "That dog belongs to my friend," I said. "He ran away a few days ago."

"No, he didn't," said the lady. "That dog has been here for almost a month."

"Nuts," I said. But I kept staring at that dog. I was getting an idea! I could take him to Annie and hope she thought he was Fritz. After all, a dog is a dog. And Annie needed any Fritz she could get. It was perfect. This sad, droopy dog would get a new home. Annie would be happy again. She would have Fritz back.

Then I began to wonder. Do dogs have warts and moles and scars and stuff like people? Could Annie tell the difference between the dogs? Maybe Fritz had a pimple that I didn't know about that Annie knew about. Still, he'd been gone for a few days. Who knows what a dog can get and get rid of?

I wanted this dog, Journal. Now, how to take him home?

It was easier than you'd think.

Zitts's dad had to sign a paper and pay a few dollars for Zitts's dog. (Zitts's dog in its previous life was named Brussels Sprouts. Zitts changed it to Wolf right then and there.) I said to Zitts's dad, "My mother and father want me to pick out a dog, too."

"No they don't," said Zitts's dad.

"Yes they do," I said. "They told me that if I found one I wanted, I could bring it home. And I found one."

"No they don't," said Zitts's dad again. He wasn't exactly listening.

"I love that black-and-white dog," I said.

"Love is what counts," said the animal shelter person.

I also had a dollar with me, and I told Zitts's father I'd pay him the rest next week. Then Zitts started with his *Please, please, Pops* routine that he's famous for in our neighborhood because it works.

Zitts's dad signed for two dogs.

I held my breath when Zitts saw my dog. Would he notice how much he looked like Fritz? But Zitts was too busy with Wolf.

My dog's name in his (yes, it was a *his,* I had forgotten to think about that) previous life was Duchess. Wild. How could a boy dog get the name of Duchess?

"What are you going to name your dog?" Zitts asked on the way home.

"Brussels Sprouts," I said.

"Brussels Sprouts? That's stupid," Zitts yelled. "That's why I took my dog. I figured he must have had a stupid life with stupid people who would name him Brussels Sprouts. I want to give this dog a new life. Right, Wolf?"

Wolf and my dog were panting and drooling and moving around in the backseat. It was a crazy ride home. When we got to my house, I rushed out of the car and pulled my dog after me.

I started to walk to Annie's house. I had to give this dog — *return* him — to Annie right away. Before my mother and father knew I had him.

50

That walk to Annie's was the best walk ever. Because I, Richie Carr, was returning Fritz to Annie. Well, maybe it wasn't exactly Fritz, but it was close enough. All dogs have wet noses and fleas and they sniff and they wag their tails. Annie would think it was Fritz and she'd be so happy she couldn't stand it.

But what if Annie just knew that this sad long thing following me down the street was in real life Duchess? Duchess of the dog pound. Poor Annie. Without a Fritz.

Duchess followed close behind me. He seemed to like me. He should. I was getting him a new home, and a lot of instant love.

I rang Annie's doorbell. Nobody answered. I rang five times. Duchess barked. Uh-oh, I hoped his bark was like Fritz's. I hadn't thought about that.

I left a note at Annie's house. It was a super note. I knew she'd call me as soon as she read it. Then Duchess and I went home.

I tried to sneak Duchess up to my room.

"Who is that?" my mother asked.

Some question.

"I'm showing Duchess my room," I said.

"What if she ...?" my mother asked. My mother hadn't noticed that Duchess was a he.

"Duchess is a he and he's housebroken," I said. (The lady at the animal shelter told me he was. She also said Duchess was friendly, very good-natured, intelligent, obedient, and wonderful with children. She said the exact same thing about Zitts's dog. I think it's a commercial.)

"Well, you have to clean your room if she messes it," my mother said. "Whom does she belong to?"

"He didn't tell me," I said.

The rest of the day I waited for Annie to call me. Duchess slept most of the time. At suppertime I left Duchess in my room and went downstairs. My mother didn't ask about him. I guess she thought he'd left.

"EEEEEK!"

That was my mother when she felt something warm and furry rubbing against her leg. It was Duchess. Then Duchess made this little puddle on the floor. Trouble, Journal. It went like this.

"Get rid of her at once!": my mother.

"Out! Out!": my father.

"I have to keep him a little longer," I said. "Just a little longer."

"Why?": my mother.

"Why?": my father.

"Because.": me.

I cleaned up the puddle.

Then I took Duchess for a long walk. He needed it. When we got home Duchess went up to my mother as if he liked her. This made a big hit, Journal. My mother bent down and patted Duchess and said, "Well, she is cute."

Duchess sat down and waited for lots of pats.

My father said, "Yes, she's a nice dog."

I hadn't even thought about Duchess that way. Cute, nice — who cares? I only thought about the Duchess who was going to be Fritz. We all gave him a few pats because he expected them. Then my father said, "Time to take her home."

My father didn't know that Duchess was a he or that Duchess's home was our home. At least for the night. Because Annie hadn't called. I waited until my mother and father were watching TV and then I snuck Duchess upstairs to my room.

Well, I tried to keep that dog from barking. I tried to keep my rug dry. I tried to sleep with a wet nose near my face. There was more, but I can't write another word except to say that my father discovered Duchess at half past one in the morning and that belongs in my next day, Journal.

May 9 **Annie**

Dear Diary,

Today I thought about Fritz's ears, both of them. They were always warm, and sometimes they quivered. Except for that, it was the same old Saturday stuff. Visited with Aunt Fan and Uncle Mack. Came home smelling of cigar smoke. Found a dumb note from Richie Carr. It said, BIG IMPORTANT NEWS! CALL ME. He probably wants to show me a new fish picture. Ho hum. I'm going to bed.

May 10 **Richie**

Dear Journal,

My father isn't the kind of father who would send a dog away in the middle of the night. He's the kind of father who would take away my allowance for a week instead. I guess that's fair. Except my allowance was going to pay back Zitts's dad.

Anyway, my father said, "I am too tired to ask you why you have this dog in your room, why it isn't home, where its home is, where you got it, and will it be gone by tomorrow morning." My father drooped out of the room.

Duchess climbed up on my bed. And we fell asleep.

In the morning Duchess and I went out. My mother and father said, "Good-by, Duchess," as if they felt that *good-by* was the key word.

I went straight to Annie's house. I rang her bell. Duchess was standing behind me. Annie answered the door. This was it!!!

"Guess who I found," I said.

Annie saw Duchess. She looked surprised. Then she squealed. She ran past me and hugged Duchess. Duchess yelped. Annie has a boa constrictor hug. "Oh, Fritz!" she cried. "You're back, you're back, you're back! I love you, I love you, I love you!"

Do you have to tell dogs things three times? Annie patted Duchess and looked him all over. This was the test! Warts, moles, what would Annie find that Duchess had that Fritz didn't have? Or what did Fritz have that Duchess didn't have? Annie said, "He smells funny."

I hadn't thought of that. I said, "Well, who knows where he's been?" I felt on top of things, like I knew everything.

Then Annie asked, "Where did you find Fritz?"

I hadn't thought of that either. Dummo! I said, "It was tough. Tough. But anyone who can spell *microgroove* without checking the dictionary can find a dog."

"But *where,* Richie?"

"*There,*" I said, pointing backward. "Way over there."

"What was he doing?"

"Well, he was just sort of being a dog. You know."

I guess Annie knew. No more questions.

"Well, thanks a lot, Richie," she said.

I, Richie Carr, knew that *thanks a lot* means more than thanks a lot. I knew that Annie was thinking I'm the greatest. I knew that Annie wanted to kiss me. But Duchess came over for pats.

When I left Annie's house, Duchess started to follow me.

Annie had to run after him and grab him. I turned around. Annie was holding Duchess. And Duchess was squirming to get free. They both were sorry to see me go.

May 10 Annie

Dear Diary,

I got Fritz back! Richie Carr found him. Fritz smells funny, and we have to housebreak him all over again. Do dogs forget things like that? I guess so.

I'm not sure Fritz loves me anymore.

May 11 **Richie**

Dear Journal,

Went to school. Saw Annie twice. She smiled at me both times.

May 11 **Annie**

Dear Diary,
Can't figure out Fritz. The smell won't go away, after two baths. He jumps up on furniture, and he chews socks. And I'm tired of cleaning up the puddles. Frances called it a "personality change." I didn't know dogs had that.

May 12 **Richie**

Dear Journal,
Three smiles!!!

May 12 **Annie**

Dear Diary,
I just noticed that Fritz has one brown eye and one yellow eye. How come I never noticed that before?

May 13 **Richie**

Dear Journal,
Today was boring. My mother and father talked about Duchess. "A sweet thing," my mother said. I think they like him better now that he isn't here. So do I. Why is that? Maybe they miss him. Maybe I miss him.

May 13 **Annie**

Dear Diary,
Dumb is what I am.

That's why I never noticed that Fritz has a funny bump on his leg that won't wash out in his bath.

May 14 Richie

Dear Journal,
Saw Annie five times in school. Got five smiles. Five out of five. Something big is happening!

May 14 Annie

Dear Diary,
I've been thinking about Richie. I'm going to buy him a nice present for finding Fritz. Maybe a game or a book. Maybe a book about high divers. That would make Richie feel good because he is one. When I think of bugs and itches and liver, I will no longer think of Richie at the same time.

But I'd better ask him some more questions about finding Fritz. That might help me know why Fritz seems so strange. I don't suppose it will help me figure out why his tail seems shorter.

May 15 Richie

Dear Journal,
Hooray! How do you spell that? Maybe it's hurrah. Who cares? Here it is in big letters.

ANNIE TOLD ME SHE BOUGHT ME A PRESENT AND SHE WANTS ME TO GO TO HER HOUSE TOMORROW TO GET IT.

This is really it. I hope Duchess will be at the door to meet me, because I MISS him in big letters, too.

May 15 **Annie**

Dear Diary,
The high diver book cost me two weeks' allowance. I bought a thank-you card, too. Fritz almost threw up over the present after I gave him his favorite dinner. I guess his favorite dinner isn't his favorite dinner anymore.

May 16 **Richie**

Dear Journal,
I almost left a blank page for today. Blank is better than what happened to me. I got all dressed up to go to Annie's house to get my present. I wore my shark T-shirt. This was Richie Carr Day. A present for Richie Carr. Annie *liking* Richie Carr a lot. And no more chasing after Annie. Annie was chasing after Richie Carr, sort of. Buying me a present. Asking me over.

I thought about Annie and me all the way to her house. How much I wanted her to like me. How hard I tried. Like finding Fritz for her.

Then it hit me. Right in the stomach. On the way to Annie's house. I didn't find Fritz. All I did was play a trick on Annie, that's what I did. I was phony Richie Carr. Pretending Duchess was Fritz. And now I was getting a present for a dirty trick. I wanted to go back home. Maybe Annie liked Richie Carr, but I didn't. Even worse, poor little Duchess liked me. I must be a great phony, fooling a dog. (I read somewhere that it's hard to fool dogs.)

Well, my feet kept walking toward Annie's house. When I got there, my fingers rang the bell. Annie answered. My feet walked inside.

Duchess ran toward me and jumped all over me. Then he sat down and waited for his pats. Annie was looking at me like I was an A on her report card. Like I was the greatest. She had my present in her hand. Then she held it in front of my eyes. She could hardly wait to give it to me.

But now (and I'm gritting my teeth as I write this) I had to *be* the greatest. By telling the truth, Journal, by telling the truth. Annie would hate me. But it was better than me hating me.

Duchess was sitting there watching us. Good. I needed a friend. I was getting up my courage. Annie looked so happy, so friendly, that I wanted to memorize that look forever, like the alphabet. She said, "Richie, I . . ."

She stopped. She was looking behind me. I looked behind me. The door was still open.

Coming up the walk, sniffing all the good old scents of home sweet home, was Fritz.

May 16 **Annie**

Dear Diary,

Two Fritzes! Got to think. Richie ran off. Odd.

May 17 **Richie**

Dear Journal,

Shock is a bad thing. Even *I* don't deserve shock.

Yes, it was Fritz, the genuine real one-hundred-percent Fritz.

First thing, he sniffed Duchess. Seeing them together made my eyeballs shudder. Then Fritz slunk up to Annie and cried. And cried.

I ran home. It wasn't a smart thing to do. But it felt very good.

I haven't mentioned today. I spent today trying to forget yesterday.

May 17 **Annie**

Dear Diary,

Number Two is *my* Fritz. I knew it right away. But I have to be very fair about this. Just because Number One Fritz was wrecking my house isn't why I decided against him. There's the smell, the bump, the eyes, the tail. The bark is a little off, too, when I think about it.

So who is he and where did Richie get him? And why did Richie run off? I wonder if stores take back books and thank-you cards.

May 18 **Richie**

Dear Journal,

I think I died today. I was in school. And Zitts comes up to me. And Annie comes up to me at the same time.

Zitts asks, "How is Brussels Sprouts?"

Annie asks, "Who is Brussels Sprouts?"

"An ugly vegetable that shouldn't have been born, ha ha," I say. And I walk away.

Zitts and Annie keep on talking. Did I die on the spot?

May 18 **Annie**

Dear Diary,

Are you ready for weird? Here it is. Zitts told me that Richie got a dog from the animal shelter. He named it Brussels Sprouts. Zitts said that I'd be just crazy about Brussels Sprouts. I thought it was a vegetable joke when he said it. Now I'm not sure.

Here's some sad news. I was saving it until last.

My folks say I can't have two dogs. Number One Fritz has to go. But where?

May 19 **Richie**

Dear Journal,

I'm not dead yet, but I'm getting there. Soon. Zitts says his dad wants to talk to me. Something about honor and owing money. And Frances says Annie wants to talk to me. Something about Fritzes Numbers One and Two.

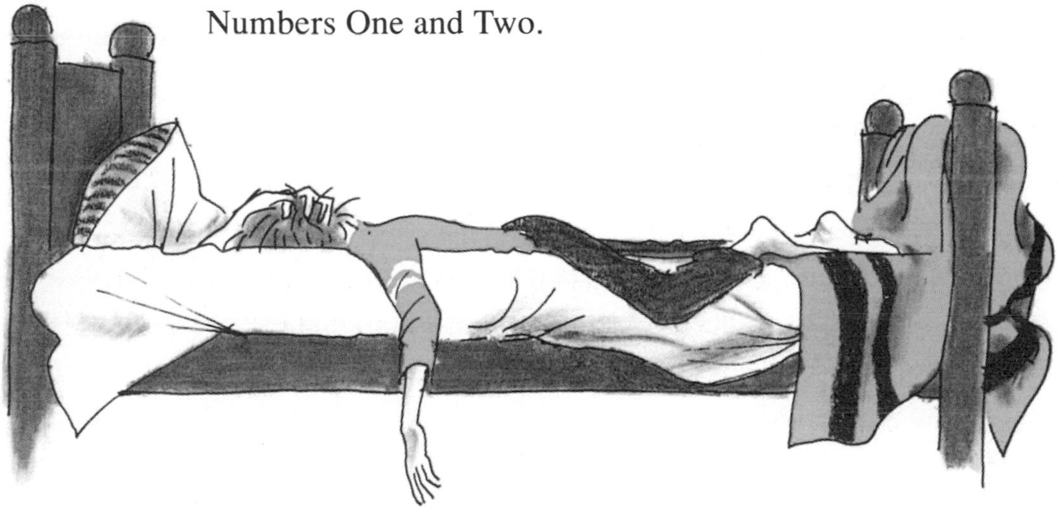

May 19 **Annie**

Dear Diary,

Decision. Tomorrow I'm going over to Richie's house with Fritz Number One and Fritz Number Two. There's something fishy going on. With Brussels Sprouts. With Richie running away. With two Fritzes. Tomorrow will be a big day.

May 20 Richie

Dear Journal,
What happened today? I finally died.

May 20 Annie

Dear Diary,
I hate Richie Carr. More than bugs, more than itches, more than liver.

May 21 Richie

Dear Journal,
What happened yesterday?

When Annie and Fritz and Duchess came over after school, Annie didn't even say hello. She looked like one of those characters in comic books who can turn into something else, some kind of monster. She looked like she was turning.

I invited her and the dogs inside. Duchess came over and sat for pats. Annie asked, "Where did you find the dog you said was Fritz? Why did you run away when the real Fritz came home? Who is Brussels Sprouts? Do you have a big secret?"

Just then my mother peeked into the room. Duchess ran over for pats. My mother said, "Nice Duchess. Good Duchess." Then my mother left.

Now Annie had a new question. "Duchess? *Duchess?*" It was all over.

"Duchess is Brussels Sprouts is Number One Fritz," I said. "I got him from the animal shelter. I got him because he looks like Fritz and I wanted to find Fritz for you."

Now Annie was out of questions. And into statements. "Richie Carr, you're rotten," she said. And she picked up Fritz and left.

Duchess came over to me for more pats. Well, somebody likes me.

May 21 **Annie**

Dear Diary,
I'm still too mad to write anything.

May 22 **Richie**

Dear Journal,
I want to write something good right away so I'll tell you that I paid Zitts's father the minute I got my allowance. Also, I told Zitts everything. Then I told my mother and father everything. I think they're getting a lecture ready for me. But I don't care because they're letting me keep Duchess. I have plenty of cleaning up to do, but I'm getting busy training him. I take him for long hikes. I love him. He loves me, too. I don't even have to *try* to impress him.

May 22 **Annie**

Dear Diary,
I keep thinking about the dirty trick Richie Carr played on me.

May 23 **Richie**

Dear Journal,
Duchess is the best dog in the world and sometimes I think I'm lucky, but not very. I won't mention Annie because I don't want to.

May 23 **Annie**

Dear Diary,
A perfect day because I didn't see Richie Carr. I guess he's busy with his new dog Duchess.

May 24 Richie

Dear Journal,
No puddles today.

May 24 Annie

Dear Diary,
Today I saw Richie Carr playing with Duchess. Duchess rolled over for stomach rubs and Richie gave him at least nine. You'd almost think that Richie was some kind of good person if you didn't know better.

May 25 Richie

Dear Journal,
Still no puddles.

May 25 Annie

Dear Diary,
Guess who I saw again. He was walking along, kicking pebbles, talking to Duchess, not showing off. I must be crazy but I almost liked him when I looked at him. Maybe Richie is a dog person just like me. Maybe the next time I see him, or the time after that, I'll speak to him.

May 26 Richie

Dear Journal,
Annie spoke to me! She said, "Hello." And we walked together down an alley. I told her I was training Duchess and that Duchess already knows what *sit* means. Annie patted Duchess and I patted Fritz.

Well, it's a start. Richie Carr may rise again.

May 26 **Annie**

Dear Diary,
I'm sure, I'm positive, that there are worse people in this world than Richie Carr.

Today we went for a walk. It was nice. Maybe someday I'll look at the fish scrapbook he keeps talking about.

May 27 **Richie**

Dear Journal,
Annie came over today. I only had to ask once. She looked at every fish in my scrapbook. She went wild over my piranha. Then we raced around the block twice with Fritz and Duchess. Annie said to me, "Richie, you're a dog person!"

I, Richie Carr, am a dog person? Annie Alpert *really* likes me, Journal.

And I haven't even told her yet that I can multiply 3,000 by 464 in my head and get the right answer!

DOG DAYS

May 16 was the day the real Fritz came home and the fake Fritz (Duchess) was exposed. If the two dogs could talk, what would they say about each other?

Write two journal entries for that day: one by Fritz and one by Duchess.

When Marjorie Sharmat was eight years old, she made up her own newspaper called *The Snooper's Gazette*. She filled it with news obtained by spying on grownups in the neighborhood. That was Sharmat's start as a writer.

Sharmat's early days as a spy and reporter may have prompted her to write *Mysteriously Yours, Maggie Marmelstein*, about a girl secretly writing for her school paper.

Sharmat often gets ideas for characters in her stories from people and sometimes pets in her own life. In fact, Fritz, the dog in *Chasing After Annie*, was named after her own dog.

Marjorie Weinman Sharmat

TAKE A PEEK AT THESE BOOKS

Class President
by Johanna Hurwitz
Julio is thinking about running for class president, but will anyone vote for him?

Bà-Năm
written and illustrated by Jeanne M. Lee
A graveyard, a thunderstorm, and a scary old woman named Bà-Năm await Nan when she honors Thanh-Minh Day with her family.

The Secret Moose
by Jean Rogers
When Gerald follows the tracks of a moose, he never dreams what he'll discover about this secret creature.

Me, Mop, and the Moondance Kid
by Walter Dean Myers
T.J. has problems: His best friend is going to have to move away unless she gets adopted, and his baseball team can't beat anybody.

Mom Can't See Me
by Sally Hobart Alexander
Being blind doesn't stop Leslie's mom from tap-dancing, riding a bike, and playing baseball.

Pueblo Boy
by Marcia Keegan
Timmy likes belonging to two cultures. At school he uses a computer, but at home he takes part in ancient ceremonial dances.

The Sioux

A Plains Indian Nation

Thinking Focus

What was life like for the Sioux in the early 1800's?

Key Words

plain
Native Americans
culture
tepee

As daybreak came to the Great Plains, the Sioux were finishing preparations to move out of camp. During the night, a group of scouts had come riding into camp, awakening everyone with their cries. "Buffalo!" they had shouted. A herd of buffalo, perhaps numbering more than a hundred, had been spotted several miles away. It had been months since the last hunt, but tonight there would be fresh buffalo meat. Within a few short hours, each family's belongings had been loaded onto a travois, an A-shaped frame fastened behind a horse. The entire village was ready to move out.

This scene could have taken place many years ago in the region of the United States that today we call the Great Plains. In this lesson you will learn what life was like in the 1800's for the Sioux, a group of people who lived on the Great Plains.

The Great Plains

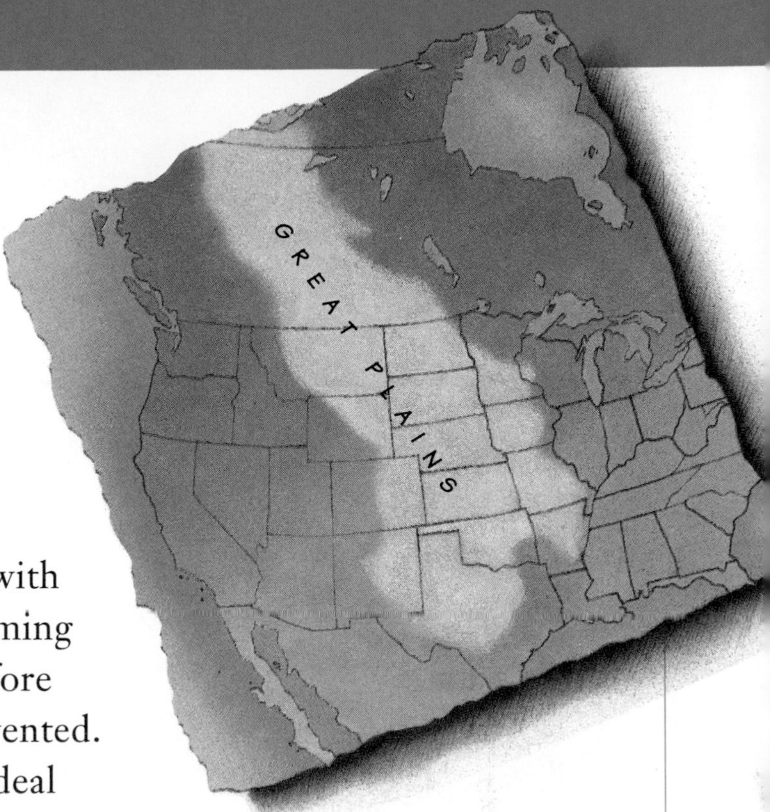

The Great Plains extends south from south central Canada to southern Texas and east from the Rocky Mountains for about 400 miles, covering parts of about fourteen states.

A Grassy Region

The Great Plains is a grassy region in the central United States and Canada. A **plain** is a wide, flat or gently rolling area of land covered with thick grasses. The grasses made farming difficult two hundred years ago, before modern farming equipment was invented. However, the Great Plains was an ideal grazing land for animals such as the buffalo.

People of the Plains

The people who lived in North America before the first Europeans arrived are called **Native Americans**. *Native* means "from this area" or "born there." Native Americans are sometimes called Indians.

The Native Americans who live on the Great Plains are known as the Plains Indians. In the early 1800's, there were at least ten major tribes, or nations, of Plains Indians living on the Great Plains. Some of these nations were the Blackfoot, the Crow, and the Comanche. Another was the Great Lakota Nation, or Sioux Nation. Members of a nation spoke the same language.

A travois.

Stop and Think

1. What have you learned about the Great Plains?
2. Why are the Sioux called Native Americans?

A Culture Based on the Buffalo

When Sioux babies were born, they were wrapped in the soft skin of a buffalo calf. When a Sioux died, he or she was wrapped in a buffalo hide. From birth to death, the Sioux culture was based on the buffalo.

***Culture** is the way of life of a group of people. It includes the homes they live in, the food they eat, their activities, their customs, and their beliefs.*

This scene of a Sioux camp shows how the Sioux used the buffalo for making clothes, dwellings, and tools — almost anything they needed.

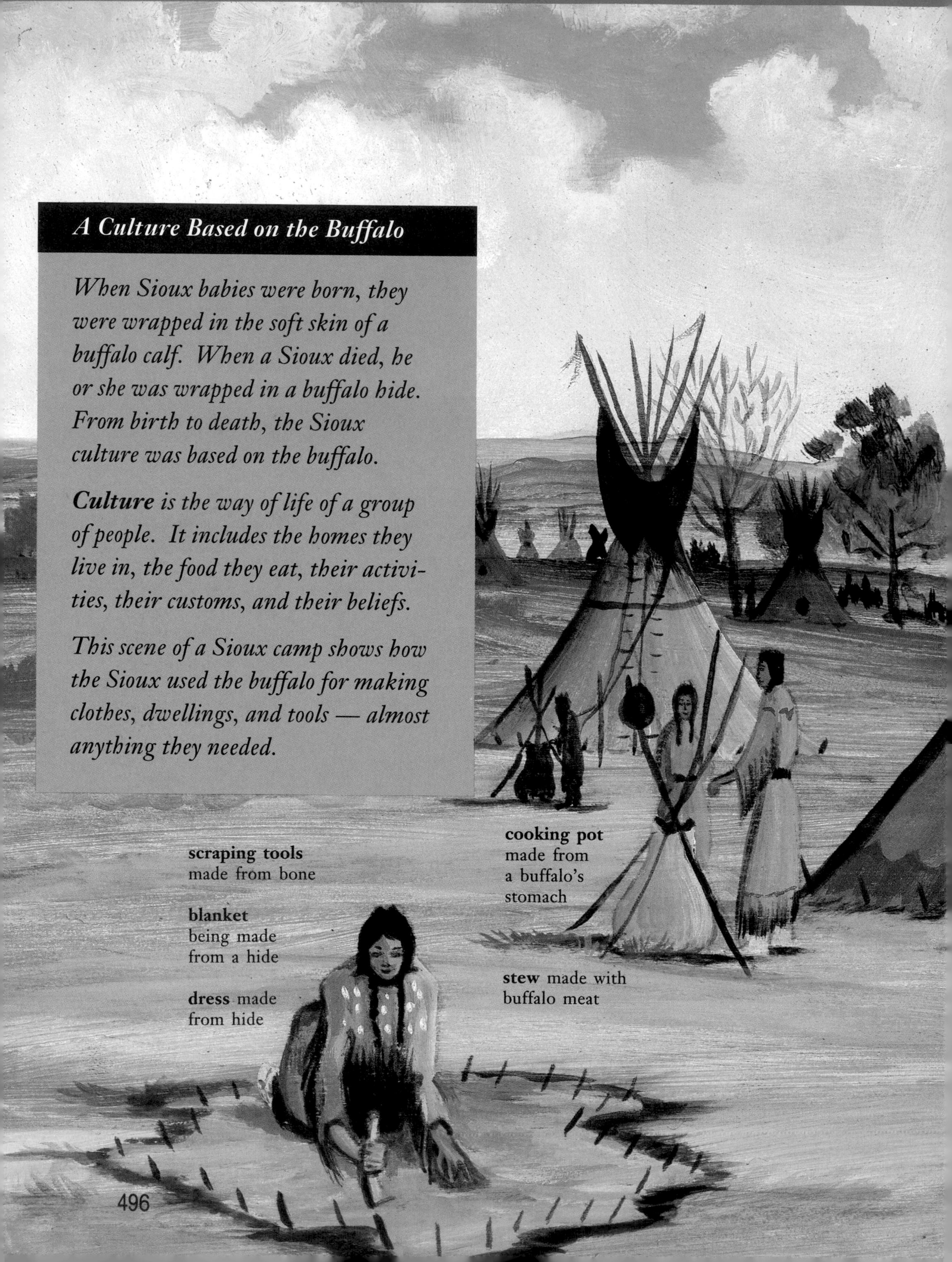

Sioux Life

The Ideal Home

Because the Sioux moved from place to place following the buffalo, they needed homes that they could take with them. The **tepee** was the ideal home, or dwelling, because it could be put up or taken down in less than an hour. *Tepee* comes from the Sioux word *tipi*, meaning "they dwell" or "dwelling." A tepee was a sturdy tentlike structure with a wooden frame and a covering made from buffalo hides. It took fifteen to thirty buffalo hides to make one cover. The hides were stitched together with a buffalo-bone needle and thread made from the tendons of a buffalo.

In the center of the tepee was a fire pit, which was used for heat during the cold winters and for cooking year round. Flaps at the top of the tepee could be opened to let the smoke out.

Sioux women sometimes kept small gardens. They grew corn, beans, squash, and other vegetables. They also gathered berries and vegetables that grew wild.

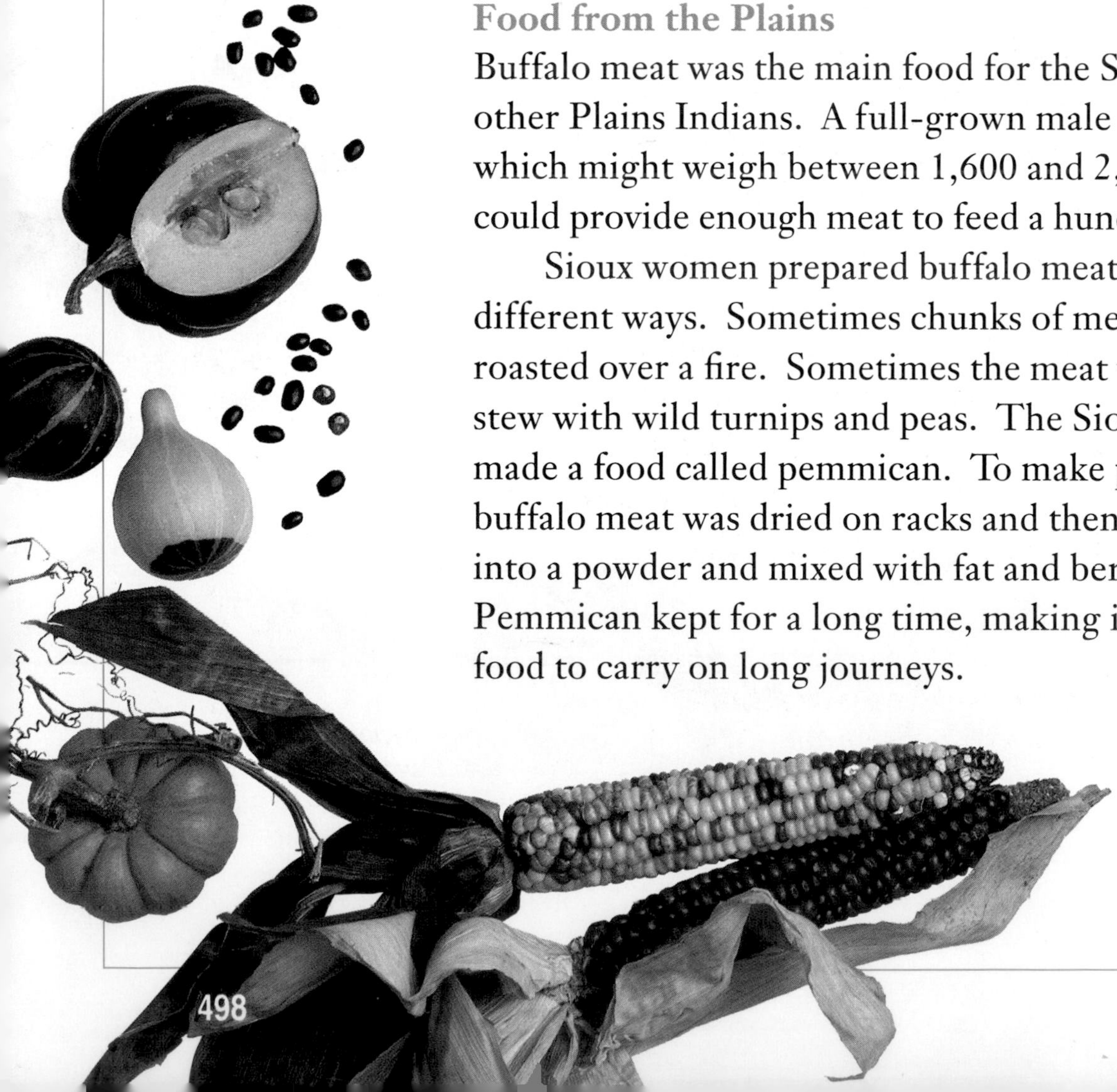

Food from the Plains

Buffalo meat was the main food for the Sioux and other Plains Indians. A full-grown male buffalo, which might weigh between 1,600 and 2,000 pounds, could provide enough meat to feed a hundred people.

Sioux women prepared buffalo meat in many different ways. Sometimes chunks of meat were roasted over a fire. Sometimes the meat was added to stew with wild turnips and peas. The Sioux also made a food called pemmican. To make pemmican, buffalo meat was dried on racks and then pounded into a powder and mixed with fat and berries. Pemmican kept for a long time, making it a good food to carry on long journeys.

A Buffalo Hunt

In the summer the Sioux hunted buffalo. When a herd of buffalo was located, the band would move its camp closer to the herd. Then the men would hunt. Hunters on horseback would approach a herd from two sides. When the buffalo began to stampede, the men attacked with bows and arrows or with spears. Although the entire hunt might last no more than fifteen minutes, it was very dangerous. Men and ponies were often killed or badly injured.

The painting at left shows a Native American buffalo hunt. It is titled Buffalo Chase, a Surround by the Hidatsa. *The Hidatsa were an upper Missouri tribe, neighbors of the Sioux. The painting was made in 1832–33 by George Catlin.*

After the hunt, the women skinned and cut up the animals. The man who had killed the buffalo got to keep its hide. In a few hours the entire buffalo was cut up into sections, loaded onto a travois, and carried back to camp. Sometimes the hearts of the buffalo were left behind on the plains because the Sioux believed that the hearts would help new buffalo to grow.

Sioux boys learned how to ride a horse and shoot a bow and arrow at a very young age. Usually a boy began to go hunting with the men when he was about thirteen years old, but he was not considered a man until he had killed his first buffalo.

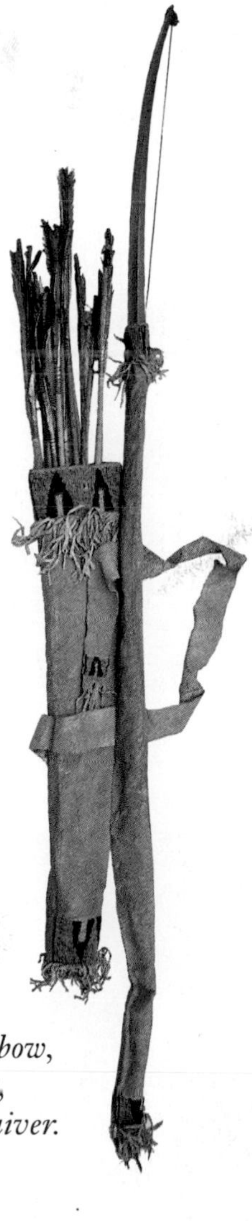

Sioux bow, arrows, and quiver.

Stop and Think

1. Why was a tepee the ideal home for the Sioux?
2. How did the Sioux hunt for buffalo?

Exploring Primary Sources

Standing Bear, who lived from 1868 to 1939, was a chief of the Oglala Tribe of the Sioux Nation. In his 1928 autobiography, My People the Sioux, *he recalled the preparations for his first buffalo hunt when he was a boy.*

"I had been out with my father and grandfather many times on buffalo hunts, but they had always attended to the killing, and I had only assisted in the eating afterward. But this time I was going as a hunter. I was determined to try to kill a buffalo all by myself if possible. My father had made me a special bow and some steel-pointed arrows with which to kill big game, and this was to be my first chance to see what sort of hunter I was.

"A scout had been sent out, and one morning, very early, he reported that there were some buffalo near. Everybody, including myself, began to get ready. While one of my stepmothers was helping me, she said, 'Son, when you kill a buffalo, save me the kidney and the skin.' I didn't know whether she was trying to poke fun at me or to give me encouragement. But it made me feel proud to have her talk like that to me."

A portrait of Chief Standing Bear

The End of a Way of Life

Stuffed buffalo heads displayed outside the offices of the Kansas Pacific Railroad in 1870.

In 1850 there were about twenty million buffalo roaming the Great Plains. By 1890 there were fewer than a thousand. The great herds that once roamed the plains had been almost completely wiped out.

How did this happen in such a short period of time? One reason was the coming of the railroad across the plains. In the 1860's a railroad line was built from Omaha, Nebraska, to Sacramento, California. In the decade following the building of the railroad, professional hunters killed millions of buffalo for their hides, which could be sold for a high price.

By the late 1800's, the Sioux and the other Plains Indians had lost the buffalo — and their way of life.

Stop and Think

1. What happened to the buffalo between 1850 and 1890?
2. How did the coming of the railroad to the Great Plains affect the Sioux's way of life?

Review

1. Describe the life of the Sioux on the Great Plains in the 1800's.
2. In what ways was the buffalo important to Sioux culture?
3. How might the Sioux's culture have been different if there had never been any buffalo on the Great Plains?

Rivers

Thinking Focus

How do rivers shape the land?

Key Words

erosion
canyons
tributaries
meanders

Somewhere near the northwest corner of Minnesota an icicle begins to melt. Drop after drop splashes onto smooth rocks below. All around, other icicles are melting. Soon the many drops join to form tiny rushing streams. These streams are so small you could easily jump across them.

Soon, two, three, or four tiny streams come together to make bigger streams. This water runs downward into valleys and lakes. From one of these lakes gushes a clear, beautiful stream. It will flow 2,348 miles before it empties into the Gulf of Mexico far to the south. During its journey, it will be joined by many other streams. Together these streams will make a mighty river, the Mississippi River. It is the longest river in the United States.

All over the world, rivers — long and short, young and old — wind over hills and form valleys. In this lesson you will learn how rivers change the land through which they flow.

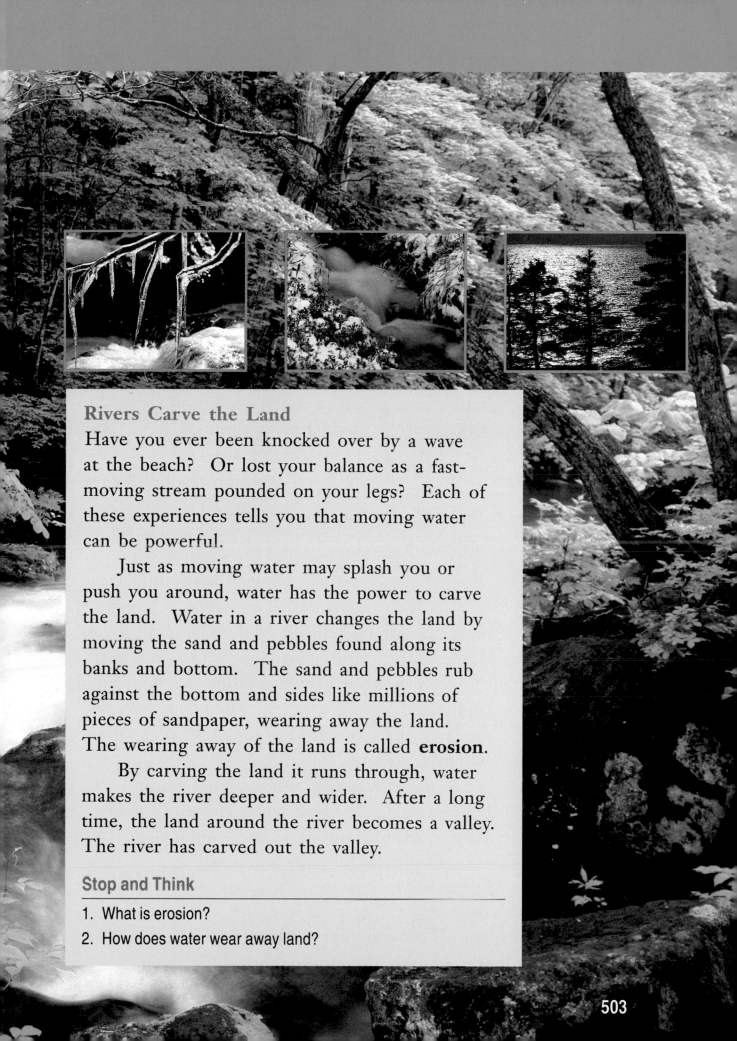

Rivers Carve the Land

Have you ever been knocked over by a wave at the beach? Or lost your balance as a fast-moving stream pounded on your legs? Each of these experiences tells you that moving water can be powerful.

Just as moving water may splash you or push you around, water has the power to carve the land. Water in a river changes the land by moving the sand and pebbles found along its banks and bottom. The sand and pebbles rub against the bottom and sides like millions of pieces of sandpaper, wearing away the land. The wearing away of the land is called **erosion**.

By carving the land it runs through, water makes the river deeper and wider. After a long time, the land around the river becomes a valley. The river has carved out the valley.

Stop and Think

1. What is erosion?
2. How does water wear away land?

Different rivers carve the land in different ways. Like people, some rivers are young. Others are middle-aged. And still others are old. You can tell the age of a river by its shape and by the shape of the valley it makes.

Young Rivers Carve Steep Shapes

Because the water in young rivers has not had time to wear away the surrounding land and flatten it, a young river runs down hills and mountains that are still very steep. Because water flows faster down a steep hill than down a hill that is less steep, young rivers move very rapidly. If its speed is fast enough, the force of the water will carve very deep valleys with clifflike walls, called **canyons**. One of these, the Grand Canyon of the Colorado River, is one of the world's most spectacular wonders.

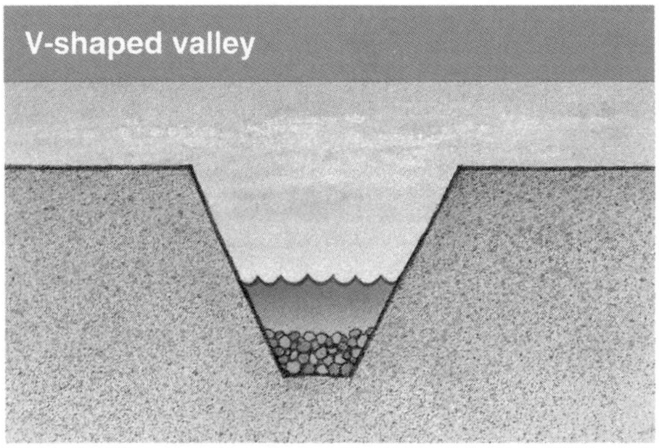

A young river may also erode the surrounding land into a V-shaped valley. Here, the banks of the river are very steep, rising above it on either side in a V-shape.

The photo below shows the Colorado River flowing through the clifflike walls of the Grand Canyon.

A young river has other special features. Because the river hasn't had a chance to wear away its bottom, the floor of a young river is not smooth, but full of large and small rocks. Also, in some places young rivers flow over slopes that are especially steep. Here, the water seems to leap all around. These waters are called rapids.

Middle-Aged Rivers: Wider and Calmer

The photo above shows a tributary flowing into the Tennessee River.

Over time, a young river wears away the surrounding land. As it becomes middle-aged the hills between which the river now flows are not as steep. The water moves more slowly. But a middle-aged river contains more water. That's because over time many smaller streams and rivers, called **tributaries,** have added their waters to the middle-aged river.

The water of the middle-aged river grinds more slowly and with smaller grains of sand and gravel than the young river carries. The land gets less carving as a result. It wears away its banks from side to side. This kind of river doesn't get much deeper as it continues to age. But when it floods over its more shallow banks it wears them away. For this reason, a middle-aged river can become very wide.

Now the valley the river has carved is more U-shaped. Gentle hills roll down to the water. Gradually, the large rocks have been worn away, and there are no longer any rapids.

Old Rivers Carve Less

As a river continues to age, it wears down the land even more. No longer does it flow down curving hills. The land through which an old river flows is now only slightly tilted. Old rivers often swing around in great flat loops called **meanders**. When heavy rains come in the spring, or an early warm spell melts lots of ice and snow, these rivers can flood their wide valleys.

Old rivers such as the Rappahannock River, shown below, meander across the land.

The river now flows so slowly that soil mixed in the water falls to the bottom. The river becomes shallower and shallower. If the process continues, parts of the river may turn into great swamps.

But these shallow old rivers are far from dead rivers. Their waters become homes for a wide variety of plants and animals. Because the water moves very slowly, birds and other animals can build nests that won't be swept away. Fish and frogs and other small animals can hide among the plants that cover large patches of water.

Stop and Think

1. What are tributaries?
2. Why do old rivers carve the land less?
3. How are young rivers different from middle-aged rivers and old rivers?

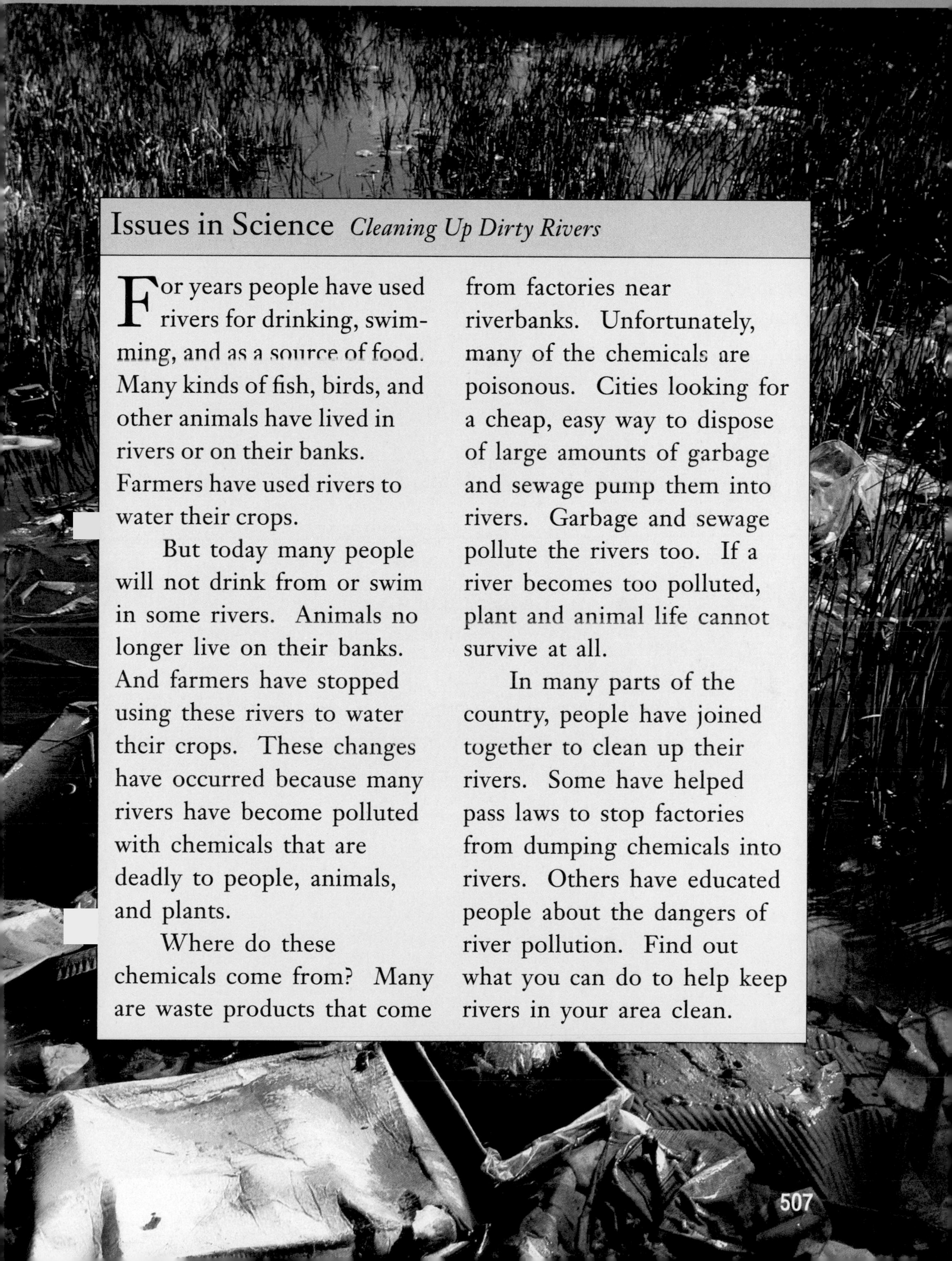

Issues in Science *Cleaning Up Dirty Rivers*

For years people have used rivers for drinking, swimming, and as a source of food. Many kinds of fish, birds, and other animals have lived in rivers or on their banks. Farmers have used rivers to water their crops.

But today many people will not drink from or swim in some rivers. Animals no longer live on their banks. And farmers have stopped using these rivers to water their crops. These changes have occurred because many rivers have become polluted with chemicals that are deadly to people, animals, and plants.

Where do these chemicals come from? Many are waste products that come from factories near riverbanks. Unfortunately, many of the chemicals are poisonous. Cities looking for a cheap, easy way to dispose of large amounts of garbage and sewage pump them into rivers. Garbage and sewage pollute the rivers too. If a river becomes too polluted, plant and animal life cannot survive at all.

In many parts of the country, people have joined together to clean up their rivers. Some have helped pass laws to stop factories from dumping chemicals into rivers. Others have educated people about the dangers of river pollution. Find out what you can do to help keep rivers in your area clean.

Try This! How Water Carves the Land

Purpose

To discover how different speeds of water shape land.

Materials

- 1 medium-sized bag of sand
- gravel or small pebbles
- 1 large paint pan
- pots and pans of different sizes
- sink stopper

Procedure

1 Put a stopper over the drain in a large sink.

2 Line the bottom of the paint pan with gravel or pebbles. Then cover the pebbles with sand and make a shallow groove in the sand with your finger. See the first drawing.

3 Place a small pot, face down, under the water faucet in the sink.

4 Place the end of the pan on the pot. Let it tilt downward in the sink. See the second drawing.

5 Turn on the water so it just trickles onto the "land." Let it run for three minutes.

6 Draw a picture of what happens to the sand. If you have a camera, you can photograph what happens.

7 Repeat the procedure, but increase the slope of the pan by putting a bigger pot under the end of the pan nearest the faucet. See the third drawing.

8 Repeat the procedure two more times, each time using a larger pot to increase the slope of the pan.

Conclusions

1. How does the slope of the pan affect the speed at which the water flows?
2. How does the speed of the water affect the erosion of the "land"?
3. Which part of the experiment represents a young river? a middle-aged river? an old river?

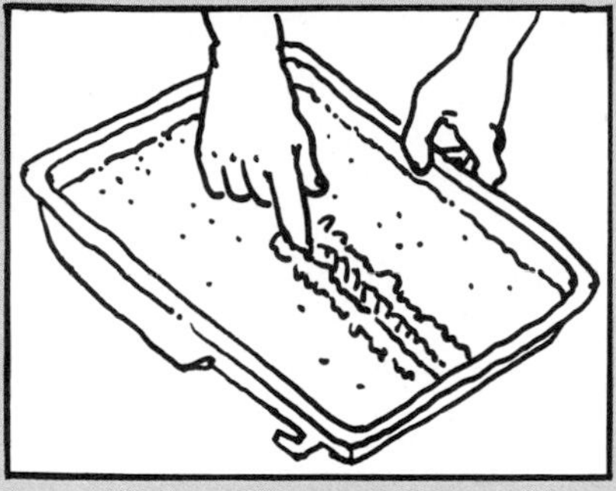

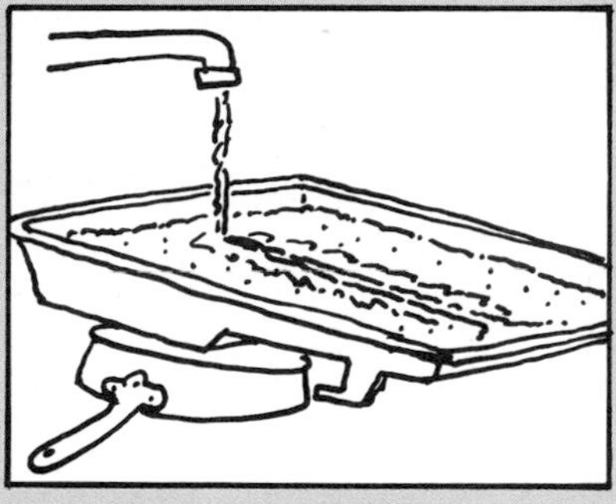

Important Ideas

- Rivers are made by many streams pouring into them.
- Rivers wear away and carve the land by erosion.
- Rivers can be young, middle-aged, or old.
- Young rivers move very fast, making canyons and V-shaped valleys.
- Middle-aged rivers move more slowly and make U-shaped valleys.
- Old rivers move least rapidly through flat valleys and carve the land less.

Review

1. How does a river shape the land?
2. How does the speed of flowing water affect the land?

Glossary

Some of the words in this book may have pronunciations or meanings you do not know. This glossary can help you by telling you how to pronounce those words and by telling you the meanings with which those words are used in this book.

You can find out the correct pronunciation of any glossary word by using the special spelling after the word and the pronunciation key that runs across the bottom of the glossary pages.

The full pronunciation key opposite shows how to pronounce each consonant and vowel in a special spelling. The pronunciation key at the bottom of the glossary pages is a shortened form of the full key.

FULL PRONUNCIATION KEY

Consonant Sounds

b	**b**i**b**	k	**c**at, **k**ic**k**, pi**que**	th	pa**th**, **th**in
ch	**ch**ur**ch**	l	**l**id, need**le**	*th*	ba**th**e, **th**is
d	**d**ee**d**	m	a**m**, **m**an, **m**u**m**	v	ca**v**e, **v**al**v**e,
f	**f**ast, **f**i**f**e, o**ff**,	n	**n**o, sudde**n**		**v**ine
	phase, rou**gh**	ng	thi**ng**	w	**w**ith
g	**g**a**g**	p	**p**o**p**	y	**y**es
h	**h**at	r	**r**oa**r**	z	ro**s**e, si**z**e,
hw	**wh**ich	s	mi**ss**, **s**au**c**e, **s**ee		**x**ylophone,
j	**j**u**dg**e	sh	di**sh**, **sh**ip		**z**ebra
		t	**t**igh**t**	zh	gara**g**e,
					plea**s**ure, vi**s**ion

Vowel Sounds

ă	p**a**t	î	d**ea**r, d**ee**r,	ou	c**ow**, **ou**t
ā	**ai**d, th**ey**, p**ay**		f**ie**rce, m**e**re	ŭ	c**u**t, r**ou**gh
â	**ai**r, c**a**re, w**ea**r	ŏ	p**o**t, h**o**rrible	û	f**i**rm, h**ea**rd,
ä	f**a**ther	ō	g**o**, r**ow**, t**oe**		t**e**rm, t**u**rn,
ĕ	p**e**t, pl**ea**sure	ô	**a**lter, c**au**ght,		w**o**rd
ē	b**e**, b**ee**, **ea**s**y**,		f**o**r, p**aw**	yo͞o	ab**u**se, **u**se
	s**ei**ze	oi	b**oy**, n**oi**se, **oi**l	ə	**a**bout, sil**e**nt,
ĭ	p**i**t	o͝o	b**oo**k		penc**i**l, lem**o**n,
ī	b**y**, g**uy**, p**ie**	o͞o	b**oo**t		circ**u**s
				ər	butt**er**

STRESS MARKS

Primary Stress ′	*Secondary Stress ′*
bi•ol•o•gy [bī **ŏl′** ə jē]	bi•o•log•i•cal [bī′ə **lŏj′** ĭ kəl]

A

ac•com•pa•nist (ə **kŭm**´ pə nĭst) *n.* A performer, such as a pianist, who plays an instrument for the lead performer: *The singer sang while her **accompanist** played the piano.*

ac•com•plice (ə **kŏm**´ plĭs) *n.*, *pl.* **accomplices.** A person who helps another to do something wrong or illegal: *The robber's **accomplice** hid the money that he stole.*

ad•mire (ăd **mīr**´) *v.* To look at with delight: *We stopped to **admire** the beautiful garden.*

aim•less (**ām**´ lĭs) *adj.* Without a purpose or goal: *My brother led an **aimless** and lazy life until he found a good job.*

air•brush (**âr**´ brŭsh´) *n.* A tool that uses compressed air to spray paint or other liquids onto a surface.

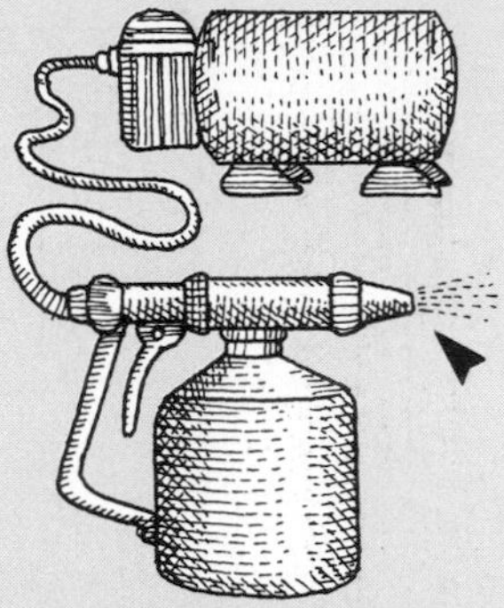

airbrush

AUTHENTIC

To the ancient Greeks, an *authentes* was a master. An authentic piece of work was "created by the master," not copied.

an•i•mal shel•ter (**ăn**´ ə məl **shĕl**´ tər) *n.* A place for homeless animals to stay: *Richie went to the **animal shelter** to find a pet that needed a home.*

an•i•ma•tor (**ăn**´ ə mā´ tər) *n.* A person who draws the pictures for an animated cartoon.

ap•pre•ci•ate (ə **prē**´ shē āt´) *v.* **1.** To be grateful for: *I **appreciated** your cheering me up when I was feeling sad.* **2.** To recognize the worth or importance of something.

ar•mor (**är**´ mər) *n.* A hard protective covering: *The hard shell of a turtle is **armor** that protects it from its enemies.*

au•then•tic (ô **thĕn**´ tĭk) *adj.* Real; true; genuine. If something is authentic, it is real and not a fake.

awe (ô) *n.* A feeling of wonder and respect: *The crowd stared at the astronaut with **awe**.*

B

bar•gain (**bär**´ gĭn) *v.* To try to agree about a price for something: *If I **bargain** with the landlord, maybe he will lower the rent.* —*n.* An agreement between two sides about a payment or trade.

ă pat / ā pay / â care / ä father / ĕ pet / ē be / ĭ pit / ī pie / î fierce / ŏ pot / ō go / ô paw, for /

bit•ter•ness (**bĭt´** ər nĭs) *n.* Angry or hurt feelings: *She never got over her **bitterness** at being cheated out of her life savings.*

bluff (blŭf) *v.* To fool someone with a false show of strength or confidence: *Peter said he had solved the case, but he was **bluffing**.*

brag•gart (**brăg´** ərt) *n.* Someone who speaks with too much pride about himself or herself in an attempt to show off: *Amy was a **braggart** when she said that she was the smartest person in school.*

C

ca•reer (kə **rîr´**) *n.* The kind of work that a person chooses to do; a profession: *Marian chose a **career** as a singer.*

car•toon•ist (kär **to͞o´** nĭst) *n.* A person who sketches or draws cartoons: *Mickey Mouse was drawn by the **cartoonist** Walt Disney.*

cast (kăst) *n.* The throwing or flinging of the line on a fishing rod: *My brother's first **cast** put his line halfway across the pond.*

ca•tas•tro•phe (kə **tăs´** trə fē) *n.* A disaster that causes great damage and often loss of life: *Scientists think a great **catastrophe** may have killed the dinosaurs.*

cau•tious (**kô´** shəs) *adj.* Not willing to take chances: *George is **cautious** about what he says to strangers.*

cel•lu•loid (**sĕl´** yə loid´) *n.* A clear shiny material used for making animated motion pictures: *A cartoonist draws the characters for animated movies on sheets of **celluloid**.*

cer•tain•ty (**sûr´** tn tē) *n., pl.* **certainties.** The feeling of being sure. "The boy said it with certainty" means he felt sure of what he was saying.

cham•pi•on•ship (**chăm´** pē ən shĭp´) *n.* The award for a person or team that is accepted as the best of all: *The Pirates beat the Orioles and won the baseball **championship**.*

CHAMPIONSHIP

The old Latin word for battlefield, *campus*, is in the word *championship*. Today's champions win battles on playing fields.

oi **oil** / o͝o **book** / o͞o **boot** / ou **out** / ŭ **cut** / û **fur** / *th* **the** / th **thin** / hw **which** / zh **vision** / ə **ago, item, pencil, atom, circus**

cli•mate (**klī**´ mĭt) *n.* The weather that usually occurs in a place: *People who live in a cold **climate** need to dress warmly.*

col•lec•tive work (kə **lĕk**´ tĭv wûrk) *n.* Work that is done by a group. Club members might use collective work to build a new building for club meetings.

com•mand (kə **mănd**´) *n.* An order or direction: *The conductor gave the **command** and the band began to play.*

com•pet•i•tor (kəm **pĕt**´ ĭ tər) *n.* A person or group that tries to be more successful than another: *Walt Disney tried to make better animated movies than his **competitors**.*

con•ceal (kən **sēl**´) *v.* To hide someone or something: *The key to the back door was **concealed** beneath the mat.*

con•cert (**kŏn**´ sûrt´) *n.* A performance of music given by one or more singers or musicians: *Thousands of people filled the stadium to hear the singer's **concert**.*

con•fi•dent (**kŏn**´ fĭ dənt) *adj.* Feeling sure of oneself: *Lynn is **confident** that she will do well on her spelling test.*

con•sent (kən **sĕnt**´) *v.* To agree or give approval: *If she does **consent** to marry him, they will become husband and wife.*

con•tract (**kŏn**´ trăkt´) *n.* An official paper that shows the conditions of an agreement: *According to the **contract** you must pay me one thousand dollars.*

cue (kyo͞o) *n.* A word or signal to tell a performer to begin: *She raised her hand as a **cue** for the dancers to start.*

D

dan•dy (**dăn**´ dē) *n.* A man who takes too much pride in his fancy clothes: *Iktomi looks like such a **dandy** when he wears his finest clothes.*

de•cay (dĭ **kā**´) *v.* To rot away: *The flesh of the dinosaurs **decayed**, so now we have only their bones to study.*

ă pat / ā pay / â care / ä father / ĕ pet / ē be / ĭ pit / ī pie / î fierce / ŏ pot / ō go / ô paw, for /

de•ci•pher (dĭ **sī**´ fər) *v.* To make out the meaning of something that is hard to understand or is not clear: *After the note fell in a puddle, the words were difficult to* ***decipher****.*

de•code (dē **kōd**´) *v.* To change from code into the original language: *The detective tried to* ***decode*** *the puzzling message.*

de•cree (dĭ **krē**´) *v.* To give an official order or decision: *The judges have* ***decreed*** *that the merchant's daughter must marry Taro.*

de•duce (dĭ **do͞os**´) *v.* To figure out by reasoning: *The detective tried to* ***deduce*** *from the clues where the missing baseball was.*

de•duc•tion (dĭ **dŭk**´ shən) *n.* The drawing of a conclusion by reasoning: *Meg's list of* ***deductions*** *showed what she had learned about the clues.*

de•sire (dĭ **zīr**´) *n.* A strong wish; a longing: *Roberto's* ***desire*** *to play baseball was like a hunger for food.*

des•per•ate (**dĕs**´ pər ĭt) *adj.* Feeling nearly hopeless: *Chris was* ***desperate*** *to find a way to keep his family from moving.*

de•tect (dĭ **tĕkt**´) *v.* To discover or notice something: *I* ***detect*** *a dimple in your cheek whenever you smile.*

de•tec•tive (dĭ **tĕk**´ tĭv) *n.* A person whose work is gathering information about crimes and trying to solve them.

de•test (dĭ **tĕst**´) *v.* To dislike very much. "They detest each other" means they hate each other.

dis•tract (dĭ **străkt**´) *v.* To draw away the attention of: *While you* ***distract*** *the dog with food, I will open the gate.*

du•et (do͞o **ĕt**´) *n.* A musical piece for two voices or two instruments: *The two girls sang a* ***duet*** *together.*

DETECT, DETECTIVE

Detect comes from the Latin word *detectus*, meaning "uncovered." A good detective uncovers hidden facts.

oi **oil** / o͝o **book** / o͞o **boot** / ou **out** / ŭ **cut** / û **fur** / *th* **the** / th **thin** / hw **which** / zh **vision** / ə **a**go, it**e**m, penc**i**l, at**o**m, circ**u**s

E

el•o•quent (ĕl´ ə kwənt) *adj.* Using language in a clear, forceful, and effective way: *The man's speech was so **eloquent** that he talked many people into voting for him.*

em•bar•rass•ing (ĕm **băr**´ əs ĭng) *adj.* Causing to feel uncomfortable and nervous: *It was very **embarrassing** for me when you started to snore in the middle of the movie.*

en•cour•age (ĕn **kûr**´ ĭj) *v.* To give hope or confidence to: *John didn't think he could bowl very well, but Uncle Joe **encouraged** him to try.*

ENTHUSIASM

Someone with enthusiasm seems to have a special spirit inside. The old Greek word *entheos* meant "having a god inside" or "inspired by one of the gods."

en•thu•si•asm (en **thōō**´ zē ăz´ əm) *n.* Strong interest or feeling for something: *Sue looked forward to the track meet with **enthusiasm**.*

en•trust (ĕn **trŭst**´) *v.* To give to another for protection or care: *That woman often **entrusts** her coin collection to her daughter.*

e•qual (ē´ kwəl) *n.* Someone who has the same rights and privileges as another. To accept someone as an equal is to feel that person should have the same rights as you.

ex•pe•di•tion (ĕk´ spĭ **dĭsh**´ ən) *n.* A journey made for a definite purpose: *The scientists went on an **expedition** to look for the bones of dinosaurs.*

ex•tinct (ĭk **stĭngkt**´) *adj.* No longer existing in living form: *Woolly mammoths once lived on Earth, but today they are **extinct**.*

F

fee•ble (fē´ bəl) *adj.* Lacking strength: *After the operation, he was too **feeble** to lift the heavy boxes.*

fierce (fîrs) *adj.* **1.** Wild; dangerous: *The **fierce** expression on Taro's face scared the merchant.* **2.** Very strong or extreme.

flail (flāl) *v.* To wave wildly: *The child tried **flailing** her arms to get the teacher's attention.*

ă pat / ā pay / â care / ä father / ĕ pet / ē be / ĭ pit / ī pie / î fierce / ŏ pot / ō go / ô paw, for /

fly (flī) *n., pl.* **flies.** A fishhook made to look like a fly: *We tied little green feathers to the hook to make a **fly**.*

fu•ri•ous (fyo͝or´ ē əs) *adj.* Filled with anger: *My mother was **furious** when I broke the front window.*

G

gap•ing (gā´ pĭng) *adj.* Opened wide: *The alligator, with its **gaping** jaws, appeared to be yawning.*

gen•u•ine (jĕn´ yo͞o ĭn) *adj.* Not false; real: *Annie could tell that this dog was the **genuine** Fritz, and not a fake.*

gill (gĭl) *n., pl.* **gills.** A body part of certain water animals, such as fish, used for taking oxygen from the water: *That opening near the fish's head is a **gill**.*

gos•sip (gŏs´ əp) *n.* **1.** Stories and news, often not true, that people repeat; rumors. **2.** A person who likes to tell and hear such stories and news.

grad•u•al•ly (grăj´ o͞o əl ē) *adv.* Happening little by little: *The dinosaurs may have died off **gradually**, over a long period of time.*

guide (gīd) *n.* Someone or something that shows the way, directs, or teaches: *The **guide** led us safely through the jungle.*

H

Hall of Fame (hôl ŭv fām) *n.* A group of persons judged outstanding in a sport or profession: *Roberto Clemente is in baseball's **Hall of Fame** because he was one of baseball's greatest players.*

hon•or (ŏn´ ər) *n.* A sign of someone's excellence or worth; a mark of respect: *One of the **honors** the singer received was a medal from the queen of England.*

hov•er (hŭv´ ər) *v.* To stay in one place in the air: *The children saw hundreds of mosquitos **hovering** over the pond.*

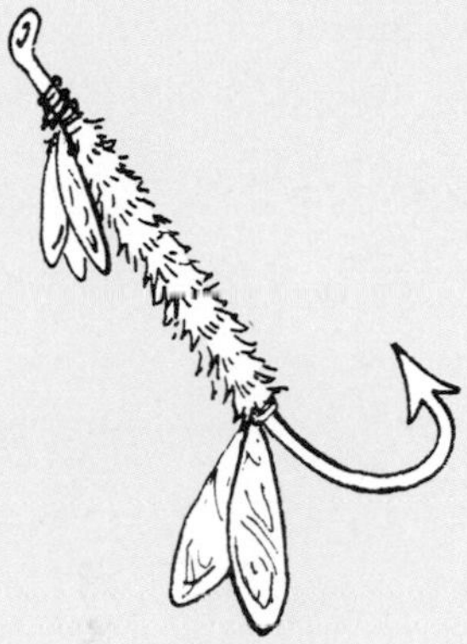
fly

oi **oil** / o͝o **book** / o͞o **boot** / ou **out** / ŭ **cut** / û **fur** / *th* **the** / th **thin** / hw **which** / zh **vision** / ə **ago, item, pencil, atom, circus**

HUMBLE

Humble comes from the Latin word *humus*, meaning "the ground." To be humble once meant "to lower yourself to the ground."

hum•ble (hŭm´ bəl) *adj.* Not thinking or speaking too highly about one's own talents or accomplishments: *The man is so* ***humble*** *that he never talks about his wealth.*

I

i•dle (īd´ l) *adj.* Staying away from work; lazy: *That* ***idle*** *boy just sits on the street corner all day.*

im•pa•tient•ly (ĭm **pā**´ shənt lē) *adv.* Lacking patience or the ability to put up with something calmly: *She pounded* ***impatiently*** *on the door when no one came.*

im•pos•si•ble (ĭm **pŏs**´ ə bəl) *adj.* **1.** Difficult to deal with or put up with: *My baby sister is* ***impossible*** *when she doesn't get her way.* **2.** Not capable of happening or existing.

in•field (ĭn´ fēld´) *n.* The part of a baseball field that includes the bases and the area inside them: *If the pitcher had not caught the ball, it would have gone out of the* ***infield.***

in•form (ĭn **fôrm**´) *v.* To tell about something: *I will* ***inform*** *our friends when we will visit them.*

in•ning (ĭn´ ĭng) *n.* One of nine divisions of a baseball game during which each team comes to bat: *Both teams came to bat in the eighth* ***inning*** *and scored a run.*

in•struc•tions (ĭn **strŭk**´ shənz) *n.* Directions; orders: *According to the* ***instructions,*** *the first player to reach the blue square is the winner.*

in•tro•duc•tion (ĭn´ trə **dŭk**´ shən) *n.* A beginning part, like that of a song, that leads into the main part: *When the band played the* ***introduction*** *to their most famous song, everyone cheered.*

INVESTIGATE

Investigate goes back to the Latin word *vestigium*, or "footprint." A detective who investigates a mystery is following footprints.

in•ves•ti•gate (ĭn **vĕs**´ tĭ gāt´) *v.* To look into carefully: *The detective decided to* ***investigate*** *the mystery.*

ă pat / ā pay / â care / ä father / ĕ pet / ē be / ĭ pit / ī pie / î fierce / ŏ pot / ō go / ô paw, for /

J

jinxed (jĭngksd) *adj.* Struck with bad luck: *When hail ruined his garden again, Herbert felt **jinxed**.*

L

land•lord (lănd´ lôrd´) *n.* A person who owns property, such as a house or apartment, that is rented out: *Mendel became a **landlord** after he rented a room to the stranger.*

lead (lēd) *n.* A hint or clue that helps to solve a mystery: *The only **lead** we have is a hair from the thief's head.*

lick•ing (lĭk´ ĭng) *n.* A punishment of being hit or struck again and again.

lime•light (līm´ līt´) *n.* The center of attention: *Her beautiful voice sent her into the **limelight** at a young age.*

limp (lĭmp) *adj.* Not firm or lively: *When she fainted, we carried her **limp** body to the couch.*

liz•ard (lĭz´ ərd) *n.* An animal that has a scaly body, four legs, and a long tail: *The largest **lizards** the world has known are the dinosaurs.*

lure (lo͝or) *n., pl.* **lures**. A human-made bait used to attract and catch fish: *I bought a bright, new **lure** for my fishing line.*

M

mag•ni•fy•ing glass (măg´ nə fī´ ĭng glăs) *n.* A lens that makes things look bigger.

ma•jor leagues (mā´ jər lēgz) *n.* A group of the highest class of professional baseball teams in the United States: *The young pitcher dreamed of playing on a team in the **major leagues** someday.*

mer•chan•dise (mûr´ chən dīz´) *n.* Things that are bought and sold: *The store's owner placed the new **merchandise** in the front window.*

LIMELIGHT

A limelight is an especially bright light used in the theater. It shines on one character to focus the audience's attention. A person who is the center of attention is said to be "in the limelight."

lizard

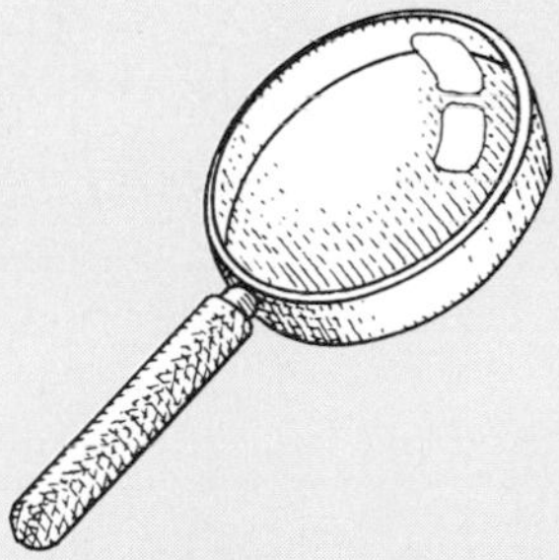

magnifying glass

oi **oil** / o͝o **book** / o͞o **boot** / ou **out** / ŭ **cut** / û **fur** / *th* **the** / th **thin** / hw **which** / zh **vision** / ə **ago, item, pencil, atom, circus**

might•y (mī´ tē) *adj.* **mightier, mightiest.** Great in size, strength, or importance: *Other dinosaurs ran for cover when they saw the **mighty** Tyrannosaurus coming.*

mis•chief-ma•ker (**mĭs´** chĭf mā´ kər) *n.* A person who plays tricks or causes trouble: *My cousin is a **mischief-maker** who is always in trouble for something.*

orchestra conductor

mis•tress (**mĭs´** trĭs) *n.* A woman or girl in a position of authority, control, or ownership: *Charlotte is the dog's **mistress** because she takes care of him.*

mon•soon (mŏn **sōōn´**) *n.* A wind in southern Asia that brings heavy rain from the ocean: *During the season when the **monsoon** blows, the rain falls almost every day.*

O

ob•nox•ious (əb **nŏk´** shəs) *adj.* Extremely unpleasant: *The princess spoke in an **obnoxious** way when she didn't get what she wanted.*

ob•serve (əb **zûrv´**) *v.* To celebrate in a certain way. People observe a holiday by following certain traditions, such as being with family and friends and eating certain foods.

ob•vi•ous (**ŏb´** vē əs) *adj.* Easy to see or understand: *The **obvious** plan was to wait until sunrise to start for home.*

or•ches•tra con•duc•tor (**ôr´** kĭ strə kən **dŭk´** tər) *n.* A person who leads or conducts a group of musicians who play various instruments.

out•field (**out´** fēld´) *n.* The grassy part of a baseball field outside the bases: *Roberto ran to the edge of the **outfield** and caught the ball before it went over the fence.*

o•ver•qual•i•fied (ō´ vər **kwŏl´** ə fīd´) *adj.* Having more skills than are needed to do a job: *A bank president would be **overqualified** to be a teller.*

o•ver•whelm (ō´ vər **hwĕlm´**) *v.* To be struck with a powerful feeling: *The hot and crowded room **overwhelmed** the young child.*

ă pat / ā pay / â care / ä father / ĕ pet / ē be / ĭ pit / ī pie / î fierce / ŏ pot / ō go / ô paw, for /

P

pan•to•mime (**păn´** tə mīm´) *n.* Body movements used to express a message or meaning without speech: *His **pantomime** of the record was so good we thought he was really singing.* —*v.* To move the face and body as if speaking or singing a recording.

part•ner (**pärt´** nər) *n.* One of two or more persons joined in a business: *When the job became too hard for one person, the detective worked with a **partner**.*

pa•thet•ic (pə **thĕt´** ĭk) *adj.* Causing one to feel pity, sorrow, or sympathy: *The little boy seemed **pathetic**, sitting alone on the bench weeping.*

pa•tient (**pā´** shənt) *adj.* Putting up with trouble, delay, or pain without complaining or getting angry: *Roberto asked the Pirates to be **patient** and give the new player time to get used to the team.*

pa•tron (**pā´** trən) *n.* The guardian or protector of a nation, place, person, or group: *Ujigami is the town's **patron** because the people believe he protects them.*

per•son•al•i•ty (pûr´ sə **năl´** ĭ tē) *n., pl.* **personalities**. All the kinds of behavior and feelings a person has that make that person different from everyone else. A "personality change" is a change from the way someone usually acts.

PERSONALITY

In ancient Greek drama, a *persona* was the special mask an actor wore. In time it led to *personality*.

plead (plēd) *v.* To ask for urgently: *She **pleaded** with the officer to help find her dog.*

pre•tend (prĭ **tĕnd´**) *v.* To put on a false show: *Annie really likes me, but she **pretends** she hates me.*

pre•vi•ous (**prē´** vē əs) *adj.* Coming before something else; earlier: *I am a teacher now, but my **previous** job was playing baseball.*

prin•ci•ple (**prĭn´** sə pəl) *n., pl.* **principles**. A basic rule or truth: *The **principle** that we believe in is equality.*

pro•duc•tion (prə **dŭk´** shən) *n.* The act or process of making something. The production costs are the money needed for making a movie.

pro•fes•sion•al (prə **fĕsh´** ə nəl) *adj.* Performing an activity as a job, for money. A professional singer is someone who is paid for singing.

prof•it (**prŏf´** ĭt) *n.* The amount of money left after the costs of operating a business have been subtracted from all the money earned: *I earned thirty dollars, but I spent ten dollars on the job, so my* ***profit*** *was twenty dollars.*

pro•ject (prə **jĕkt´**) *v.* To cause light to throw a picture on a screen: *I flipped the switch and the cartoon of Mickey Mouse was* ***projected*** *on the screen.* (**prŏj´** ĕkt´) — *n.* A special experiment or study.

proof (pro͞of) *n.* Evidence or facts that show that something is true: *The fact that Meg solved the mystery was* ***proof*** *that she was a good detective.*

PROJECT

The Latin word *projectus* means "thrown forward." Moving pictures are thrown forward when we project them on a screen.

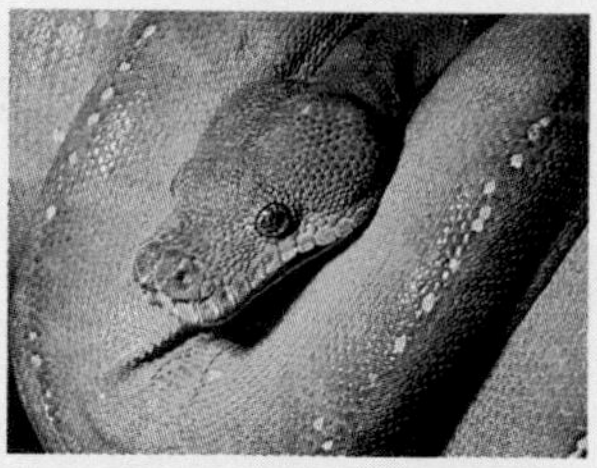

python

pros•per•ous (**prŏs´** pər əs) *adj.* Enjoying or marked by wealth or success. Someone who is prosperous-looking looks successful or wealthy.

py•thon (**pī´** thŏn´) *n.* A very large snake of Africa, Asia, and Australia, which coils around and crushes the animals it eats.

R

rea•son (**rē´** zən) *v.* **1.** To talk or argue in order to make sense of something: *The detective* ***reasoned*** *that if it snowed last night, the thief must have left footprints.* **2.** To use the ability to think clearly.

re•fer (rĭ **fûr´**) *v.* To talk about or call attention to: *The teacher was* ***referring*** *to you when she talked about good students.*

re•hears•al (rĭ **hûr´** səl) *n.* A private practicing of a show, such as a concert or play, before performing in public: *At the* ***rehearsal****, the symphony practiced the two new pieces.*

re•luc•tant•ly (rĭ lŭk′ tənt lē) *adv.* Without really wanting to: *She* ***reluctantly*** *gave back the lost kitten.*

rep•tile (rĕp′ tīl′) *n.* One of a group of cold-blooded animals that are usually covered with scaly skin: *Snakes, turtles, and dinosaurs are all* ***reptiles****.*

re•sem•blance (rĭ zĕm′ bləns) *n.* Similarity in looks; likeness. Family resemblance means that the members of a family look like one another.

re•spon•si•ble (rĭ spŏn′ sə bəl) *adj.* **1.** Having a duty or obligation: *I am* ***responsible*** *for my little brother when we go to the movies.* **2.** Being the cause of something: *Who is* ***responsible*** *for this mess?*

re•veal (rĭ vēl′) *v.* To make known: *His dirty clothes* ***revealed*** *that he had been hiding in the chimney.*

rit•u•al (rĭch′ o͞o əl) *n.* A ceremony with rules that are followed each time it is done: *Singing a song of thanks is one part of our Thanksgiving* ***ritual****.*

roam (rōm) *v.* To move or wander over an area: *Dinosaurs* ***roamed*** *from place to place in search of food.*

rou•tine (ro͞o tēn′) *n.* The usual or regular way of doing things. A comfortable routine means a regular way of doing things that you are satisfied with.

ru•ins (ro͞o′ ĭnz) *n.* The remains of a building that has been destroyed or fallen into pieces from age: *Scientists can learn about the past from the* ***ruins*** *of old buildings.*

S

sam•u•rai war•ri•or (săm′ə rī′ wôr′ē ər) *n.* A member of a special class of people in Japan who were experienced in war or fighting.

scal•y (skā′ lē) *adj.* **scalier, scaliest.** Covered with the small, thin plates that form the skin of a fish or a reptile: *The* ***scaly*** *skin of a lizard feels bumpy to the touch.*

REPTILE

Reptiles get their name from the Latin word *reptilis*, which means "creeping."

ROUTINE

Routine comes from the French word *route*, which means "a road that is well traveled."

oi **oil** / o͝o **book** / o͞o **boot** / ou **out** / ŭ **cut** / û **fur** / *th* **the** / th **thin** / hw **which** / zh **vision** / ə **a**go, it**e**m, penc**i**l, at**o**m, circ**u**s

scan•dal (skăn′ dl) *n.* Harmful talk or gossip: *The story about the king caused a **scandal** that turned the people against him.*

scene of the crime (sēn ŭv *thə* krīm) *n.* The place where an unlawful activity occurred. When there is a bank robbery, the bank is the scene of the crime.

scoun•drel (**skoun**′ drəl) *n.* A very wicked person: *The man with the fine manners was actually a **scoundrel**.*

scowl (skoul) *n.* An angry frown: *We could tell the boy was angry from the **scowl** on his face.*

se•lect (sĭ **lĕkt**′) *v.* To choose; pick out: *Before the game begins, each player **selects** a card from the pile.*

se•ries (**sîr**′ ēz) *n.* A number of similar things that occur in a row or follow one another: *Walt Disney could make a **series** of drawings look like a mouse dancing.*

shock (shŏk) *n.* Something sudden that disturbs or upsets the mind or feelings: *The loss of their homes was a terrible **shock** to the people.*

short•cut (**shôrt**′ kŭt′) *n.* A shorter, faster route than the usual one: *If you use the **shortcut**, you can get home in half the time it usually takes.*

shrine (shrīn) *n.* A place where people may worship or remember an important person or event.

sig•nif•i•cance (sĭg **nĭf**′ ĭ kəns) *n.* The thing or quality that makes something important: *The Emancipation Proclamation has great **significance** for African Americans.*

sin•cer•i•ty (sĭn **sĕr**′ ĭ tē) *n.* The quality of being honest or genuine: *The look of **sincerity** on her face told me she was not lying.*

smart (smärt) *v.* To cause to feel a sharp mental or physical pain: *My sister's mean comments **smarted**, or hurt my feelings.*

ă pat / ā pay / â care / ä father / ĕ pet / ē be / ĭ pit / ī pie / î fierce / ŏ pot / ō go / ô paw, for /

smol•der (smōl´ dər) *v.* To think angrily about something over and over: *He is still **smoldering** over the D he got on his English test.*

spir•i•tu•al (spĭr´ ĭ cho͞o əl) *n.* A religious folk song of African American origin.

sta•di•um (stā´ dē əm) *n.* A large building, often without a roof, where athletic events are held.

stake•out (stāk´ out´) *n.* A way of secretly watching a person or a place to catch someone doing something: *To catch the thieves, the police set up a **stakeout** outside the jewelry store.*

strive (strīv) *v.* To try very hard: *Always **strive** to do your best.*

stroke (strōk) *n.* A single complete movement: *He swung the tennis racket with a smooth **stroke**.*

sus•pect (sŭs´ pĕkt´) *n.* A person who, without proof, is thought to be guilty of a crime: *The boy was a **suspect** because he was in the building around the time the skates were stolen.*

sus•pi•cious (sə **spĭsh´** əs) *adj.* Looking as if something is wrong or out of place. A suspicious person looks like he or she is out of place or about to break the law.

sym•pa•thy (sĭm´ pə thē) *n.* A feeling of pity or sadness for the problem of another person: *Many people in the crowd felt **sympathy** for the rider who fell in the horse race.*

stadium

T

tal•ent (tăl´ ənt) *n.* A natural ability to do something well: *Marian had a great **talent** as a singer, but she had to develop it with study and practice.*

tar pit (tär pĭt) *n.* A hole in the ground filled with a thick, dark, sticky substance: *Most animals who fell into **tar pits** could not get out.*

TAR PIT

Tar comes from *treow*, an old English word for "tree." In those days tar came from the wood of trees.

tell•tale (tĕl´ tāl´) *adj.* Indicating or revealing information: *The footprints were a **telltale** sign that someone had been there.*

oi **oil** / o͝o **book** / o͞o **boot** / ou **out** / ŭ **cut** / û **fur** / *th* **the** / th **thin** / hw **which** / zh **vision** / ə **ago, item, pencil, atom, circus**

TENSION

When you feel tension, you probably feel like your nerves are stretched to the breaking point. *Tension* comes from the Latin word *tendere*, meaning "to stretch out."

ten•ant (tĕn´ ənt) *n.* A person who pays rent to live on property owned by another: *Mendel's new **tenant** made his home in Mendel's shop.*

ten•sion (tĕn´ shən) *n.* A feeling of strain among people: *After our argument, there was **tension** between us.*

trace (trās) *v.* To copy by following lines seen through thin paper: *The animator copied the cartoon rabbit by **tracing** it onto paper.*

trunk

trip (trĭp) *v.* **1.** To trap or catch in a mistake: *The thief was **tripped** when he lied about where he had been.* **2.** To strike the foot against something and stumble.

trunk (trŭngk) *n.* The long, flexible snout of an elephant, used for grasping and feeding.

tset•se fly (tsĕt´ sē flī) *n.* A bloodsucking African fly whose bite gives disease to human beings.

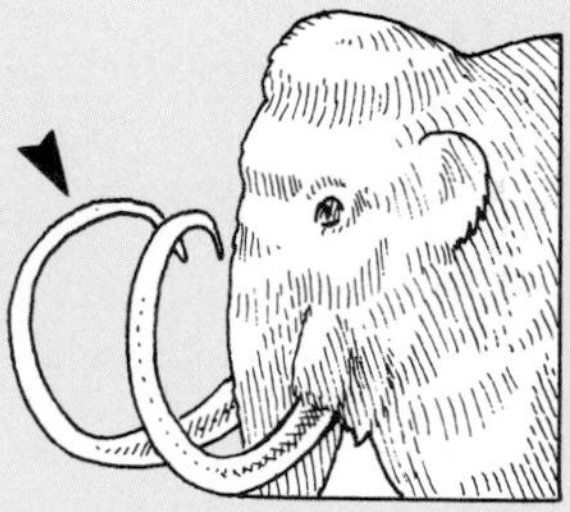

tusk

tusk (tŭsk) *n.* A long, pointed tooth, usually of a pair, reaching outside of the mouth of certain animals.

U

u•ni•ty (yo͞o´nĭ tē) *n.* The state of people joining and working together: *The team's **unity** helped them to overcome many problems.*

un•so•cia•ble (ŭn´ sō´ shə bəl) *adj.* Not liking to be with people: *That **unsociable** woman never joins in group activities.*

W

weap•on (wĕp´ ən) *n.* Something that is used in defense or attack: *The tiger's **weapons** are its sharp teeth and claws.*

World Se•ries (wûrld sîr´ ēz) *n.* The series of baseball games played each fall between the championship teams of the American and National Leagues.

Y

yearn (yûrn) *v.* To want something strongly: *She **yearned** to travel to Europe.*

ă pat / ā pay / â care / ä father / ĕ pet / ē be / ĭ pit / ī pie / î fierce / ŏ pot / ō go / ô paw, for / oi oil / o͝o book / o͞o boot / ou out / ŭ cut / û fur / *th* the / th thin / hw which / zh vision / ə ago, item, pencil, atom, circus

Acknowledgments

For each of the selections listed below, grateful acknowledgment is made for permission to excerpt and/or reprint original or copyrighted material as follows:

Major Selections

The Boy of the Three-Year Nap, by Dianne Snyder, illustrated by Allen Say. Text copyright © 1988 by Dianne Snyder. Illustrations copyright © 1988 by Allen Say. Reprinted by permission of Houghton Mifflin Company.

"The Case of the Missing Roller Skates," from *Encyclopedia Brown: Boy Detective*, by Donald J. Sobol. Copyright © 1963 by Donald J. Sobol. Reprinted by permission of the publisher, Lodestar Books, an affiliate of Dutton Children's books, a division of Penguin Books USA, Inc.

Chasing After Annie, by Marjorie Weinman Sharmat, illustrated by Marc Simont. Text copyright © 1981 by Marjorie Weinman Sharmat. Illustrations copyright © 1981 by Marc Simont. Reprinted by permission of Harper & Row, Publishers, Inc.

"Digging In," from *3-2-1 Contact* magazine, January/February 1991. Copyright © 1991 Children's Television Workshop (New York, New York). All rights reserved.

Have a Happy . . ., by Mildred Pitts Walter, illustrated by Carole Byard. Text copyright © 1989 by Mildred Pitts Walter. Illustrations copyright © 1989 by Carole Byard. Reprinted by permission of William Morrow & Company, Inc./Publishers, New York, and the author.

Iktomi and the Boulder: A Plains Indian Story, retold and illustrated by Paul Goble. Text and illustrations copyright © 1988 by Paul Goble. All rights reserved. Reprinted by permission of Orchard Books, New York.

Jumanji, by Chris Van Allsburg. Copyright © 1981 by Chris Van Allsburg. Reprinted by permission of Houghton Mifflin Company.

"La Bamba," from *Baseball in April*, by Gary Soto, copyright © 1990 by Gary Soto, reprinted by permission of Harcourt Brace Jovanovich, Inc. Lyrics from the song "La Bamba" (adaptation and arrangement by Ritchie Valens) © 1958 Picture Our Music (renewed). All rights administered by Windswept Pacific Entertainment Co. d/b/a Longitude Music Co., 4450 Lakeside Drive, Suite 200, Burbank, California 91505. All rights reserved. Used by permission.

"Louella's Song," by Eloise Greenfield. Appeared in *Ebony Jr.* magazine, May 1975. Copyright © 1988 by Eloise Greenfield. Reprinted by permission of Marie Brown Associates.

Making Room for Uncle Joe, by Ada B. Litchfield. Text copyright © 1984 by Ada B. Litchfield. Illustrations copyright © 1984 by Gail Owens. Reprinted by permission of Albert Whitman & Co.

Marian Anderson, by Tobi Tobias (Thomas Y. Crowell). Text copyright © 1972 by Tobi Tobias. Reprinted by permission of Harper & Row, Publishers, Inc.

Meg Mackintosh and The Case of the Missing Babe Ruth Baseball, by Lucinda Landon. Text copyright © 1986 by Lucinda Landon. Reprinted by permission of Little, Brown and Company.

"The Mysterious Girl in the Garden," from the book by Judith St. George. Text copyright © 1981 by Judith St. George. Reprinted by permission of G. P. Putnam's Sons.

Mystery in the Park, (Misterio en el Parque) from *La Legion de la Tarantula* by Pedro Bayona. D.R. © 1986, Ediciones del Ermitano, S.A. de C.V. Reprinted by permission.

A River Dream, by Allen Say. Copyright © 1988 by Allen Say. Reprinted by permission of Houghton Mifflin Company.

Roberto Clemente, by Kenneth Rudeen (Thomas Y. Crowell). Text copyright © 1974 by Kenneth Rudeen. Reprinted by permission of Harper & Row, Publishers, Inc.

The Sign in Mendel's Window, by Mildred Phillips, with illustrations by Margot Zemach. Text copyright © 1985 by Mildred Phillips. Illustrations copyright © 1985 by Margot Zemach. Reprinted by arrangement with Macmillan Publishing Company.

Strange Creatures That Really Lived, by Millicent Selsam. Text copyright © 1987 by Millicent Selsam. Reprinted by permission of Scholastic, Inc.

Tyrannosaurus, by Janet Riehecky. Copyright © 1988 by The Child's World, Inc. Reprinted by permission of The Child's World, Elgin, IL, Jane Buerger, President.

"Walt Disney: Master of Make-Believe," from the book by Elizabeth Rider Montgomery. Copyright © 1971 by Elizabeth Rider Montgomery. Reprinted by permission of Arthur Julesberg.

Wild and Woolly Mammoths, by Aliki. Copyright © 1977 by Aliki Brandenberg. Reprinted by permission of Harper & Row, Publishers, Inc.

Poetry

"The Cat Heard the Cat-Bird," from *I Met a Man*, by John Ciardi. Copyright © 1961 by John Ciardi. Reprinted by permission of Houghton Mifflin Company. All rights reserved.

"Donkey," by Eloise Greenfield, from *Under the Sunday Tree.* Illustrated by Mr. Amos Ferguson. Paintings copyright © 1988 by Amos Ferguson and text copyright © 1988 by Eloise Greenfield. Reprinted by permission of Harper & Row, Publishers, Inc. and Marie Brown Associates.

"Dreams," by Langston Hughes, from *The Dream Keeper and Other Poems.* Copyright © 1932 by Alfred A. Knopf, Inc., and renewed 1960 by Langston Hughes. Reprinted by permission of Alfred A. Knopf, Inc. and Harold Ober Associates Incorporated.

"The Early Bird," from *Mummy Took Cooking Lessons*, by John Ciardi. Copyright © 1990 by Judith C. Ciardi. Reprinted by permission of Houghton Mifflin Company. All rights reserved.

"Flower," "Moon," "Snow," haiku from *Flower Moon Snow*, by Kazue Mizumura. Copyright © 1977 by Kazue Mizumura. Reprinted by permission of Harper/Collins, Inc.

"Fossils," by Lilian Moore, from *Something New Begins*. Copyright © 1982 by Lilian Moore. Reprinted with permission of Atheneum Publishers, an imprint of Macmillan Publishing Company.

"Gertrude," by Gwendolyn Brooks from *Bronzeville Boys and Girls*. Copyright © 1956 by Gwendolyn Brooks Blakely. Reprinted by permission of Harper & Row, Publishers, Inc.

"Hold Fast Your Dreams," by Louise Driscoll, from *The New York Times*. Copyright © 1918 by The New York Times Company. Reprinted by permission.

"How to Assemble a Toy," from *Mummy Took Cooking Lessons*, by John Ciardi. Copyright © 1990 by Judith C. Ciardi. Reprinted by permission of Houghton Mifflin Company. All rights reserved.

"The Mastodon," by Michael Braude, from *Dinosaurs and Beasts of Yore*, edited by William Cole. Copyright © 1979 by Michael Braude and William Cole.

From *My People the Sioux*, by Luther Standing Bear. Copyright © 1928 by Luther Standing Bear. Reprinted by permission of Geoffrey Standing Bear.

"Poor Old Lion," from *Aesop's Fables*, retold by Tom Paxton, illustrated by Robert Rayevsky. Text copyright © 1988 by Tom Paxton. Illustrations copyright © 1988 by Robert Rayevsky. Reprinted by permission of Morrow Jr. Books, a division of William Morrow and Co., Inc., and Wendy Lipkind Agency.

"The Shark," from *Fast and Slow: Poems for Advanced Children and Beginning Parents*, by John Ciardi. Copyright © 1975 by John Ciardi. Reprinted by permission of Houghton Mifflin Company. All rights reserved.

"S'no Fun," by William Cole, from *Dinosaurs and Beasts of Yore*, edited by William Cole. Copyright © 1979 by Michael Braude and William Cole.

"There once was a Plesiosaurus," author unknown, from *Laughable Limericks*. Copyright © 1965 by Sara and John E. Brewton (Harper & Row, Publishers, Inc.).

"Tyrannosaurus," by Jack Prelutsky, from *Tyrannosaurus Was a Beast*. Copyright © 1988 by Jack Prelutsky. Reprinted by permission of Greenwillow Books (a division of William Morrow & Co., Inc.).

"What If . . . ," by Isabel Joshlin Glaser. Used by permission of the author, who controls all rights.

Quotations from Authors/Illustrators

Walt Disney (p. 378), quotation from *The New York Times*, December 16, 1966.

Paul Goble (p. 65), quotation from the book jacket of *Iktomi and the Ducks*, by Paul Goble. Published by Orchard Books, a division of Franklin Watts, Inc.

Eloise Greenfield (pp. 68-69), quotation from *Childtimes: A Three-Generation Memoir*, by Eloise Greenfield. Published by Thomas Y. Crowell, New York.

Kazue Mizumura (p. 422), quotation from the book jacket of *Flower Moon Snow*, by Kazue Mizumura. Published by Harper & Row, Publishers, Inc.

Kazue Mizumura (p. 422), quotation from *Third Book Of Junior Authors*, edited by Doris de Montreville and Donna Hill. Published by The H. W. Wilson Company.

Allen Say (p. 33), quotation from *The Boy of the Three-Year Nap*, from *The Horn Book Magazine*, March/April 1989, pp. 174-175. Reprinted by permission of The Horn Book, Inc., 14 Beacon St., Boston, MA 02108.

Millicent Selsam (p. 141), quotation from *Books Are by People* by Lee Bennett Hopkins. Copyright © 1969 by Scholastic, Inc. Reprinted by permission of Scholastic, Inc.

Donald J. Sobol (p. 346), quotations from *Something About the Author*, Vols. 32, 31. Copyright © 1983 by Gale Research, Inc. Reprinted by permission of the publisher.

Margot Zemach (p. 87), quotation from *Something About the Author*, Vol. 21. Copyright © 1980 by Gale Research, Inc. Reprinted by permission of the publisher.

Additional Acknowledgments

Marian Anderson (p. 378), quotation from *American Heritage*, Vol. 28, no. 2. Copyright © 1977 by The American Heritage Publishing Co., Inc. Reprinted by permission of the publisher.

Roberto Clemente (p. 416), quotations from *Who Was Roberto? A Biography of Roberto Clemente*, by Phil Musick. Copyright © 1974 by Associated Features Inc. Reprinted by permission of Doubleday & Company, Inc.

Mildred Pitts Walter (pp. 148-149), from *Brother to the Wind*, by Mildred Pitts Walter, illustrated by Diane and Leo Dillon. Copyright © 1985 Mildred Pitts Walter; illustrations copyright © 1985 Diane and Leo Dillon. Reprinted by permission of Lothrop, Lee & Shepard Books, a division of William Morrow & Company, Inc.

Mildred Pitts Walter (pp. 150-151), from *Mariah Keeps Cool*, by Mildred Pitts Walter, illustrated by Pat Cummings. Text copyright © 1990 by Mildred Pitts Walter. Illustrations copyright © 1990 by Pat Cummings. Reprinted by permission of Bradbury Press, an affiliate of Macmillan, Inc.

Credits

Program Design Carbone Smolan Associates

Cover Design Carbone Smolan Associates

Design **12–89, 280–283, 314–321, 345–349, 494–509** Carbone Smolan Associates; **90–143, 284–311, 322–344** Pronk & Associates; **144–219** Williams & Short Associates; **220–223** Joy Chu Design; **224–279** Landesberg Design Associates; **422–425** Louise Fili Design; **426–437, 453–465** Cheryl Miller Design; **438–452, 466–489** Joshua Hayes

Introduction (left to right) 1st row: James L. Ballard; Bing Chapelle; Ian Carr; 2nd row: Cyd Moore; Paul Van Munching; Greg Douglas; 3rd row: Carlos Castellanos; Olive Jar Animation; David Shopper; 4th row: Shennen Bersani; National Baseball Hall of Fame; Kristina Rodanas

Table of Contents **5** Kristina Rodanas; **6** Courtesy of Byron Preiss Visual Publications, Inc., copyright Bill Stout; **7** Courtesy of Mildred Pitts Walter; **8** Lynne Buschman; **9** Kurt Mundahl; John Lei/OPC; **10** Linda Phinney-Crehan; **11** Melodye Rosales

Illustration **13–14** (calligraphy) Grace Peters; **13–15** Kristina Rodanas; **16–30, 33** Allen Say; **34–65** Paul Goble; **66–67** Robert Rayevsky; **69** Amos Ferguson; **70–85, 87** Margot Zemach; **88–89** Kristina Rodanas; (calligraphy) Grace Peters; **90–91** John Gurche; **92–93** Alan Barnard; **94** (inset) Greg Douglas; **94–95** Courtesy of Byron Preiss Visual Publications, Inc., copyright Bill Stout; **97** Greg Douglas; **98** (top) Steve Van Gelder; (bottom) John Sibbick/courtesy of Salamander Books; **100** John Sibbick/courtesy of Salamander Books; **101** C. R. Knight/American Museum of Natural History; **102** Ian Carr; **103** John Gurche/courtesy of Smithsonian Institution; **106–118** Aliki Brandenberg; paper reliefs by Margo Stahl; **119** Ian Carr; **126** Alan Barnard; **126–127** (bottom) Painting by C. R. Knight/American Museum of Natural History; **127** (top) Margo Stahl; **128, 131–132** Greg Douglas; **133** The Macmillan Illustrated Encyclopedia of Dinosaurs and Prehistoric Animals; **135** Barb Massey; **138–139** Bing Chapelle; **142–143** Julie Ebberly; **149** Diane and Leo Dillon; **151** Pat Cummings; **152–153, 156–217** Carole Byard; **221–223** Cyd Moore; **225–227** Lynne Buschman; **228–243, 245** (bottom) Chris Van Allsburg; **246** (inset)**, 247–255** Allen Say; **256** Shennen Bersani; **258–275** Alexander Farquarson; **284–310** Carlos Castellanos; **312–320** Paul Van Munching; **322–344** Lucinda Landon; colorization by Pronk & Associates; **345** Amy Wasserman; **348–349** Paul Van Munching; **351** Linda Phinney-Crehan; **355–371** (lettering) Tom Canty; **360–363** Olive Jar Animation; **375** Barbara C. Morse; **378–395** (borders) Linda Phinney-Crehan; **396–397** Margery Mintz; **400** Pat Rossi; **418–419** Linda Phinney-Crehan; **420–421** Rudy Backart; **423–425** Kazue Mizumura; **427–429** Laura Tarrish; **430–435** Gil Ashby; **436–437** Laura Tarrish; **438–452** Gail Owens; **453, 454** (top) Laura Tarrish; **454–463** Melodye Rosales; **465** Laura Tarrish; **466–489** Marc Simont; **490–491** Laura Tarrish; **495** (top) Ellen Jane Kuzdro; (bottom) Victor H. Runnels; **496–497** Victor H. Runnels; **504, 505** Ellen Jane Kuzdro; **509** John Jones; **512, 519** (bottom)**, 526** (bottom) Joe Veno/Gwen Goldstein; **517** Meg Kelleher-Aubrey; **519** (top) Pam Levy

Photography **32** (all) Courtesy of Dianne Snyder; **33** Richard Allen, courtesy of Houghton Mifflin Company; **65** Courtesy Orchard Books (top); **65** Janet Goble (bottom); **86** Courtesy of Mildred Phillips (top right); **86** Courtesy of Four Winds Press, imprint of Macmillan Publishing Company (bottom); **87** Courtesy of Kaethe Zemach-Bersin (top right); **99** Royal Ontario Museum. Photo by Ian Chrysler; **104-105** Ian Chrysler (top); Chip Clark/Smithsonian Institution (bottom); **105** Chip Clark/Smithsonian Institution (top right); **120** NASA (bottom); **120-121** Curtis Slepian/Earthwatch; **122** Sheilah Crowley/Earthwatch; **123** Curtis Slepian/Earthwatch; **124** Sheilah Crowley/Earthwatch; **125** Curtis Slepian/Earthwatch; **128** Chip Clark/Smithsonian Institution (top left); **129** Royal Ontario Museum; **130** Chip Clark/Smithsonian Institution (top); **130** Royal Ontario Museum, Photo by Ian Chrysler (bottom); **131** Courtesy of George O. Polnair, Jr., Berkeley Amber Laboratory (bottom); **134** Jonathan Blair (left); **136-137** Royal Ontario Museum, Photo by Ian Chrysler; **140-141** Royal Ontario Museum, Photo by Ian Chrysler; **140** Courtesy of Janet Riehecky; **140** Courtesy of Aliki Brandenberg; **141** Courtesy Boston Properties; **145** Courtesy of Mildred Pitts Walter (opener); **220** Courtesy of Mrs. Judith Ciardi (top); **244-245** Richard Howard/People Weekly © 1989, The Time Inc. Magazine Co.; All Rights Reserved; **256-257** Mel Krieger (background); **257** Aperture (inset); **276** Topham/The Image Works; **277** A.C. Cooper Ltd. Copyright Reserved to Her Majesty Queen Elizabeth II. (top); **277** Courtesy of Judith St. George (bottom left); **277** Courtesy of Judith St. George (bottom right); **281-283** Kurt Mundahl; **321** Kurt Mundahl; **346-347** Kurt Mundahl (background); **346** Courtesy of Lucinda Landon (top); **346** Courtesy of Donald J. Sobol (bottom); **347** Courtesy of Pedro Bayona; **352** © The Walt Disney Company/RKO Radio Pictures, Inc. (top); **352** The Lester Glassner Collection (bottom); **353** The Pittsburgh Pirates; **354** © The Walt Disney Company/RKO Radio Pictures, Inc.; **367** © The Walt Disney Company; **369** © The Walt Disney Company/RKO Radio Pictures, Inc. (bottom); **373-374** © The Walt Disney Company (bottom); **376-377** Roy Bishop/

Stock Boston; **377**`© The Walt Disney Company; **378-379** The Lester Glassner Collection; **380** The Lester Glassner Collection (top left); **380** Culver Pictures (top right); **380** Culver Pictures (bottom left); **380** Paul Cordes/Culver Pictures (bottom right); **385** AP/Wide World Photos; **386** Culver Pictures; **388** FPG International; **389** The Lester Glassner Collection (bottom); **391** UPI/Bettmann Newsphotos; **392** Lisa Larsen/LIFE Magazine/Time Inc.; **393** UPI/Bettmann Newsphotos; **395** The Lester Glassner Collection; **401** Sybil Shelton/Peter Arnold, Inc. (left); **401** Jacques Janqoux/Peter Arnold, Inc. (right); **403** Courtesy of Diana D. Zorilla; **405** La Presse; **408-409** The Pittsburgh Pirates; **411-412** AP/Wide World Photos; **413** National Baseball Library, Cooperstown, N.Y.; **415** National Baseball Hall of Fame; **416** Ciudad Deportiva Roberto Clemente Inc.; **417** The Pittsburgh Pirates; **418** Peter Liddell/The Seattle Times; **419** Courtesy of Kenneth Rudeen; **422** Reprinted Courtesy of HarperCollins Children's Books; **437** Courtesy of Eloise Greenfield; **453** Paul Litchfield/Ada Litchfield; **465** Courtesy of Gary Soto; **491** Reprinted Courtesy of HarperCollins Children's Books, Photo: Deborah Grisorio; **494** Jodi Cobb/Woodfin Camp and Associates; **498** National Museum of American Art, Washington, Art Resource (top); **499** Lee Boltin; **500** Edward Sheriff Curtis/San Diego Museum of Man; **501** R. Benecke/DeGolyer Library, SMU; **502** TSW-CLICK/ Chicago Ltd.; **503** William Jacobs/Superstock (left); **503** Peter Van-Rhign/Superstock (center); **503** Mia & Klaus/ Superstock (right); **504** M. Collier/Stock Boston; **505** Jerry Howard/Stock Boston; **506** Robert Llewellyn/Superstock (top); **506** Medford Taylor/Superstock (bottom); **507** Hope Alexander/Superstock; **520** Milton Feinberg/The Picture Cube; **522** Kenneth Lucas at Steinhart Aquarium/Biological Photo Services; **525** Dan Kelley/The Picture Cube; **526** Stephen G. Maka © ; **Assignment Photographers** See Spot Run **106-118**. Kindra Clineff **427, 429, 436, 464, 492**. Tana Dubbe **498** (bottom). Kenji Kerins **145-147** (border), **154-217** (border). Susan Lapides **245** (top left). Karen Meyers **278-279**. Steve Nelson/Fay Foto, Inc. **352-353, 356-357, 398-399**. Dan Paul **311**.